Mothering an Angel

Carol,
May you always
listen to the voices
of the angels.
Blessings,
Patsy Keech

Beaver's Pond Press, Inc.
Edina, Minnesota

Patsy
Neary
Keech

Art on title page and on page 309 by Anita Moss.

ISBN 1-890676-99-3

Library of Congress Catalog Number: 2001089579

First printing: July 2001

Printed in the United States of America.

04 03 02 01   5 4 3 2 1

Beaver's Pond Press, Inc.

5125 Danen's Drive
Edina, MN 55439-1465
(952) 829-8818
www.beaverspondpress.com

To all the children I have never met,
but have grown fond of through the memories
of their parents and loved ones.

Chris Delong
Savannah Felix
Kelsey Fleming
Jonathon Friesen
Michael Gardiner
Marit Gillard
Kimberley Gratke
Brian Hortsch
Noah Heglund
Robert Island
Zachary Kanner
Madelyn Keech
Leah Lund
Chelsea Olsen
Casey Quinn
Ben Rhody
Katlin Ringhofer
Angela Rosenquist
Clint Rosauer
Jacob Salzer
Billy Scheuer
Mary Kay Scheuer
Dan Schwartz
Michael Van Epps

Drawing by Connor Keech

Dedicated in Thankfulness to:

God, for giving us the gift of Derian.

Derian for completing his life's mission.

My husband, for his belief and trust in me.

Our families for their unyielding support.

The friends who shared our journey,

and the ones we met along the way.

To the Valley Middle School students and staff from 1993–1997

*Congregation of Ss. Martha and Mary Episcopal Church
for always remembering*

And

Connor Keech, my cheerleader in life!

Opus Derian
Lyrics by Diane Anderson

Son
Little One
Derian
Derian
I see you with longing eyes—through the
Tears that I must cry
Let me hold you and dream awhile—of a time
When you were mine.

Tender Child
Radiant Child
Where you are the flowers bloom all year long
To caress your treasured face
Roam not far from me
In the garden free
Angel Child

Playful spirit within my heart—will you
Cast the pain away
Knowing the love you always bring—now
My soul can rest and sing—to you…

Used with the permission from Diane and Steven C. Anderson

Table of Contents

A note from the author

All mothers have a birth story. If you are pregnant, please allow your own story to unfold before reading about mine.

Happy pregnancy!

Although this is a true story, some of the names of the participants have been changed to protect anonymity.

The biggest lesson I learned from Derian was to find beauty in imperfection. If you should find errors in this book, assume Derian put them there to remind us all of this lesson.

Derian's wave from heaven

Movement One—

Let Me Hold You and Dream Awhile…

Chapter 1

Name: Patsy Keech
Age: 28
Occupation: Middle School Teacher
Married: Yes
Spouse's Name: Robb Keech
Age: 30
Occupation: Retail manager
Insurance: Yes

"I will just make a copy of your insurance card, Mrs. Keech."

I handed her my card and she disappeared. Robb put his hand on my belly and whispered, "I am so excited to meet you, little baby."

She returned, handed me my card. "You realize you are two weeks overdue, don't you?"

Really? I can't believe that the last nine months have just slipped by. "Yes, I am aware of that."

"Sorry, I was overdue myself – I know how annoying it is when everyone points it out to you. Your contractions are how far apart?"

"Five minutes, lasting for forty-five seconds."

"Is this your first baby?"

"Yes, actually this is the first baby on both sides of our family."

"Well, I guess this little one won't be *too* spoiled."

Robb smiled as he said, "I can almost guarantee it."

"Mom, here is your ID band, and Dad, you need to hang onto this one for the baby."

Robb smiled and said "*Dad.* That sounds wonderful. We'll stop by and introduce you to our little one on our way out."

As Robb and I waited for someone to call us to our room, a feeling of victory passed over me. We had waited nine months for this day.

"Keech."

Robb grabbed our things and we followed the nurse into the elevator to the Birth Center. She led us to a beautiful blue and mauve-colored room that looked more like a hotel room than a hospital room. This would be where our little "Skeeter" would be born.

The Birth Center has a different birthing philosophy than traditional labor and delivery. The Center is open to unique types of labor and creating a home-like atmosphere. Once "Skeeter" was born, I wanted him or her to feel relaxed and cozy, rather than blasted with bright lights. In addition to the atmosphere, I wanted to have a midwife, a doctor, and a birth plan.

Birth Plan for Patsy and Robb Keech

I've enjoyed this pregnancy immensely and have excitedly awaited this day. I have done a great deal of reading and mental preparation for birthing our child. I see labor and my delivery as the finale to a great experience. I realize I will only go through this experience a few times in my life, and I want it to be as natural and personal as possible.

I know I am heading into the unknown with this process and I'm not able to control everything that might occur during labor, but I do have some goals:

1. I want to be entirely alert during my delivery. Please do not offer me drugs.

2. Because I want this to be a natural process, I will do anything to avoid a C-section birth. I will consent to this only if alternative methods have been tried or if my child's or my own life is in danger.

Once the baby is born I have the following requests:

1. I want to keep the baby with my husband or me at all times.
2. I'd like to have the eye-ointment put into our baby's eyes while it sleeps. I want the three of us to meet each other eye-to-eye and focus clearly on those first glances.
3. I want to have the PKU test done at the baby's two-week check up. The VIT-K shot can be omitted.

At the beginning of my pregnancy, I met the wife of a co-worker who shared her birth story. She delivered her baby in her home with a doula (a trained woman who aids birthing women and couples), while her doctor was on the phone.

That conversation led me to Gail Tully, the doula, and Dr. Matt, an M.D, who both agreed to play a role in the birth of our child. I liked Gail immediately, as she had a profound way of looking at life. Robb was not quite as comfortable with birth as I was, so in bringing Gail and Robb together, I knew I would need to make sure Gail was prepped on how to win "scientific" Robb over. Four months into my pregnancy, the two of them met and hit it off. Gail became an intricate part of our journey. Our relationship seemed more like that of sisters than a client-patient relationship. During the course of nine months, Gail challenged my opinions on medicine and parenting and she taught me how to advocate for my unborn child and myself. She also helped me tap into a part of myself I had never examined before. Her challenges helped me develop skills I would need following the pregnancy.

Gail arrived at the hospital a few hours after we did. By the time she came, my labor had completely stopped. In addition to helping us with our birth of "Skeeter," Gail was making final preparations for her wedding that would take place the following evening. It was already early evening and nothing was happening. Our time was critical. Gail got me out of bed and the two of us walked up and down the hospital halls, trying to get my labor to pick up. Around 9 p.m. Gail ran home to get her wedding dress. She hemmed it between contractions. Robb and I continued walking, hopeful that I would be in hard labor by the time she returned.

No such luck. The reality of my slow labor and Gail's wedding day had collided. The soon-to-be bride was exhausted. It wasn't fair to keep her any longer, as her wedding would take place in just sixteen hours. We knew it was time for her to go. She came over to me, caressed my hands, and ever so quietly whispered, "Patsy, I know you can deliver this baby. I will be thinking of you and will be anxious to meet your baby when I get back from my honeymoon." As she spoke, I cried. I had always imagined the three of us greeting this child together. Gail recognized my fear and disappointment. She told me she wasn't about to let Robb and me experience "Skeeter's" birth alone. She had already contacted Rolla, another doula and a good friend, who had agreed to fill in for her.

When Gail left the room, a triangle of light from the hallway brightened the room, and then faded as the door closed. In the darkness of the hospital room, I was left alone with my sleeping husband. Feelings of disappointment, frustration, and failure surrounded me. I turned on the light next to the bed and grabbed the notes I had written earlier to "Skeeter" and to God.

Dear "Skeeter",

I keep thinking about the first few minutes we will have together. I can't believe you'll really be my baby – that I'll be a mom. I can't wait to look into your eyes for the first time. I wonder what you will look like. If you'll be happy? What it will feel like to have you squeeze my hand? I wonder how you will express yourself, what your cry will sound like, when your active and sleepy times of day will be. I can't wait to feel the softness and newness of your skin, to hear the sound of your breath. How precious the first few moments of life—you are welcome to the planet. What will your first thoughts be? What dreams will you have? You are so fresh—the bud of God's plan. What will you bloom into?

Dear God,

You have given me the gift of a child, Lord. I know You feel I am ready to be a parent. Please guide me in this journey. I can't wait to feel this child in my arms. I want to touch, smell, and hear its newborn cry. I've waited so long to meet this little one. When I hold this baby, I will be able to see the master You are and completely admire Your work. I have no doubt how much You love us. Help me to convey this message to our child each day.

Even though I couldn't sleep, I turned off the light and thought about some of the events that took place during my pregnancy. I remembered how excited Robb was when I told him he was going to be a daddy, how thrilled our parents were to be grandparents, and the efforts we put into saving for a down payment on a house. All the weekends we had driven around looking for the "right home" for our "Skeeter." It was time to sleep. Tomorrow would be a big day.

Rolla, our new doula, arrived around 7 a.m., and although I was glad to have a part of Gail with me, this was a strange way to meet someone. But Rolla's spirit was similar to Gail's. She stood next to me and asked a few questions before sitting down. Very little conversation took place, yet her presence brought peacefulness.

Dr. Matt arrived around 9 a.m. She knew I was exhausted and tired of messing around! She promised me that, one way or another, I was going to have that baby soon. She put in an order for Pitocin, and a few minutes later, a nurse hooked up an IV. I hadn't cared how much labor was going to hurt–until I really got into it. Although my goal was natural birth, my fatigue was obvious to Dr. Matt and Rolla. While they both respected my goal, they let me know it would be okay to change my plans mid-course. I hesitated because I had worked so hard preparing my birth plan, rehearsed those first moments with our child so many times. I didn't want to miss anything because I was drugged. However, realizing I could spare myself some pain, I agreed to have a shot of Nubian.

Labor continued building hard and fast. Now my contractions were one minute long and one minute apart. I felt as though the base of my body was being pried apart. But I reasoned that the harder things got, the closer I was to having all this birth stuff over! The morning slipped into afternoon, and while my contractions were still intense, my body was fighting hard to hang onto this baby. I was exhausted...Robb was disappointed...and our families were standing by the telephone, waiting for news. No pressure!

Robb's parents called and wanted to come up for a late lunch. Robb asked if I would mind. I let him know it was fine if he wanted to leave for a while, but that I didn't feel like having people in for a picnic. A while later, a nurse came in and said I had a few visitors. I couldn't imagine who it would be...until she described Robb's mom, sister, and aunt. The nurse asked if it was okay to invite them in. I glared at Robb and responded sharply. "No, it is not! Tell them they are not to wait at the hospital—they should go home, and we will call them when the baby arrives!" I was in pain, and upset with Robb. Rolla jumped to my assistance and helped explain to Robb that his family would have to leave. Heather, Robb's sister called out, "Hi, Patsy" as the door was closing.

A few hours later, my labor shifted. When I started to push, Dr. Matt sternly said, "Patsy, DO NOT PUSH!" *What? Wasn't this supposed to be the big moment? What do you mean, don't push?* Apparently, my cervix was swollen, and I had to wait until the swelling went down before I could start pushing. This was like telling a volcano not to erupt.

Once I got the go-ahead, you can bet I was only too ready. Three giant pushes and I heard the first sounds of our newborn crying. Dr. Matt and Robb proudly announced, "It's a boy! Patsy, you have a boy!" *My "Skeeter" is a boy!*

Moments later a team of doctors and nurses entered the room with a clear incubator. Meconium (newborn baby feces) was discovered in the placental sac. This group of people picked Derian up, laid him in the incubator, turned on a bright light, and pushed a tube into Derian's nose. The incubator was lined up next to my bed so I could watch as they worked on Derian.

As I looked at Derian our eyes connected. "Welcome to the world Derian. I'm your mom. We've had a tough day." I couldn't take my eyes off him. He was so beautiful!

When the team finished, they wrapped Derian tightly in a polka-dotted hospital baby blanket and handed him to Robb. Robb cradled him for a few moments, before he reverently laid him on my stomach. "Derian, this is your mommy." We looked at each other through blurry eyes as we touched our much-awaited baby. We'd done it!

Our hallmark moment lasted a few minutes before Robb ran to the phone to announce Derian's August 2, 8:08 p.m. arrival. Rolla and I admired Derian. She congratulated me one more time and slipped out of the room.

Now I had Derian all to myself. I rubbed his silky skin next to mine, leaned my ear next to his mouth, and listened to the sounds of his baby breaths. I opened the blanket to see his ten little toes. I counted his ten little fingers, two arms and two legs, one cute pug nose, and gazed into his dark brown eyes. He was beautiful. He was my baby.

After Robb finished making the calls, he came back into the room. He was beside himself; I had never seen him like this before! He crawled into the bed, laid his head on my shoulder and kissed me. As he wrapped Derian's small fingers around his, he said, "Patsy, you did a good job. You made me the happiest man in the world!" While the three of us snuggled together, I could hear the sound of three heartbeats. Derian brought such warmth between us; the turmoil from the afternoon dissipated into the stillness of the room.

It was exciting to introduce Derian that evening to our families. Each person holding him noticed different things. Our dads commented on his big hands. When it was my brother Tim's turn to hold Derian, he unwrapped the blanket and peeked at Derian's toes saying, "I just love to look at babies' feet!" Our moms held him without saying anything—I could tell they had been waiting for this day for a long time. By 10 p.m. I could barely keep my eyes open and everyone left so I could rest. They scheduled different times to come the next day so they could each enjoy more holding time with Derian.

Tuesday was a day of activity. In between visitors and phone calls, we took classes and talked with nurses about new-parent stuff. Later Robb slipped out to hang up an "It's a Boy!" sign in front of our house. At one point, I awoke to find Robb sleeping on the couch with Derian on his bare chest. Robb told me later that he had caught himself bursting into tears several times as he held Derian. His birth and presence moved Robb in a profound way. I was pleased to see this new part of him; this child was bringing us closer than we had been before.

By the end of the day, we were anxious to get home and have everyone over for a formal, "Meet Derian" party. I couldn't wait to acquaint

Derian with his room and his new home. How wonderful it would be to wake up with the sound of a baby in the house! The evening nurse acknowledged my birth plan but discouraged me from keeping Derian in our room overnight. "Honey, you need to rest now; you'll have plenty of sleepless nights once you get home." Perhaps she was right. Robb and I dreamed that night of the new life we were about to begin.

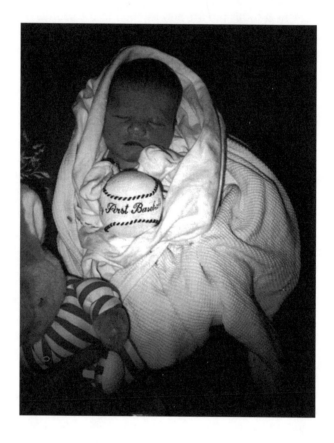

Chapter 2

Around 2 a.m. our dreams were interrupted by a quiet knock at the door. A nurse told us Derian was having a few problems breathing and had been moved to the NICU (Neonatal Intensive Care Unit). She was very relaxed, reassuring us that the neonatologist was checking him over. It didn't seem to be a big deal. Still exhausted from labor but calmed by the nurse's manner, we went back to sleep, too naive to be alarmed.

At 4 a.m., there was a louder knock on our door. I was frustrated that my sleep was being interrupted again. The nurse turned on the lights this time and a doctor joined her. I couldn't imagine what was going on. The doctor introduced himself as Dr. Miller, a neonatologist. I didn't even know what a neonatologist was. Dr. Miller proceeded to tell us that Derian had a heart problem, but was unsure of the type, so he'd put a call into a cardiologist who would run some tests and then make a diagnosis. He clasped his hands together as he said; "I've scheduled Derian for heart surgery tomorrow morning."

Robb and I looked at each other in complete disbelief. This couldn't be happening! Not to our baby! Not to us! We were so stunned by this news that nothing else registered.

When the doctor finished speaking, I asked if I could see Derian. United Hospital is attached to Children's Hospital so the nurse led Robb and me down the hall toward the NIC Unit. On a pre-birth hospital tour, I remembered feeling sad learning that some pregnancies ended up there. Rows of cribs, beeping machines, and lullabies soothing naked babies whose skin hung from their tiny skeletons never left my mind. Some of those babies cried newborn cries, while others cried without making sounds. Many were sleeping attached to a machine. One baby was wearing her dad's wedding ring—on her wrist. It was strange I didn't recall Robb and I ever speaking about "those people" or "those babies" following the tour. *How ironic that we had become one of "those" people with one of "those" babies.*

The NICU had a cubby-like entrance off the main hall. A huge sign over the doorway had the following rules:

1. Wash hands with soap thoroughly

2. Put on gown

3. Ring buzzer and identify yourself

We followed the instructions, and the double doors opened as a nurse greeted us. I searched the long row of incubators for our child. The nurses smiled at us as we made our way toward Derian. Some of Derian's chest peeked out in between the thick stickers that were attached to wires. Each wire was attached to a machine. Derian's nurse explained that the machine was monitoring and recording the rate of his heart.

This new environment put me into a dazed state; thinking and feeling seemed impossible. It looked so complicated…machines, wires, tubes, and the sounds of different beeps that filled the air. *Why did Derian have to be here?* I kept a safe distance from our baby in the incubator. I didn't want to get too close to him. *What if he would die?*

Robb and I held hands as we looked at Derian. There was nothing to say. We didn't know him, we didn't know what to do and even if we did, it was obvious from the sight of everything that we couldn't do anything for this child. The care he needed was way too advanced for us. I wanted to get out of this place. I looked down at Derian one more time and made my way back to the entrance. I couldn't help but notice the other babies on my way out; each was attached to different equipment. Some babies were only inches long, and had tubes sticking out of them. Many had paper cups protecting the IV placed in their heads. What kind of paraphernalia would our child end up with?

Our heads hung low as we made our way back to our room. We called our parents and let them know what was going on. Robb made his call first. I heard strength in his voice. He was trying to be brave for his parents and me, but his pain won out. He began to sob as he told them about Derian. I saw the dad in Robb. For the first time we were more than husband and wife—we were parents. When I called my parents, I got as far as saying "Mom" before I began to sob. Robb took the phone and explained what was going on. I had never seen so much strength in Robb before.

I felt like a small child resting in Robb's arms as we waited. Even though it was the middle of summer, my teeth chattered and my body shivered uncontrollably. This was FEAR. I hadn't known what it was until this moment. My fear was growing at such a fast rate I couldn't process what was going on. The only thing I understood was that our little baby wasn't going home. He was having heart surgery in less than twenty-four hours.

I knew it was in poor taste to call a bride before noon the morning after her wedding night, but I knew Gail would want to know what was going on with our "Skeeter." I wept as I spoke with her. Gail could listen but had no cure. We had not prepared for this!

Our families arrived at the hospital around 6 a.m. for our meeting with the doctor. We had never greeted each other with tears before. We held hands, and our two families merged into one as we prayed for our Derian.

A doctor came in to tell us that Dr. Hesslein would be the cardiologist performing a heart catheter procedure. That test would determine what was wrong with Derian's heart and, therefore, what would need to be done to correct it. If all went as planned, Dr. Hesslein would have the test results by four that afternoon. Since the hospital discharge time was 10 a.m., our families began to pack up our suitcases, flowers, and gifts and load them into the car. Somehow, we felt we needed to abide by those rules.

Dr. Matt called just before we were discharged. Apparently she had turned her pager off and hadn't realized what was going on until moments ago. I began crying as she told me how sorry she was and that she understood how leaving Derian in the hospital would be the hardest thing I would ever do. When I heard those words, something deep within me bellowed. I didn't care that the room door was open. I didn't care that people could hear me crying. This wasn't fair. I had done everything right. Dr. Matt said she would meet us at the hospital that afternoon for the cardiologist's report. I was glad she would be there.

After I hung up, a nurse came in to discharge me. She went through a checklist that explained what we would need to do for the care of our newborn at home. As she ran down the list, I realized none of these instructions would apply to me. I wouldn't be taking his temperature, giving him a bath or caring for his umbilical cord. Why did we have to go through this stuff? It was apparent to this nurse as well. I looked at her with tears in my eyes as she continued down the list. We connected as women and as mothers, and the pain of the situation allowed the nurse to cry with me.

When we finished with the discharge papers, she walked me down the hall to the car. This was not the way I had envisioned leaving the hospital. I expected a cart full of flowers, balloons, and most importantly, a baby. So many thoughts filled my mind that, at one point, I stopped and asked the nurse, "Are people going to feel uncomfortable around me now? How are they going to treat us?" Tears welled in her eyes as she reached for my hand and sandwiched them between her own. "You will find your way, Patsy Keech. You will find your own way to deal with all this." I hoped she was right. When I opened the car door and saw the empty car seat, the woman I had been and the mother I had become collided.

The car ride was filled with disappointment. Robb and I held hands, but our hearts bled in silence. Pulling into the driveway, seeing the "It's a Boy" sign on the garage would have been an exciting sight, had things gone as we planned. All the preparation we did to welcome our child into the world were reminders of the way things should have been. I had failed to have a healthy baby. *I must have done something wrong to make my baby sick. Did I think or say something that could have caused this? Why had my body betrayed me?*

At home, I inched my way to the cradle, slid my finger along the rail and picked up the crisp white baby quilt. The silky edges felt cool between my fingers, I could smell the sent of baby powder as I buried my face into it. Robb put his arm around me as we knelt in front of the empty cradle and wept. This was the first time we had ever cried together. When we could cry no more, Robb helped me stand up, and tucked me into bed. As close as we might have felt in those moments, we needed time to be alone. We had to deal with our emotions in different ways.

While Robb needed quiet, I needed to talk to someone! I called Pastor George from our church and told him about Derian. We were some-what new to this church, yet George offered to meet us at the hospital for the cardiologist's report. A few more calls, a few more hours passed. The phone rang. It was Heather, Robb's sister. We were in the begin-ning stage of our relationship. "Patsy, I just got off the phone with my mom. I am praying for you and little Derian. I know we have bumped heads many times, so Derian has to be as stubborn as we are. I know he will fight his way through this." I wanted to believe what she told me.

Resting was not doing a thing for me. I called out for Robb...no answer. I called out again and received no answer. I wandered out of our room to look for him. I heard the television downstairs. Robb was lying on the floor watching *Hook*—one of our favorite movies. I sat next to him and tuned into the part of the movie where Pan is trying to find his "happy thought," the thought that would enable him to fly. Tinker Bell is trying to help him, but without a happy thought, he can't get off the ground. After several failed attempts, he remembers the birth of his first child. As Pan thinks of this moment, he begins to soar. His happy thought was being a daddy. Robb turned to me and tearfully said. "Patsy, being a daddy is my happy thought, too." I put his hand on my babyless belly and told him he was.

Linda Pots, a counselor at the school I worked at, phoned later that afternoon. "Patsy, I just heard about your baby, and I wanted to let you know I walked in your same shoes twenty years ago." *Your same shoes— she knew how it felt? And she made it!* How wonderful to know someone else who understood. From that moment she became my soul mate. She offered me support in ways no one else could.

At 3:30 p.m. we headed back to the hospital for our meeting with the cardiologist. The family waiting room was a good-sized room with lots of chairs, a television, and a small leather couch. Our parents were there; as well as my sister Colleen and her boy friend Joe, my brother Tom and his fiancée Kathy, my brother Tim and his girlfriend Jeannie, Dr. Matt, and Pastor George. Robb's sister and Aunt Jean lived in Wisconsin, but were waiting for a call following the meeting.

Five, ten, then fifteen minutes passed. Finally the door opened and a thin, middle-aged man wearing wire-rimmed glasses and a wild tie walked in. I sensed a gentleness in this man as he made his way to the center of the room, I could tell he was visually rounding us up. No doubt he felt outnumbered.

He asked if any of us worked in the medical profession and then grinned and said, "I hope you aren't all lawyers!" With that, the intensity of the room lightened up. We liked this guy. He introduced himself as Dr. Hesslein. "Which of you are Derian's parents?" This was a transitional moment, the first time Robb and I introduced ourselves as

Derian's parents.

As we stepped forward in front of our families and claimed Derian, a separation was established. We were responsible for this child. Prior to this moment I had secretly regressed back to childhood. I assumed our parents would be the ones the doctors would speak with and explain things to. But that wasn't happening. From the beginning of Derian's crisis, the staff had been speaking directly to Robb and me...now Dr. Hesslein was doing the same thing. Looking back on this, I am grateful the hospital staff helped shape me into becoming Derian's mom.

Since none of us had a medical background, Dr. Hesslein drew us pictures of a normal heart and then showed us what Derian's heart looked like. I was amazed at his teaching ability and how clearly everyone seemed to understand his findings.

I, on the other hand, could not concentrate. I didn't feel like learning about my son's heart. I wanted to be at home, getting to know who he was. I kept looking at the doctor, nodding my head like I understood what was going on—even though I didn't. Frankly, it was more important to me that I liked and trusted him. After all, I was turning my baby over to him. The stakes were high. I wanted to see this doctor's soul and make sure he was the person to whom I should entrust Derian.

It was obvious Dr. Hesslein loved his job, and cared about children. I was sure he would do the best he could for Derian. He was optimistic that Derian would do fine and assured us that he would live a very normal life. Realizing that he'd given us an incredible amount of information, Dr. Hesslein invited questions. He promised he would explain things as often as we needed.

"When will Derian be able to come home?" I asked.

"In seven to ten days."

It wasn't all that long, but I felt ripped off. I buried my face in my sister Colleen's lap and cried. I was exhausted. My feet were swollen, so swollen that the skin around my ankles was bruised. I was supposed to be resting, taking care of myself. Instead, I was in the trenches, pushing myself—I had to be there for my baby. If I didn't initiate a relationship with Derian now, I might never get the chance. Robb and I went to the NICU and kissed Derian goodnight. Fear followed us home. We lay frozen in bed that night, staring at the ceiling, wondering what tomorrow would bring.

Chapter 3

Robb woke me up with a kiss and whispered, "Happy Anniversary, Patsy." In the midst of our whirlwind crisis, I had completely forgotten. From now on we would have two special days to mark on August's calendar: August 2—Derian's birthday and August 4—our anniversary.

Derian was awake when we got to the NICU. His brown eyes pulled me in. I looked away—too afraid of getting close. When I looked back, his eyes stared deeply into mine. *Did he know me? Did he know I was his mommy? What was he thinking?* I spotted a yellow box with our names on it behind Derian's incubator. I opened the card:

> *Dear Patsy and Robb,*
>
> *You are in my thoughts and prayers. Patsy, I remember you talking about Mary, the mother of Jesus during one of our walks. This statue reminded me of the three of you—beginning your own family journey. Robb, you must lead your family just as Joseph led his family. I will keep the three of you in my prayers. We will get together when I return from my honeymoon.*
>
> *All my love,*
>
> *Gail*

She had been here and had seen Derian. I could feel her presence.

The nurse notified us when our families had arrived. Derian was only allowed three visitors at a time and was not to be held. Robb decided to wait in the waiting room so everyone would get a chance to see Derian before surgery. My dad and Colleen were the first ones to meet Derian that morning. The three of us huddled together as we scanned Derian's newborn body. My dad held his feet and Colleen stroked his wisps of baby hair. I looked at his smooth chest. This would be the last time I would see it like this. In a few hours, he would forever bare a scar that would remind us of this day.

"Have you baptized Derian, Patsy?" my dad asked.

I hadn't thought of it! I panicked. *I know he needs to be baptized so he can go to heaven.* "Dad, I don't know how to do it."

My dad took control of the situation. "Get some water."

I obediently asked Derian's nurse, who handed me a small bottle of sterile water. Dad cupped his hand and poured in the water. With wet fingers, he traced a cross on Derian's forehead. "God, we ask you to protect Derian today. We thank you for the gift of him. We bless you, Derian, in the name of the Father, Son, and Holy Spirit."

That was it—Derian was baptized. Colleen and my dad gave Derian a gentle kiss on his newly baptized forehead, squeezed his hand and told him they loved him. The rest of the family had some time with Derian before Robb and I returned.

Robb and I held Derian's hands as we waited for things to happen. Three people dressed in white gowns wearing blue puffy hairnets gathered around us and introduced themselves as the anesthesiologist, surgery assistant, and nurse. They briefly re-summarized what was going to happen to Derian during the surgery and handed us a consent form to sign. We were allowed to give Derian one more hug before the team picked him up and whisked him away. Tunneled in confusion, terror, despair, and anger, we watched as they maneuvered their way through the unit with our baby. As the team went out the door, the anesthesiologist turned his head and said in a confident voice, "We'll take good care of him, Mom and Dad." Hearing those words offered comfort. They cared about our baby.

At that moment Robb's and my relationship changed. We never needed each other as much as we did at that moment. No one else could feel the way we felt. We grew into a connected force: Derian's parents. In an effort to bond with Derian I reached into his clear crib and felt the warmth his body left behind, picked up the blanket that was under him, and smelled it. The sweet baby smell I anticipated was buried under the harsh burnt smell of the heat lamp. I had nothing of his, not even his smell!

We left the NICU with Derian's hospital blanket, and met our families in the waiting room. The television was on and everyone was pretty quiet. We were lost in our own thoughts until the surgeon entered the room. Dr. Nichols was dressed in dark blue scrubs and seemed to be in a hurry. He quickly shook our hands as he introduced himself. I found my eyes drawn to his hands. *Did he have any idea the important job those hands were about to perform?* I didn't want to let go of his hand. I wanted to hold onto the hand that would soon enter Derian's heart. Dr. Nichols went over the procedure once again. It all had been explained to us several times. I wondered if he was having a good day? Did he eat breakfast? Was his mind primed to do a good job for Derian? The surgery was going to last between five and seven hours. I was relieved to hear him say a cardiac nurse would give us a report each hour. He paused to see if we had any last questions and then promptly went on his way.

We began our five-hour wait and increased our prayers.

An hour into surgery, Nancy, one of the cardiac nurses, stopped by to tell us everything was going fine. She was an experienced nurse with a kind personality. Her insights and report kept us connected to Derian.

Two more hours passed, two more positive reports.

The next time Nancy stopped by with a report she brought several tubes along with her. She explained the purpose of each tube and where it was located on Derian's body. As we listened, I wondered if Derian's body was big enough for so many attachments.

Nancy's last report brought great news! "The surgery is over; Derian did just fine." Thank you, God! Everyone loosened up and breathed a deep breath of relief. Nancy let us know Dr. Nichols would be stopping by to give us a report.

Minutes later, Dr. Nichols surprised us with his quiet entrance. As we listened to his report, we couldn't help but be distracted as Dr. Nichols referred to Derian as "she." No one corrected him. That oversight served as a much needed laugh when someone made the comment, "I guess specialists are so specialized they don't notice anything other then the part of the body they're working on."

It became obvious to Robb and me that we both had picked up on different things from Dr. Nichols' report. Robb focused on the technical stuff of surgery, while I zeroed in on things like how long Derian would be in the hospital, and what recovery involved. With so much information, there was no way any one person could absorb it all, so if we both listened to specific things we had a better chance of getting most of it.

"Derian is on his way. Go out into the hallway if you want to see him," Nancy announced. We hurried into the hallway to greet our hero. The heaviness of the equipment vibrated under our feet as several nurses pushed it down the carpeted hall. Derian was in the center of this parade on a full-sized gurney. His chest was stitched from his sternum bone to just below his rib cage. Tubes extended from his heart…a catheter protruded his penis…and IVs stuck out of his neck…his entire body was connected to machines.

Although Nancy had prepared us, seeing Derian like this terrified everyone. My dad breathed heavily—something he did when he was overwhelmed. The surgical team got Derian and all of his machines into the elevator. They were bringing him to the PICU—the Pediatric Intensive Care Unit—where they would hook him up to more machines. After what seemed like another hour, Nancy brought us to see Derian.

I could smell vanilla. It was strange to smell something so comforting as I scanned Derian's body. His newborn skin that was once soft to touch was now so puffy and swollen that it shone. A blue accordion-looking tube protruded from his mouth and his lips were taped in a fish-face position. Ointment was globbed on his eyelids and lips to keep them moist under the heating lamp. Gauze was placed over Derian's incision —and covered the trunk of his body. The vanilla-smelling chest tube stuck out from the base of the gauze. This tube ran from Derian's chest down to the floor. As the medicine required total darkness, the tube was wrapped in tin foil. This tube needed to be stripped every half an hour to allow excess blood to pass through it. A small Velcro strip attached to his big toe monitored his heart. Every breath, every heartbeat, was monitored. Underneath all the equipment was the baby I had carried.

I wasn't overwhelmed with the motherly love everyone talks about as I looked at our baby. He was connected to so many things—yet the most natural connection of all wasn't hooked up. I needed to protect my heart; I didn't want to love him until I knew he was going to be okay. Before Robb and I left for the evening, Derian's nurse let me know it was okay to call and check on him in the middle of the night. Knowing I could connect with him from home made me feel welcomed in this strange new environment.

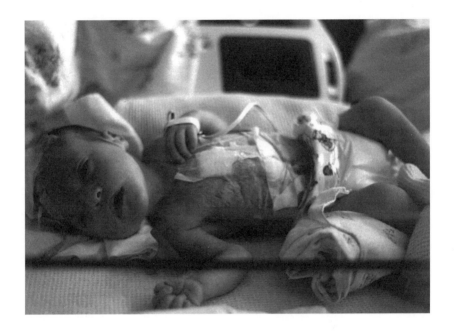

Chapter 4

August 5—Day 3

I was unable to get out of bed the next morning. I called the hospital to check on Derian and told the nurse I wasn't sure what time I would get there. To my horror, I ended up sleeping most of the day.

That evening Robb called Dr. Matt to see if this was normal. Since my hemoglobin was low when I was discharged, she wanted me to be seen. Robb was worried I would be admitted, and he would be running between Derian and me. He helped me to the car, and we set off for the hospital.

As wiped out as I was, a surge of energy sprang forth as we got closer to the hospital. Once we arrived, I felt fine. I was sure it was because we were close to Derian. The tests came back normal; no one could explain what happened. Perhaps I was simply emotionally and physically exhausted.

I felt positively giddy as we walked to the Pediatric Intensive Care Unit. I was thrilled to be able to see the new little man in our life. We checked on Derian and chatted with his nurse. It was a fulfilling visit for me. As I held the little foot that used to kick the inside of my belly something inside me changed. By the end of that visit, I was ready to take a risk with Derian.

That morning in church, Pastor George invited Robb and me in front of the congregation of Saints Martha and Mary's Episcopal Church. George explained what was going on with our baby and led a prayer that asked for strength to get through this struggle. He ended by asking everyone to keep us in their prayers throughout the week. Having the congregation's prayer support meant so much.

August 6—Day 4

Robb dropped me off at the hospital that morning and I spent the day with Derian. While I was there, I got to know the nurses who were working with Derian. His day nurse was named Eda. At first, I thought she was kind of rough—but as I continued to watch her care for him, I viewed her differently. During the course of 12 hours, Eda painted pictures of who my son was by saying little things like, "He's got a temper!" "He's a wild man!" "He's being naughty." I became proud of the fact that he was a fighter, even if he gave her trouble once in awhile. I liked Eda and appreciated the care she gave to my son.

It was during that 12-hour day that my breast milk came in. Eda showed me to a hospital room. Since I had originally planned on nursing, I was committed to pumping and freezing my milk. This was something I could control in the middle of this uncontrollable situation. I wanted Derian to have the best formula of all and from what I had heard about breast milk—it could cure anything. I felt proud I could do something for Derian that no one else could.

I was glad to see Robb when he came back to the hospital to get me that night. It had been a long day! Robb got the day's report, greeted Derian, and took us home.

August 7—Day 5, very early in the morning

"Ring, Ring, Ring." As I fumbled to answer the phone, I noticed it was 1 a.m. *Who would be calling us at this time in the morning?* "Hello."

"Patsy Keech?"

"This is the Keechs."

"Patsy, Derian's condition is declining rapidly. Come to the hospital immediately!"

"We'll be right there!" We quickly dressed and ran out to the car.

Robb and I had never prayed out loud together prior to this moment. I got down on my knees in the Escort and pleaded for Derian's life. In the middle of the prayer that spewed from my lips, I looked at Robb. I was embarrassed he had seen me pray like that, so I sat back down and put my head on his shoulder. "Patsy, don't give up on him. Keep praying!" I got back down on my knees and prayed—this time for both of us.

Robb whipped the car into an ER parking spot. We bolted out of the car and ran up to the third floor. As we turned the corner of the unit, I felt relief in the air. I could tell the medical staff was relieved—the crisis was over. The nurses that hovered over Derian somberly smiled at us as we entered the unit. We had no idea what to expect, but whatever it was it had to be bad—the hospital doesn't call in the middle of the night for nothing. I felt more lost at that moment than I had that whole week. We waited in the middle of the room for someone to come. A few minutes passed before Dr. James approached us. Before he spoke, he brought his hands together and breathed deeply. I couldn't foresee anything but serious trouble. Sweat began to run down my back and my arms; I squeezed Robb's hand as hard as I could. Dr. James sounded like an FM radio announcer working the late night shift. In soothing tones, he calmly told us Derian's heart had stopped. They worked on him for ten minutes before his heart began to beat on its own. He ordered a few tests and x-rays and hoped the results would shed light on what was happening.

He had been dead for ten minutes! My heart felt like it was being shredded on a cheese grater. I couldn't take any more news like this. I became numb; my soul was vacant. I looked at Robb and faded from the conversation. I couldn't understand all the technical jargon involved in keeping my son alive. I wanted to be dumb to all of it; I just wanted to know him as a little boy, a human being, a person, our son.

I needed to talk to my mom. Hearing the sound of her voice made me feel better. I hung up and stood next to the child I wanted to mother. This baby of ours was so fragile. His skin was stained with the blue tinge of death, his body felt cool. I sensed he was not going to be my baby for very long. I felt like taking back the bond we had formed—Derian was far too scary to love.

Robb came over to Derian's crib, took my arm and said, "Let's go." I was jolted by those words; I wasn't sure leaving was the right thing to do. "Patsy, we can't do anything more here." Somehow, that made sense to me. But before I left, I had to let Derian know what love felt like. In his four days of life most of what he had know was pokes, IVs, stitches, and the sounds of machines. If Derian really were to die, I wanted to be sure he felt love while he was on this earth. So I touched him, I stroked his few baby hairs, picked up his feet, and wiggled and kissed each toe.

Love was the only thing in this technical mess that Robb and I could give him. That night was my farewell to Derian.

We walked with heavy hearts into the darkness of the morning. Once again, we were going home without our baby; this time the chill of death hung in the air.

I woke later to the sound of running water. In my sleepy state, it took me a while to recognize the sound of the shower. Robb must be going to work. I couldn't believe he could think of going to work! As far as I was concerned, the outside world just didn't matter anymore—but it did for Robb. He needed to get to work; he needed something else to think about—he needed a different place to be. He kissed me and told me to take good care of our boy and be sure to call him with updates. I said good-bye without getting out of bed. The previous night was still fresh in my mind and my heart.

Pastor George gasped in horror when I called to tell him about Derian's cardiac arrest. I asked him to give Derian Last Rites. He agreed to meet at the hospital later that morning. As we hung up, I flipped through the pages in my little phone book and ran across the number of Sheila, one of the wisest women I knew. She had helped me work through difficult situations in the past. I was certain she would know what to do now. As I tearfully told her what had happened, she sensed I'd lost hope for Derian. She asked me to sit down and put together a list of all the good things Derian had brought into my life before returning to the hospital. We prayed over the phone and asked God to do His will, no matter what it was. I would not fight for my baby if God wanted him back—but if He was going to take him, he needed to take him now, before he suffered anymore. When we finished our prayer, she told me I was a good mom. I promised to call her as soon as I got any word on the test results.

I sat facing the empty cradle and composed my *"What Derian has given me"* list:

Robb and I bought a house.

We experienced the joy of preparing for the birth of our child.

I felt a baby move inside of me during pregnancy.

Robb and I experienced a deeper faith together—we bonded as a couple.

We fell in love a little bit more.

When I finished my list, I went to the mirror, took off my nightgown, and examined my stomach. The stretched-out skin was the evidence of a baby. As I traced the lines, I remembered the way Derian moved. God, I missed being connected with him. My soul cried.

Somehow, I managed to get myself to the hospital to meet Pastor George. I was late for our 11 a.m. meeting, but I didn't care. George was friendly, introducing himself to the hospital staff and got updated on Derian's condition. From the reports he was confident Derian didn't need Last Rites. It didn't sound as if Derian was dying. I had been deceived by that kind of reassurance once before. Derian's body was touched by death last night; I wanted him to be blessed no matter what the doctors said. George was sensitive to my needs and anointed Derian, while insisting I see to my own well being. "Patsy, make sure you are taking care of yourself! Derian will be keeping you so busy once he gets out of here." George was so hopeful, while I was sure Derian was going to die, that day.

I spent the entire day at Derian's bedside. My mom came to the hospital around dinnertime. She coaxed me to the cafeteria to get something to eat. I was nervous about leaving, but the nurses told me they would call me if I needed to come back—since everything was improving, they didn't expect anything to change. As Mom and I talked, I picked at my food. My mom tried to chip away at the darkness I felt. She had always been a big believer in affirmations, so throughout our meal she kept stressing how important it was to be positive and affirming to Derian. "You need to say things like…'Look how strong you're getting, Derian. You are a healthy, lovable boy.'" She also told me I needed to have a positive frame of mind when I was around him. I squinted at the light she cast my way. I felt safer in the darkness. I wanted and deserved to feel exactly the way I did and I resented her trying to take that away from me. When I couldn't stand her ministrations anymore, I politely suggested we go back upstairs. She continued talking, affirming all the way back.

When we got back to the unit, Derian's nurse asked if I would like to hold him. I couldn't believe it! I smiled a disbelieving smile and nodded "yes." It had been four days since I held him. All the tubes made me nervous; I didn't want to hurt him. I sat in the rocker and waited for the nurse to bring Derian to me.

How wonderful it was to feel the weight of his body resting on mine. Feeling him this close put me back together. The ache lost its grip. I marveled at his deep brown eyes. I traced his pug nose with my finger and stroked his feet. Tears dripped down my face, but this time they were happy tears. Without his touch, I felt empty. As I looked at Derian, I knew he knew I was the woman who loved him the most—I was his mom. It was then that I invited him into my heart. No longer was I afraid to love this child of mine; I would never give up on him again. He gave me the courage I needed. I held Derian for as long as the nurse would let me. How wonderful to feel like a "normal" mom! My mom's affirmations must have worked. We were both encouraged by Derian's responses.

I left the hospital on an absolute high that evening! Robb and I arrived home at the same time; he stared at me until he figured out what was different. "You're smiling. This is the first time I've seen you smile in days; what's going on?"

"Robb, I got to hold Derian tonight! The nurse helped me."

"Really! Do you think they'll let me hold him?"

"I don't know—why don't you call and find out?" This was the best conversation we had had in our driveway for a long time. Robb ran into the house to call the hospital. He came out wearing the same satisfied smile I had. "I can hold him as long as he's stable! I get to hold my son tomorrow!"

The clock couldn't tick fast enough for Robb. He was dressed and on this way to the hospital by 6 a.m. He didn't need to be at work until 9 a.m., so he had plenty of time to hang out with his son. Being able to hold Derian made the hospital bearable. We wondered if all parents got this excited about holding their children.

Strange as it may be, the trauma that surrounded the first few days of Derian's life drew Robb and me closer than we had ever been. When we had said our wedding vows three years earlier, I was hopeful I could live up to such a promise. Yet, Derian's birth reconfirmed the depth of my vows. I was a different woman now.

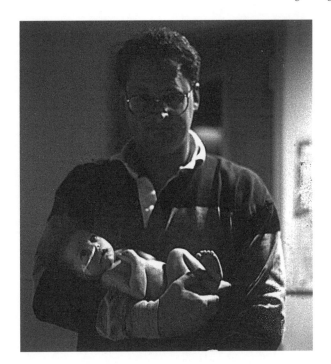

Chapter 5

The days blended into each other. Because of Derian's setback, he needed to stay in the PICU longer than what was first expected. I pumped several times each day; in fact, our freezer at home was filled with breast milk. Robb even showed off my frozen milk supply when people came to visit. I was frustrated spending so much time pumping in the hospital and at home in the middle of the night, and yet Derian was never able to have my milk. I kept asking day after day, "When will Derian be ready to start taking my milk?"

A young male doctor eloquently answered that question one day. "Mom, I know this is the one thing you alone can do for Derian, and you want to help him. Right now, you are doing everything you can. But we just have to wait and see when the timing is best for Derian." I was grateful he understood and had acknowledged my part in all of this. Motherhood was secondary to the medical world. "Keep your milk supply going so you will be able to help Derian when the time is right."

The hospital was becoming my new home. Because I was spending far more time there than at home, I got to know the staff. We had shared many conversations in the hours we spent together; I felt close to many of Derian's nurses and felt more comfortable with his doctors. Each morning I attended rounds, and from those doctors, began to understand how the monitoring of weight, fluid intake, and fluid output helped the doctors determine what drugs and dosages were needed. In addition to getting an update of our child's condition and a peek into the medical plan, we could ask questions about where home fit into 'the plan'. Robb and I made a point to have one of us there each day.

Our days were filled with visits from family and friends. I realized that not every child or parent had as much support as we did. Some children didn't have any visitors; no one stopped by night or day to hold them. They were completely alone. This made me sad. It wasn't that their parents didn't care about them; many of them lived far away and had other children to care for. I was lucky to have the summer off so I could spend each day in the hospital with Derian. What would I have done if Derian were born during the school year, when I was teaching?

August 25th–Day 23

Teachers' workshops were scheduled to begin within a week. At this rate, my entire maternity leave would be gone before Derian was out of the hospital. I had to figure out a way to stay with Derian! I needed to learn about what kind of help was available to mothers in my situation. I quizzed social workers and others in a position to help. No one had any answers. I couldn't believe that nothing was designed to help families in our situation.

Since there was no sign of Derian going home, my principal suggested I extend my leave through the first trimester. Hiring a sub was the easy part of the puzzle; how to pay for it was another. As I thought this out, I realized Derian's health problems could complicate my ever going back to work, and yet I carried all the insurance benefits for our family. Derian was branded with the curse of a pre-existing condition. What medical insurance company would pick him up? Because of this, I knew there was no way I would ever be able to leave my job.

We used every cent we saved for the closing on our house. Since I was the one who wrote out our monthly bills, this financial issue rested heavy on my mind. I searched my brain for ideas on how to solve this problem. Each day I spent in the hospital I was determined I would figure out a way to be with Derian. I had no intention of letting him spend the day by himself.

One day, I came up with an idea. I would throw my own benefit in order to buy myself some time with Derian. I spoke with Robb's sister that evening and told her about my idea. Heather seemed pleased that I figured out a solution but was horrified to think that Robb and I had reached such a desperate state. In order to save our dignity, she intervened. She must have called Robb's Aunt Jean after we hung up the phone and told her of my plan.

Jean called later that evening and requested both of us to get on the line. "I want you to stay home with Derian. I am prepared to give you the money you would be paid if you were teaching." How would we ever thank her for such a gift? She bought us time to be with our son. I vowed to someday pass on the same gift to another family.

We moved out of the PICU and moved back to the NICU a week later. We made a big deal out of this graduation. Robb brought in bagels, juice, and a beautiful bouquet of flowers as a way to thank the staff that had taken care of Derian. We so appreciated all they had done, both for him and for us. Derian's last hurdle was eating. *How hard could that be?* We were sure it would be only a few more days until we could bring him home.

It took a few days to readjust to the NICU's routine and get to know the nurses. The best part of being in the NICU was that we had the opportunity to become normal parents. We could be as involved in Derian's care as we wanted—and WE WANTED! We changed diapers, took his temperature, and gave him baths. During rounds one day, I heard the nurses say they wanted to try Derian on the breast to see how he would do. I couldn't believe it! I ran to the phone to call Robb. He knew this was a big deal and was happy for me. I promised to call him and let him know how it went. Derian's nurse called the lactation specialist in for me. None of my friends ever had to go through breast-feeding training! All of the things that came so easily with other parents required planning and careful training for us. Gail returned from her honeymoon and came to visit that morning. It was wonderful and fitting to have her with me on this day. We both had experienced so much since Derian's birth.

The nurse wheeled a thin portable curtain stand behind me; this was considered privacy in the NICU. The lactation specialist gave me instructions on how to get Derian to latch on. "Latch on." Hmmm, that was a new term for me, and it didn't sound very comfortable. Once everything was explained, the nurse, Gail and the lactation specialist looked at me with "go ahead eyes."

Go ahead nothing! I can't pull my shirt up in public—this curtain thing is not going to do it for me.

I had moments to talk myself through this privacy issue. *Patsy, you have been waiting for this day forever. Do you want to pump in the dark with that stupid machine for the next year? Get over it, you're in the hospital and you're a mom, so who cares. Me!*

I took a deep breath, clenched my teeth, pulled up my shirt, and began to squeeze my nipple together like the lactation specialist said, and stuck it in Derian's mouth. It slipped out. After several tries, I was so frustrated that the lactation specialist did it for me. *Yeah, I had come a long way in a short period of time. Modesty was a thing of the past.* Derian was hungry and crying. I was frustrated and so was my audience. Together we decided to throw in the towel and resorted to plan B—the gavage feeding tube. We hoped tomorrow, things would be better.

Robb could hear my disappointment when I called him, but he assured me that next time things would go better. The lactation specialist was concerned Derian didn't have a strong suck, so she asked a speech specialist to examine him the following morning.

Two speech clinicians showed up the next morning to examine Derian's face. Their conclusion was that Derian had facial palsy. They would help figure out a way to compensate for the weakness in his oral muscles. I vaguely remembered hearing a doctor speak of this condition. But since it wasn't obvious, I didn't think it would be a big deal. Now, I had to deal with it.

Derian's heart problems were fixable and on the inside—no one could see them. Everyone would notice a facial palsy. This meant teasing in school and stares from strangers. Each time I heard "facial palsy", my ears stung. I liked Derian's face just the way it was. It hurt to hear it described as a medical defect.

In order to determine what modifications could be made for Derian to be successful at breast-feeding, the clinicians wanted to watch me nurse him. Picture this: New mom, hungry baby, two speech clinicians, a lactation specialist, and a nurse all watching me. Boy, motherhood had yanked me out of my comfort zone. Just as I squeezed my nipple to place it in Derian's mouth, a team of doctors rounded the corner. Milk shot from my breast across the room and hit the lead doctor in the arm. He looked around to see what hit him before he continued speaking. I broke into an embarrassed laugh, I never had thought of my breasts as squirt guns.

Now I was really determined to figure this out! To my amazement, Derian latched on and I felt gentle wet squeezes on my breast. I shared my excitement with the whole crew. I was doing it! I was feeding him! It was a small step, but it was indeed a step. Derian and I were becoming a team.

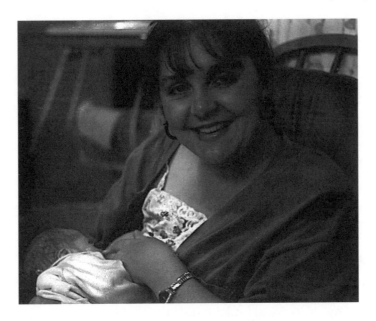

After a few days we got the hang of it, yet Derian wasn't gaining weight. Since he had a gavage tube the staff could measure what Derian had eaten after each feeding and then send it back down his tummy. He was lucky to get an ounce of milk and that just wasn't enough. So a new feeding schedule was made: we would rotate nursing and the bottle for each feeding. Robb felt bad that things weren't working like I had hoped…but he couldn't hide his excitement either. Now he would be able to feed Derian! We would still use my milk; I just wouldn't nurse him as often.

That night Robb gave Derian his first bottle. The nurse handed him a tiny cylinder that looked like a doll bottle containing three ounces of breast milk. Robb got comfortable and snuggled Derian into his side. The nurse gave him detailed instructions on where to place the bottle in Derian's month and how to hold it. *Are we just weird parents or what? How come we need so much help to do such simple things for our child? Even kids can put a bottle in a baby's mouth.* Derian couldn't get anything out of the bottle so Robb switched to a different nipple and tried again. Still no progress. We left the hospital that evening extremely frustrated! We thought eating would be so easy. Before Derian could go home he would have to be able to drink at least six ounces per feeding. Six ounces seemed impossible!

A few days later Robb called me from the hospital after feeding Derian the first bottle of the day. Pride boomed through the telephone. "Patsy, Derian drank three ounces of milk for me this morning!" I was excited for him—and a little jealous. Now there was pressure for me to do just as well.

Just as I had feared, Derian would only take an ounce from me. He wanted to nurse, so we did a bottle/breast combination until we got to two ounces. Then we quit. Both times that day, Derian drank only a few ounces for me. But when Robb came that night, Derian drank three ounces. GRRR! Maybe I wasn't pushing Derian hard enough. The next day, Derian was back to his usual non-eating habits and put all of us in our place.

Within a few days we were close to reaching our six-ounce goal. In fact, the word "home" came up more and more in our conversations with the doctors. My dad affectionately referred to my daily hospital reports as the "Derian Daily."

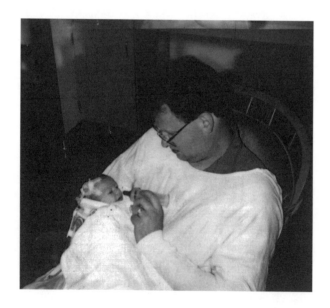

Chapter 6

"Home" was a carrot that dangled before us. We did everything we needed to do in order to get there. One of those things was to take an infant CPR class with our parents. The next was to learn how to insert the gavage tube in Derian's nose and feed him through it. For weeks I had promised Derian he wouldn't have to have that tube when he went home. Now it was going to go home with us. On my day of training I confessed to the nurse, "I don't think I can stick that thing in my child's nose."

"Well, you won't be able to bring Derian home unless you can, Patsy" Since I was left without a choice, I picked up the tube, prepared the supplies, and stood over Derian. Derian looked up at me with eyes that seemed to say, "Don't tell me you're going to hurt me, too!" He wiggled his head around as I began to push the eight-inch tube into his left nostril. It killed me to do this to him. The nurse could tell I was freaking out. I was a mom first and a nurse second. She shouted out, "Keep going Patsy, you can do this." Derian continued thrashing his head. Since I was afraid I would hurt him, I stopped.

I looked at the disappointed nurse. "I know I can do this but I need to do it differently than you." I held Derian's face in my hands "Derian, if there is anything I could do to get out of this, I would. I don't ever want to hurt you. But I want you to come home and this is the only way I can do it. Can you work with me on this?" He must have understood. The next time he kept his body still enough for me to get the tube in, feed him through it, and take it out. This was success!

We went through the same procedure the next day on the alternate nostril. I pushed it in just like the day before, but couldn't find the spot that allowed the tube to loop over the bone in the nostril. I tried to do it twice, then the nurse tried; she couldn't get it either. Derian was going crazy by that time so we put it back to the other nostril. Another try and still no luck. Why wouldn't this work? What was wrong with his nostril? The answer to these questions would be revealed to us at a later date.

Days later, Dr. Glenn, the chief of NICU, asked me if we would like to take Derian home Labor Day weekend. I couldn't believe it. "What?" He asked me again, "Would you like to take Derian home this week-end?" My heart beat wildly. I needed to jump or yell. I had so many peo-ple to tell! Wow! This sounded unreal. I skipped to the phone and deliv-ered an upbeat "Derian Daily" to Robb. This was it! This was what we had been waiting for!

My friends from college were coming to visit that weekend. The idea of showing them our house and having them meet our baby thrilled me. The hours couldn't pass fast enough. I was at home preparing for Derian's homecoming when the phone rang. I was surprised when I heard Dr. Hesslein's voice on the phone. He never called us at home. "Hi, Patsy, I'm afraid I'm not going to be able to let Derian go home tomorrow."

"Why not? What's going on?"

"The x-rays and echo cardiogram all show that Derian's heart is signif-icantly enlarged with fluid. Patsy, I've scheduled Derian for heart sur-gery tomorrow. We have to drain that fluid before Derian gets into trou-ble again." He apologized before I dropped the phone.

I knew it was a trick. Why did I think Derian would ever be able to come home? I lay on the bed next to the phone and sobbed for several min-utes before I realized I was not alone. Dr. Hesslein was still on the phone. "Whatever is best for Derian," I whispered.

"Patsy I share in your disappointment. I'm so sorry. I'm going to call Robb at work and have him call you back." Dr. Hesslein took care of all of us that day.

I called my parents with the new "Derian Daily." "Not again!" Another stretch of eternity. Robb called a few minutes later. He seemed strong despite his disappointment.

Our families met again in the same hospital waiting area while Robb and I signed the surgery consent, kissed Derian good-bye, and sent him back into surgery. I was so mad at God that morning. *I told you I would give Derian back to you earlier—but I will be really angry if you decide to take him now!* I was open with Robb about my anger with God.

"Patsy, today's really not the best day to make God mad," he sternly said.

We met with our parents and settled in for another long wait. My dad looked around the room and said, "We really have to find a better place to meet." Surprisingly, this surgery was much shorter then the previous one. The nurses' reports were all positive. When the surgery was completed, we watched them wheel Derian to the third floor, and met him later in the PICU unit.

My aunt and uncle brought their four little girls to meet Derian the next day. Each of the girls had chosen a special gift for their new cousin; one by one I lifted them so they could present their gift to Derian. This scene reminded me of how Mary must have felt when the wise men presented her son with their gifts. I was touched by the respect they had for Derian. They took me out of the hospital for lunch that afternoon. I think I smiled the entire time. Their visit gave me hope—I was determined Derian would make it and be home soon.

The tubes in Derian's chest drained almost two ounces of fluid from his heart. Apparently, the first tubes had been pulled out too soon, and some of the fluid became trapped in the sac around the heart. Two days later the tubes were removed. I stopped asking about going home. I realized Derian was complicated; he would have to let us know when he was ready.

Chapter 7

On September 5, thirty-four days after Derian was born, Dr. Glenn asked if we were ready to take him home. "You mean for good? Are you serious?" I was ready, but felt that we were rushing things; he had had heart surgery just five days earlier. Dr. Glenn understood my hesitancy and suggested that we spend a couple of nights in the hospital outside of the unit with Derian. Apparently the NICU had a few sleeping rooms just for this purpose. We would be on our own but would have the hospital for back up in case we needed it. I couldn't wait to tell Robb!

Robb was as thrilled with this plan as I was—even if it meant two more days in the hospital. "Home" was on the horizon. Robb got on the loud speaker at work and shouted, "Derian's coming home! He's really coming home!" He headed to the hospital after work that night.

The nurse showed us to our room, once a broom closet. A tiny single bed was pushed up against the wall, a small corner table held a lamp, and—if everything was left this way—we would have just enough room for Derian's isolate. As small as that little room was, it represented something huge—INDEPENDENCE. This was the first time we had Derian to ourselves, without any doctors, nurses, or machines around. We could hear the sounds of Derian breathing within inches of us. What if he stopped breathing? It was humbling to think we would soon be the sole providers for Derian. We felt safe knowing help was a hallway away, but how about when we were home? Were we really ready for this?

When Robb's alarm went off, I reached over and checked on Derian. He was awake and cooing. Wow, what a cool way to wake up. We did it! We made it through the night. That morning I made a decision about what type of mother I was going to be. I wasn't a type A personality—even with a child like Derian. I just wasn't made that way. Worrying every day about germs and overprotecting Derian could never be a part of the way I lived. I thought it was important for kids to eat dirt, get dirty playing, and explore their surroundings. I was carefree and spontaneous. I knew I would be a good mom to Derian, but I also knew I was not ultimately responsible for this little guy's life—even the smartest minds almost lost him in their care. I gave myself permission to still be Patsy in addition to Derian's mom.

As we wheeled Derian back to the NICU, we felt confident we could take care of him ourselves. But we were plenty glad to have just one more night in the hospital. After spending 36 days in the hospital, Derian Keech was discharged on September 7, 1993—the first day of school!

The air felt light as I packed Derian's things and prepared for our departure. I had never had such a feeling of victory! We said our good-byes as the staff wished us luck. Our nightmare had ended. I believed we had put in our 36 days of hell and would be finished with hospitals when we left...well, at least for twelve years, when Derian would need his last heart repair.

The discharge nurse handed me a stack of papers with our doctor appointments for the next few weeks. Derian was scheduled to see the cardiologist, optometrist, neurologist, geneticist, development specialist, and an ENT (ear, nose, and throat physician). In addition to our appointment schedule, I also received handouts on recognizing heart failure or infection, information on gavage supply, and numbers to call in case of emergency.

We stood under a pink sunset and watched Derian take his first breath of fresh air before Robb buckled him into the back seat of the car. A feeling of coziness warmed me as the three of us drove home. It was a wonderful evening of "firsts"!

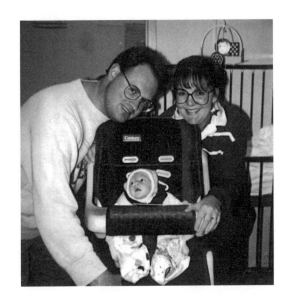

Movement Two—

Of a Time When You Were Mine…

Chapter 8

As I dressed Derian in his pajama's, I couldn't help but think about all those nights that I wondered what it would be like to tuck Derian in. I took my time putting on his pj's. No act of motherhood was taken for granted. Once he was in his pj's, I tried to bundle him in his blanket the way the nurses did. Derian looked at me as if he were saying, "Home feels so nice!" The glow from the moon shone on the floor as I rocked Derian in the quietness of home. He seemed so comfortable in the peaceful setting that he melted in my arms. It took us so long to finally have this moment. While I savored the feeling of being home, being normal, and new beginnings, Robb made a schedule of Derian's medicines and gavage-feedings.

The alarm went off at 4 a.m., time for Derian's feeding. Feeding was a two-person job in our house. One of us thawed the breast milk while the other prepared the syringe and the gavage tube. I uncapped the tube taped to his nose and attached an extension tube to the syringe. Robb poured the milk into the syringe, and we watched as it slowly dripped into Derian's tummy. Derian was oblivious to the whole thing. The process took about 30 minutes. It seemed so weird—thousands of new parents were up at this hour feeding their hungry infants; some with a bottle, some on the breast, and then there was the two of us.

We awoke to the sounds of a cooing baby that morning. I went across the hall and watched Derian interact with the bunny mobile that hung over his head. He kicked his feet freely and reached his baby hands toward the bunnies. His eyes traced the corner of his crib, the ceiling, and the objects in his room. He soaked up the sights of his home. Robb took off a couple of days so the three of us could indulge ourselves with each other's company. A home care nurse stopped by one afternoon just to make sure everything was going well. She was impressed with Robb's chart and left by saying, "Derian is in good hands." Playing the role of mommy and daddy, we spent those days on the floor with Derian. Derian was eating better than he ever had; being home agreed with him.

Derian's first big outing was going to church. Pastor George invited the three of us to the front to of the church to introduce Derian to the congregation. Everyone applauded and cheered! How wonderful it was for them to finally meet the little boy they had said so many prayers for. It felt wonderful to hold Derian and have people ask to see him. I was so proud showing him off.

I thoroughly enjoyed the fall of that year. Each day, I took Derian out for a long stroller ride to listen to the crunch of the leaves underfoot. I wanted Derian to see and experience the outdoors as we walked. Even though he couldn't understand what I was talking about, I pointed out what we saw on our way: trees, sun, grass, cars, dogs, etc. Being a mom was my favorite job!

Derian was under the watch of several doctors—we averaged five full-day appointments per month. But we could handle that because we got to bring him home. No matter where I was, hanging out with Derian each day was a gift.

At one of our doctor appointments it was suggested that we meet with a geneticist. We were nervous about what this appointment would tell us about Derian and our future children. The curtness of Dr. Snow didn't help. She began drilling us with questions about our families' medical history as soon as she walked into the office. Once she had the information she needed, she began to organize it into a genetic trait chart. I remembered studying genetics in biology; it was one of my favorite units. I had no idea that someday the principles would be applied to my life. When the chart was completed, she left the room.

While she was gone, Robb and I played with a wide-awake Derian, who was enjoying the sights in the office. There was a tone in this room that made my stomach knot. Dr. Snow was trying to discover something new for us to worry about. When she re-entered the room we sat a little straighter. Since Derian was awake, she decided to examine him. This seemed odd; she was a geneticist—why would she need to examine him? I placed Derian on the examining table and stood next to him. Robb was on entertainment duty: blowing bubbles and playing with toys to help Derian concentrate on something other than the doctor. When Robb got Derian to smile, Dr. Snow took a picture of Derian. Since she didn't express an interest in him as a little boy, it seemed odd that she would want to have a picture of him. What was she doing? I didn't like this visit. *Get to the point, lady, deliver the verdict, and leave us alone.*

When she was done with the pictures and her notes, she folded her hands and sat up very straight. Robb held my hand. We took a deep breath before she proceeded. "Derian has a syndrome called CHARGE. It is very rare, and it affects the following areas." She showed us a chart that broke down the features typical of children with CHARGE.

By the time she had finished explaining all this, I really disliked her. *She didn't know everything—we never met her before. How could she know all this about Derian with this simple exam?* She proceeded to show us pictures of children with CHARGE. I had to admit that Derian resembled some of these children. She told us many medical specialists had been involved in determining the severity of each condition Derian had. Since Derian had at least three of the conditions of CHARGE, her diagnosis was firm.

I didn't want to hear any more. "What caused this to happen?" Robb asked

"We don't know what causes CHARGE Syndrome. It's rare, affecting one in 10,000 births. We cannot predict when a child will have CHARGE. Typically, no one else in the family has similar problems. A very few families have had more than one person affected. There is no evidence that it is caused by any illness or exposure to drugs, medicines or any other substances before or during pregnancy."

Robb cut to the chase, "Could our next child have this same condition?"

She responded in a more upbeat voice. "When both parents are normal —neither has CHARGE Syndrome—the chance of a second child being born with CHARGE Syndrome is usually zero. If one parent has several features of CHARGE Syndrome, the risk of having a second affected child may be as high as 50 percent." That was reassuring, but what about Derian? *Would he ever be able to father a healthy child?*

Before we left, Dr. Snow gave us the only booklet written about CHARGE. We thanked her for her time, bundled Derian up, and left her office.

CHARGE CHARACTERISTICS

Condition	Problem Produced	Management
Coloboma of the eye	Partial vision loss—may affect peripheral vision or cause blind spots in the upper half of the visual field.	Glasses do not help visual field problems. Testing can determine if glasses are needed to near or far-sightedness and to determine the extent of the visual field loss. Special training needs vary with the visual field loss.
Heart defect	Variable—from just a murmur to being a "blue baby" and needing surgery	In some cases, the murmur goes away on its own. In other cases, drugs or surgery may be needed to correct the problem.
Atresia of the choanae	Blockage of nasal passages—child cannot breathe through nose properly.	Newborn babies may need surgery if the blockage is complete. Partial blockage may lead to increased nasal stuffiness and discharge.
Retardation of growth and/or development	Children may be short and/or mentally retarded.	Growth hormone shots may be needed for growth. Education evaluations and programs need to take vision and hearing losses into account as well as intellectual capabilities.
Genital hypoplasia	Boys—testes cannot be felt. Girls—external genital structures may be small. Both—delayed puberty.	Surgery may be necessary to bring testes down. Hormone shots or pills may be needed to induce puberty and strengthen bones.
Ear malformations	Outer ear—may look unusual. Ear canal—may be small. Middle ear—bones may be malformed. Eustachian tubes—may not work well causing ear infections. Inner ear—nerve deafness.	Surgery—on outer ears for cosmetic reasons. —on middle ear to open ear, —canal or to make bones work properly, —PE tubes to reduce recurrent infections and prevent temporary hearing loss due to fluid in the ears.

We studied the booklet as soon as we got into the elevator. We were both stunned to see a picture of a little boy who strongly resembled Derian. I looked at the information in the chart in order to prepare for what we might face. Nothing seemed as serious as the heart. As I continued flipping through the booklet, I glanced at the different categories: "Family Life." "Growth." "Maturation." "Vision." "Intelligence." I read the paragraph on intelligence:

> *"**Intelligence**: Intellectual ability may be limited. Children with CHARGE Syndrome range from normal intelligence to severe mental retardation. The level of intelligence may be difficult to assess if there is significant vision and/or hearing loss. It is absolutely essential for children with vision and/or hearing impairments to be evaluated by specialists in sensory deficits. Some individuals with CHARGE Syndrome can attend regular public schools with some special help. Others will require special school placement to get the attention and care they need to be able to learn."*

I hated this book! It offered no hope! This was obviously someone's research project and shouldn't have been given to parents. The authors didn't know my son. I refused to let them dictate what life would be like for Derian or our family. He would beat the odds and excel in each of the categories.

By the time we got home, I couldn't decide whether to keep the book or throw it out. Since it was the only information of its kind, throwing it out might not be the smartest thing to do. We decided not to share the information in this booklet with anyone. I buried it in a cupboard I never used. We simplified the diagnosis for our families and were optimistic about Derian's condition. Since CHARGE wasn't life threatening, we would be able to handle this. Nothing could top our first 36 days.

One of the most important things we had learned during that hospital stay was that doctors don't know everything. We had become confident enough to challenge the medical information we received. We respected our doctors and their knowledge, but we also knew God and his miracles were far more powerful than any doctor or prognosis.

Chapter 9

When we were not at a doctor appointment, Derian and I would hang out with Tammy, a stay-at-home mom who lived across the street from my parents. Tammy was a former elementary teacher who left teaching to be with her daughter Emily. Emily and Derian were good playmates, even though they were a year apart. Tammy was looking for a playmate for Emily, so when I asked her if she would watch Derian when I returned to work, she welcomed the idea. Derian was comfortable with Tammy, and I knew he and Emily would enjoy being together.

I returned to work right after Thanksgiving. As much as I worried about leaving Derian, I found that when the actual day arrived, I was thrilled to see everyone. Plus, Tammy kept such good notes about what she and the children did each day that I felt like I was with Derian anyway.

"Derian's going to be a Little Caesar's pizza lover! He went crazy with the paper ad. If his hair looks a little goofy in the front...sorry, Em was licking it. Derian really enjoyed watching her from the walker today."

"Derian played with his chimes for a long time today. He liked to make those growling sounds again, too. He sure is happy! Em and I get lots of smiles. He enjoyed reading books with us, especially Rudolph the Red Nose Reindeer.*"*

"Derian enjoyed looking at himself in the mirror and smiling. We went for a walk today, and he didn't enjoy it too much! He loved laying semi-nude in the sunshine—what are you two teaching this boy?"

I was a different teacher that school year. I found that by having a child of my own, I looked at life differently. This spilled over into my teaching. Because of Derian's imperfections, I was much more sensitive to

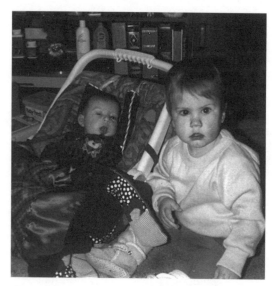

teasing. I let the students know I wouldn't tolerate any teasing because I knew how badly I would feel if someone were to tease my little boy. By promising students a safe, caring classroom, my discipline problems disappeared. They just didn't happen anymore.

Christmas was coming and we got ready for the holiday. It was going to be Derian's first Christmas and we wanted it to be unforgettable! We had a real Christmas tree so Derian could smell the fresh scent of pine. We put up outside lights and went to see Santa. As exciting as all of it was, I was exhausted ALL the time. I barely had enough energy to get through the school day and the evening with Derian.

One morning as I got out of the shower, I looked into the mirror...I really looked hard at my face. There was something too familiar to be ignored. Puffiness—my face was puffy! *Oh my God, I can't be pregnant. I just can't be!* "Robb, I think I'm pregnant."

With the hint of panic in his voice he said "WHAT! Why do you think you're pregnant?"

I responded logically. "Look at me—my face is puffy, I'm tired all the time, and I haven't gotten my period yet."

The thought of being pregnant so soon after our ordeal with Derian didn't excite me. Not because I didn't want another child, but Derian was only four months old. Robb couldn't stand not knowing one way or the other. That evening, I bought a home pregnancy test, took the test and lay down on the bed. So many thoughts flooded my mind as I waited for the results. Everything to come would be decided on the color of a dot; if it turned pink, our life would completely change. What would we do with two children? How would we afford it? What if we had another sick child?

I couldn't look. I gave Robb the box with the directions and asked him to tell me the results. He quietly came into the bedroom and gave me a long hug. I couldn't tell if he was holding me in relief or in fear. "What? What IS IT?"

"You're going to be a mommy again. I get to be another kid's dad," he said with a smile.

I could feel the color drain from my face. *"God, are you joking? How do you think I'm going to be able to be pregnant and take care of Derian at the same time?"* Robb was so good to me. He understood my fears and surprise. I was grateful for his support and immediate acceptance of this child. Without a minute of hesitation—he welcomed this news. Thank God, we had just gotten a good report from the geneticist.

I wished I could be like Robb, but labor was fresh in my mind. Each morning I awoke and thought, "Damn, I'm one day closer to labor." I was overwhelmed with the idea of two babies, plagued with another round of morning sickness and doctor appointments, and embarrassed to tell anyone I was pregnant. What were they going to think? I felt irresponsible. We just had this hair-raising, exhausting ordeal with Derian. What made us think we could afford another child? I wanted to wait before we told anyone about this pregnancy, but Robb couldn't keep such an exciting secret. He couldn't wait to let everyone know. Thankfully, people were supportive and happy for us.

I was the only one who was having a hard time accepting all of this until I told Gail. "Patsy, as soon as you said you were pregnant, I had a vision of two little angels who were going to be together." That night, I had a dream about what she said. There were two little angel boys who lived in heaven who were the best of friends. They spent their days flying around heaven, racing each other back and forth to the pearly gates. One day, one of the cherubs was called to earth to be a child. The friends tearfully said good-bye. Nine months passed and the little angel became a little boy and was welcomed into a family. Despite the love and attention he received, he missed his angel buddy, and his angel buddy missed him. The angel and boy devised a plan: Derian would return to heaven. Their plan didn't work the way they expected it to, and when God saw how miserable they were without each other, He decided they needed to be together again. From that dream on, I welcomed baby number two and considered him/her to be Derian's heavenly buddy.

At my first official baby appointment, Dr. Matt explained we could be extra cautious and take every test to ensure a healthy baby, or we could just let things be. Since terminating the pregnancy wasn't an option, she thought I might as well enjoy being pregnant and we'd handle things as they came up. She promised me at that appointment that she would deliver this baby unless there was a death in her family or one of her children was ill. I was grateful for her promise; I really wanted to have her deliver our baby. She knew so much about our family.

Derian was now able to sit, crawl, and drink a bottle on his own. He kept Robb and I so busy that we didn't have time to think about the "what ifs." Looking back now, I am very glad we just "got" pregnant. I don't think I would have ever been brave enough to choose having a baby again.

Derian loved being where the action was! Every day was a new adventure. He interacted with his environment and each person in it. He was an excitable yet easygoing baby. He made life fun for everyone around him. Derian's spirit seemed to communicate with the spirit inside of the person he was interacting with. He could coax the hero and the goodness out of anyone he connected with, whether it was a family member or someone he just met.

By nine months, Derian was trying to do everything other kids were doing. He played with such passion—he loved being a little boy! He was physically and mentally behind on a few things, but I chalked that up to losing a month of growth in the hospital. I decided to put the *What To Expect In The First Year* book away. I couldn't compare Derian's development to a healthy child's. As a way of coping, I decided to focus on Derian's progress.

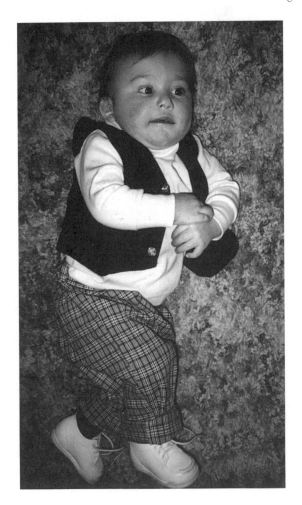

Chapter 10

That spring, Derian went for a hearing test. I was sick the day of the appointment, so Robb and Derian went without me. I was downstairs resting when they came home. Robb's feet were heavy as he touched each step. I sat up to welcome them home, but from the look on Robb's face I knew something was wrong. Before I had a chance to say anything, he gruffly spit out, "He's deaf."

Robb's anger faded into tears that dripped down his cheeks. "They said he was deaf in one ear and partially deaf in the other. They want him to wear hearing aids!" He laid his head in my lap and I held him. We looked at Derian scooting happily around the floor and wondered why.

"When do they think he will need them? How do they know for sure? Derian responds to us all the time. Maybe the test was wrong, Robb!"

"Patsy, the test he took measured the reaction of sound waves going to the brain. A hearing person would show activity on the screen. Throughout most of the test there was no activity, only a few pitches got a reaction. He's deaf." Robb was especially disturbed, perhaps because he saw this test with his own eyes; it's hard to argue with science.

I had a hard time believing the test; Derian responded to music, phones ringing, and doors shutting. The next few weeks we challenged the results of this test by purposefully making loud noises. Eight out of 10 times, Derian would look or respond accordingly. We shared the results of this test with family members; they also doubted the results. Robb and I were confident there was an error. We were going to get a second opinion.

A week later, Derian was scheduled to see Dr. Hesslein for an echocardiogram. We were sure we would get a positive report. We both took the day off for this test; experience had taught us that this procedure required the presence of both of us to be there. The information was too complicated for one person to assimilate. Besides, it was an incredibly long day.

The nurses that took care of Derian in the ICUs couldn't believe how he had grown. Derian thrived on attention; he delighted in their response as he showed them his new tricks. Then the tough stuff started. Derian was a good sport about almost everything, but despised having his blood pressure taken. Once the general tests were out of the way, the staff prepared Derian for the actual heart catheter. They applied Emla cream to his groin area where the catheter would enter the main artery. Once the cream was applied, our job was to entertain him so well that he would forget he was hungry. We watched Barney, blew bubbles, sang songs, and read books as we waited for Dr. Hesslein.

During the procedure, Dr. Hesslein would check the pressures in Derian's heart, measure its size, and take an overall look at its condition. We were much more relaxed with this procedure; it was a piece of cake compared to what he had already gone through. We gave Derian a hug and kiss and turned him over to the team. Derian welcomed the idea of meeting a new person, but when he saw we were not going with him he began to cry. The confusion in his sad cry tugged at the mother in me. I had just handed over the gold in my life. This was no simple act —even though we had given him away to surgeons before. There was no getting used to this. The truth was, each time I gave Derian to the hospital staff, I grew more uncomfortable. The more I knew about hospital life, recovery, procedure risks and surgery, the more apprehensive I became. So many times in the past, the focus began on one part of Derian's body, and then led to another part, which set us up for a brand new set of problems. Pandora's box was never closed.

Robb and I stood in the hallway listening to Derian's cries and waited until he was "safely" in the room. When the door closed, Robb put his arm around me and his hand on my pregnant belly. I loved when he did this.

We returned to Derian's room and waited. Periodically, the cardiac nurse would stop in with reports from Dr. Hesslein. All was going as planned. After several hours, Dr. Hesslein came into our room. At first, he was his usual cheerful, upbeat self, but his tone became serious as he began to tell us about Derian's heart. "The pressures in Derian's heart are much higher then they were when he left the hospital. This is very concerning to me because Derian's heart is working harder than it should. The good news is we can fix this. The bad news is the only way to correct this is through surgery. I know this is not something you were expecting or hoping for. This was a surprise to me as well."

I could feel my body getting heavier. "How long before this needs to be done? Would it be okay to wait until summer?" I asked.

"My wife is also a teacher, so I understand summers. That would be fine, but I would recommend having it done before the arrival of your new baby, perhaps in July." Baby number two was not expected until the beginning of September, so that would give us just over two months to pack in a surgery, recovery, and a new baby

We were crushed, our spirits so deflated we could barely finish our conversation with Dr. Hesslein. When he left, we closed the door and cried. This news slapped us across the face: first the hearing issue, now a heart surgery. The stress was so heavy we could hardly hold our heads up. We would deal with the hearing problem later; the heart took precedence over his ears. I hated the idea of bringing Derian back here. The last time we had started out with a single surgery and it led to other problems—36 days of problems. We were back where we started.

When we came to grips with Dr. Hesslein's news, we phoned our parents with the "Derian Daily." Disappointment blanketed our entire family. There was nothing anyone could say or do to make this better.

When Derian was wheeled back into his room, we put our feelings on hold and tended to him. He was drunk with Chloral Hydrate; his body was out of control. His arms, legs, head, and torso would flop back and forth uncontrollably; his eyes rolled into his head. It was horrible to see him like this and know more surgery lay ahead. I held him in a protective hold and waited for the drug to wear off. After several hours Derian was back to his regular self.

It was sunset before we said our good-byes to the staff and headed for home. Dr. Hesslein had told us someday that Derian's heart would require more surgery, but that wasn't supposed to take place until he was in his teens. This was happening too soon! While Robb drove, I watched the night sky swallow up the evening sun. So too, the hope of the beginning of our day was swallowed up.

There was a rose and some cookies from my mom on our doorstep when we got home. How I wished she could just take all this away. Derian slept between us that night.

Chapter 11

The morning light cast a grayish color between the blinds. Outside looked as bleak as I felt. "Robb, was yesterday a dream, or true?"

We turned on our sides to look at each other. Robb's finger caught the tears that ran down my cheek. His arm made a bridge over Derian and onto my belly. Helplessness, fear, and disappointment had invaded our lives and our children's lives. We had another person's future to think about in this mess. Bitterness poisoned my thoughts. *I've spent most of my life trying to do the 'right' thing, and this is my reward. Why is this happening to me? I did nothing to deserve this. We did nothing to deserve this. Why? Why must this blackness hover over us?*

I cried most of the way to school that morning. *How will I ever make it through the day?* I had told my students and co-workers about Derian's test. They would be wondering how things turned out. I wasn't strong enough to talk about yesterday without crying. A few friends greeted me at the front door. From my face, they knew things didn't turn out well. Before they asked anything, they hugged me. They shared my frustration as I told them of Derian's newest plight. Each time I explained the situation I felt the wind being knocked out of me. My mind kept spinning into different directions: lesson plans, set up surgery, finances, new baby, what's for dinner, etc. And my heart! My heart felt like it had a splinter in it the size of a tree branch.

During my prep time that day, I called Dr. Nichols' office to schedule a date for Derian's surgery. He had July 12 open, so I took it. I called Robb with the date so he could make arrangements at work.

The next day a co-worker met me at my classroom and gave me a rose. As she handed it to me, she whispered, "Enjoy him, Patsy." I immediately burst into tears and ran into the bathroom. I heard the warning bell ring—I had 2 minutes to gather my composure. Her brave act of kindness touched me so deeply. Once I regained my composure, I walked into my classroom with red eyes. The students could tell why I was late. They were especially quiet and cooperative that day. I was grateful my seventh graders respected me enough to give me a break. The rest of the school year was like that. My co-workers often found me in the bathroom or copy room crying. No one ever said much—just hugged me and told me they were praying for me.

One day, in my most challenging class, I lashed out at a student. He was whining about not being able to sit by his friend. "Mrs. Keech, you're not being fair." Irritated by his trivial dribble, I roared back, "What's not fair is that my kid has to have another surgery! If the worst thing that ever happens to you is that you don't get to sit by your friend, you should be so lucky!" I was losing it. Thank God, there were only eight school days left. As glad as I was for the school year to be over, I was not excited about re-entering hospital life.

I received a call a few days before school was out from Nicki, a childhood friend who lived in Arizona. Apparently, my mom had reconnected with Nicki's mother, Keri, and told her about the upcoming surgery. Nicki and Keri offered to pay half our plane fare so my mom and I could bring Derian for a visit. Robb was excited for my opportunity and encouraged me to go for it. The plan was made: we would spend a week in Arizona once school was over. This trip was a gift from friends as well as Robb. Each day we had with Derian was precious, but knowing heart surgery was coming up made the time more so. Robb gave us an extra-long hug as we boarded the plane.

I knew the flight would be long for every passenger if Derian were not entertained. Thankfully Grandma brought a "grandma goody bag" filled with little toys, crayons, coloring books, and other entertainment possibilities. When we tired of those things, Derian smiled and waved to everyone near us. Then he noticed the curtains that separated us from first class. The way the curtains waved each time someone went through them amused Derian. Soon he began to move the curtains back and forth himself. He laughed and giggled as he pushed them from side to side. The people sitting near us were amused at the joy he got out of such a little thing. Derian shared his joy freely.

We arrived and began our week of R&R. It didn't take Derian long to charm his way into our friends' hearts. They affectionately called him "Sweet Baby."

We were kept so busy the first few days I hardly had time to think about the upcoming surgery. By the fourth day, Derian and I began to miss Robb. It was obvious someone very important wasn't enjoying this vacation with us. Derian would jabber or gum the phone each time I spoke to Robb.

It was wonderful to rekindle an old friendship and share Derian. We returned home with souvenirs, suntans, and lighter spirits. I could hardly wait to put my arms around Robb and feel the three of us scrunch together in a hug. It felt great to be back together again, all 3 1/2 of us.

Chapter 12

As Derian's surgery date grew closer, my mind kept playing different scenarios: Derian dies in surgery, and we're left with one baby…things go as planned, and we adjust to two babies. Without knowing what the future held, I needed to prepare for both situations. This was an especially difficult time to be pregnant.

I remembered going for a walk with a friend a few days before surgery. Connie asked me, "So how do you feel about Derian's surgery?"

The words erupted from my mouth: "I am so afraid that God is going to take Derian, the child I love, and leave me with a child I don't know. What if that happens? How would I ever deliver this baby if his brother died?" Tears and shameful words of honesty spewed out like hot lava. Without judgment, she listened to each fearful word. I felt freed and peaceful after saying that.

One week before surgery, the geneticist called us back for another visit. We didn't know why we needed to see Dr. Snow again. She had already told us what we needed to know. Dr. Snow played with Derian for a while, and then proceeded to drill us with questions. At the end of the appointment, she told us Derian was behind in his physical and mental abilities. I knew he was behind on a few things but I attributed that to his hospital stay.

Dr. Snow recommended enrolling Derian in the Birth-Through-Three program in our community. I could feel my body temperature rise as thoughts of doubt whispered overhead: *Obviously you're not a good mom. Why else would Derian need extra help? A different school, another weekly appointment? No thanks; I can't take on anything else.* Dr. Snow's recommendation felt like a personal blow to my motherhood, and the idea of this birth-though-three class seemed too weird.

Completely distraught, I called my soulmate, Linda. My thought was that she'd let me cry on her shoulder. Instead, she piped, "Birth-Through-Three! That is the greatest program ever! We had Bill in that, and we cried the day he graduated from it. The teachers are great and so helpful. Derian will have a ball in this program. You have to sign him up!"

With that response, I changed my tune from "one more thing to do!" to "Wow, I found a great resource for my son." I called for an appointment. Since it was summer, the teachers were off, but the office would send information and an application to fill out. Now I was anxious to get started.

Robb's parents and Aunt Jean decided to treat us to a weekend in Green Lake, Wisconsin, right before the surgery. Heather, Robb's sister was also pregnant. We were quite a sight; two pregos, one with a huge belly and a toddler sitting on it, the other so tired she could hardly walk around. We stayed at a beautiful resort and were waited on hand and foot. It was a great distraction!

Chapter 13

Reality found us Monday morning when I brought Derian in for his pre-op physical. I checked in at Dr. Hesslein's office and received a checklist of tests that needed to be done: blood work, x-rays, EEG, and urine test. Once the tests were completed, I reported back to Dr. Hesslein's office where he pieced the information together and reviewed the surgery plan. As always, Dr. Hesslein was in a chipper mood, and Derian warmed up to him right away. After he examined Derian, he reviewed the surgical procedure Dr. Nichols was going to do, the equipment Derian would be attached to, and the recovery expectations.

Robb and I filled a backpack with magazines, crossword puzzles, and other mindless ways to pass the time while Derian was in surgery. I planned to tie the patchwork quilts I was making for Derian and his new little brother. Yes, it was to be another boy. I had an echocardiogram to make sure our new baby's heart was healthy, and thankfully all was well. Since we were going to have two little boys I painted a western theme in the nursery.

July 12 arrives

We woke to the voices of the morning show DJs. I wondered how they could be so happy on a morning like this. We got ready at a relaxed but deliberate pace, pausing only to offer each other a hug. We knew the road to recovery was long and unpredictable. We also knew that Derian was not a textbook example of anything; he could have complications.

When the car was loaded, we woke Derian. I changed his diaper but kept him in his pjs, hoping he would sleep on the way to the hospital. Because of the surgery, there would be no morning bottle for Derian. It

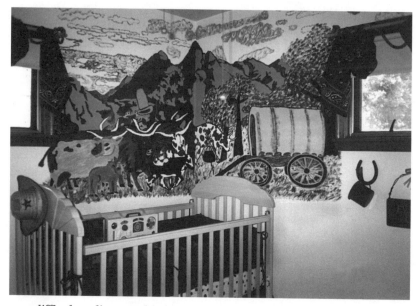

was difficult to listen to his hungry cries and not do anything. I put flavored lip-gloss on his lips in hopes that the smell might take away some of the hunger.

Baby number two kicked wildly as we pulled into the hospital parking lot. Perhaps he could sense the fear that consumed us. We both held one of Derian's hands so he could walk between us. It seemed like such an ordinary, sunny day. The morning air was filled with promise as we slowly made our way to the hospital doors.

We filled out the paperwork as Derian careened around the office. It didn't take long for 11-month-old Derian to wake up and make friends with the staff checking us in. Once the paperwork was completed, we headed to Same Day Surgery. It all seemed too damn familiar: the nurses, the feelings, and the place. I didn't want to be there. Once Derian was prepped and ready for surgery, we carried him into the elevator and headed to the second floor. The people in the elevator flirted with Derian as the elevator went up. I felt like yelling at them, *he's my baby, for god sakes, he's going in for surgery, this may be the only time I have left with him, butt out, stop talking to him, don't steal my time.*

We met a new staff once we arrived at the holding room: the anesthesiologist, his assistant, a surgery nurse, and of course, the surgeon. They briefly reviewed Derian's medical history and went over the surgery plan once more. God, how many times do we have to go over this? I could care less what you are going to do—just please bring him back to us. This was the last stop, a period at the end of the life we had been living with Derian. The past, present, and future melted together as the surgeon stood up and shook our hands. That was the signal, the kiss of betrayal; it was time to turn Derian over to them. Robb and I held him one more time and pressed his body next to ours.

Letting Derian go drained me of emotion. I couldn't cry anymore. It had been the weeks of worrying and waiting for this day. Now that it was time to live it, I was exhausted! Robb and I made our way down the hall leaning on each other physically and emotionally. Before we entered the waiting room Robb patted my belly and said hello to our new baby. Feeling an active baby offered hope. I was sure these two babies would meet each other.

We took a deep breath and tried to look confident before we met our parents. Lois, Robb's mom, was ill and unable to make it to the hospital that morning. So, Bob, Robb's dad, would call her with updates. My parents brought treats and fresh coffee. As we waited, a conversation of nothing began to snowball: "How's the weather? How is work going?"

Joan was our cardiac nurse that day. When she gave us the first report, she asked if Robb and I would like to stay overnight in the Family Center. I was relieved to know this was an option! She told us we could stay in the center as long as Derian was in the ICU unit. I felt lighter already. This was going to be all right after all. Joan would reserve a room with the ICU staff and drop off a room key for us.

It would be about six hours before Derian would be out of surgery, so the updates were helpful and made the waiting bearable. I tried to contact Derian with my mind. I wanted him to know how proud I was of him and how strong I thought he was. Maybe my mother's affirmation tendencies were rubbing off on me.

Joan stopped back with the key to our room. Since we were waiting, we thought we might check out the room and unload the extra items we brought. We could smell new carpeting and new paint as soon as we got off the elevator. The Family Center was beautiful with lots of big windows overlooking the quiet part of I-35E and the huge mansions above, hovering over the freeway. The white walls were decorated with pastel paintings that blended with the mint colored carpet. This room was divided into four sections: two had a couch and love seat, another had a table with chairs, and there was a play area. The TV was bolted to the ceiling, and tropical fish calmly swam undaunted by the stress that hovered outside their fish tank. There were free phones in three of the sections. It was a relief to think I could come up in this room and make a private call.

A light wooden doorway was at the back of the room. We put our key in and opened it to a kitchen and a light wooden dining table and chair set. A large window invited the bright sunlight, which cast a glow across the tile floor. Robb and I were taken back by this beautiful oasis. We went exploring and found two bathrooms, a linen rack filled with sheets, blankets and towels, two shower rooms, and four private bedrooms. Room #1, had our name with a reserve sign on it.

We unlocked the door, which opened up to another beautiful room. There was another large window in this room, two single beds that were neatly made, two closets, and a sink with a mirror. This was awesome! In the center of the room stood a desk with a phone on it. Only a short hallway would separate us from Derian. I could handle this!

I was immediately thankful to all the donors that made this possible for parents. They offered a beautiful physical gift, but more importantly their donation gave parents some peace of mind knowing they were only a phone call and short distance from their critical care child. Being surrounded by a pretty atmosphere made me feel special, hopeful, and taken care of. We went back to the waiting room and described the awesome quarters we were going to be staying in that night.

When the surgery was completed, Dr. Nichols met us in the waiting room. Overall he was pleased with the surgery's outcome. Except for one thing. "While I was working on Derian's heart, I accidentally cut one of the valves. I sewed it up and it all looks good for right now, but I'm not sure this won't cause future problems for Derian."

My heart sank. How could this happen? My mom worriedly asked, "Does this sort of thing happen often?" The surgeon arrogantly replied, "Not to me." Part of me wanted to pounce on him. How could he have screwed up with Derian? Like Derian needed one more problem. The other half knew he could do something for my child that I couldn't. His hands weren't perfect, but they were a hell of a lot more skilled than mine were. We would have to accept that he did the best he could, regardless of the outcome. However, if Derian needed another surgery due to his mistake, I would hate him. I knew surgeons were not the easiest people to talk to, so I decided not to get too worried about this until we talked to Dr. Hesslein. Dr. Hesslein was always optimistic, and I was sure he'd have an easy solution to this problem.

When Dr. Hesslein came into the waiting area, we bombarded him with questions. He wasn't nearly as concerned about the valve situation as the surgeon seemed. That was a relief. According to Dr. Hesslein, if the valve would be a problem, they would replace it. He decided he would watch that area regularly to be sure things were fine. Overall he was pleased with the results of the surgery and was positive, as always. I was grateful Derian had Dr. Hesslein for his doctor. Dr. Hesslein let us know Derian would be coming down the hall if we wanted to catch a glimpse of him.

I felt the now familiar rumblings of heavy equipment as it rolled across the carpeting. Each time I saw Derian in the center of such a medical entourage, I was struck by all the equipment he needed to stay alive. Derian was a high-tech kid! As I looked at all the stuff he was attached to I couldn't help but ask myself to what lengths would we go to keep him alive.

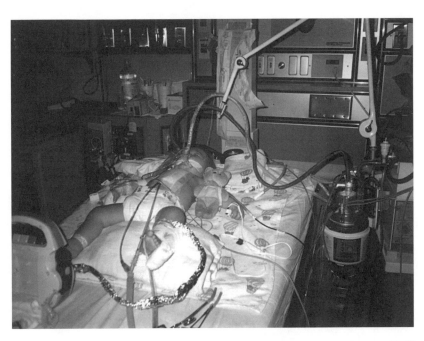

Chapter 14

After a quick lunch, we returned to the PICU and got an update from Derian's nurse. Since Derian was stabilized, the nurse led us to him. I kissed his puffy little hand and held his foot—the only part of his body that didn't have something attached to it. I saw the familiar signs of heart surgery: puffiness, the vent, IVs, chest tubes, and his lips taped together like a fish. The only thing that looked like the Derian we brought in a few hours ago was his hair.

Derian would be drugged for a few days. The machines would do his breathing until he was strong enough to do it on his own. When I knew he was settled, I took the tape recorder and the harp music I bought for him. I had read somewhere that harp music was especially relaxing for children in the hospital. I propped it against his pillow and stroked his hair while I whispered in his good ear, "Derian, I am so proud of you; you are such a little fighter." I stayed with him until the tape needed to be turned over. Exhausted, I shuffled my body down the hall and into our room in the family center. I collapsed on my bed and drifted off to sleep. It was 4 p.m. before I woke up. I jumped out of bed and dashed to see Derian. I passed through the family room and asked Robb how everything was going. Robb was playing cards with my family. "Patsy, everything is going as planned!" I went into the ICU unit to check in on Derian for myself.

"So how's the little man doing?"

"We are a little concerned. Derian is still bleeding and his hemoglobin is dropping." I couldn't believe it! Why was Robb so calm? This was serious! "What will you do if he continues to bleed or if his hemoglobin doesn't stabilize? What is the best/worst case scenario?" I asked the nurse.

She calmly replied, "Derian just received a platelet transfusion so we're waiting to see if that brings up his hemoglobin. If not, he will need to go BACK TO SURGERY."

We need God! We need prayers! I returned to the Family Center with a look that scared everyone. They put down the cards, newspapers, and turned off the TV. "Derian's bleeding; his hemoglobin is dropping. They gave him a transfusion to see if it would help him. If it doesn't, they will be calling Dr. Nichols back and bringing Derian back to surgery. We need prayers—please call everyone you know and ask them to start praying for him."

Robb went to talk to the nurse while everyone else got out their address books and started asking for prayers.

God, are you really going to take Derian? Please, God, don't. Why would you make him go through the surgery? Couldn't you have taken him without making him suffer? I pulled out my personal phone book and called Pastor George.

"Patsy, do you want to me come to the hospital? I can be there in 20 minutes."

I didn't want to have more people around, so I promised to call him with updates. The next person I called had a direct line to God. I taught with this man for many years, and I knew God would listen if Ken were praying for Derian. As soon as I told him about Derian's situation, he began to pray right on the phone. His prayer offered some peace. I was frustrated that I couldn't pray for Derian myself. I don't think I knew what to pray for. A miracle? No more suffering? A quick, painless death? What would a mother of a child like Derian ask God for?

The nurse at Derian's side looked frustrated and concerned. Before she said anything, I knew what she was going to say. "Dr. Nichols is on his way to the hospital. He will take Derian into surgery as soon as he arrives. Derian has lost a lot of blood and his vitals are dropping."

It was 10 p.m., the surgeon was returning to the hospital, and Derian was going back into surgery. *God, what do you have planned for this child?* I began to shake. Terror spread throughout my body. Robb gripped my hand. Knowing other people were praying for us made me feel that at least Derian had a chance.

In the midst of this chaos, I found comfort in the little feet that kicked wildly inside me. Baby Connor kicked me each time my emotions were locked in panic. It felt like he was tapping out a message to me: "Mom, Derian will be all right, not to worry." I began to trust those little feet inside me. If they were once angels together, he probably knew they would be together again.

Dr. Nichols hurried into the waiting room to announce he was bringing Derian back to surgery. KICK—KICK. After he left, a nurse ran in with the surgery consent form. We waited again for reports. I wondered if Dr. Hesslein knew. Not having Dr. Hesslein around made me feel especially alone. I trusted he would know what to do more than anyone else. He was like Derian's medical dad, and it didn't feel right not to have him there. We were relying solely on Dr. Nichols.

Dr. Nichols returned to the waiting room a half an hour later and told us "A stitch had worked its way out. Once it was re-sewn, the bleeding stopped. Everything is fine now."

At this point I was beginning to wonder if I should trust Derian with this surgeon again—an accident during surgery and then having a stitch come out.

Dr. Nichols left and my friend Ken entered. He had been waiting in the other family room. When we told him what the surgeon had said, he reached out and gave me a hug. I introduced Ken to our families. Before leaving, he told us he would continue to pray for us. It had been a long day and all of us were relieved we could retire for the evening knowing Derian was okay.

How I would welcome a few days of boredom. Unfortunately, I knew the next few days could all be this wild. Recovery is long and unpredictable. But, day one was over.

Before going to sleep I called George with an update. Robb and I managed to give each other a kiss before we sank into a well deserved good night's sleep.

Chapter 15

When I got up the next morning, I looked out the Family Center's window—I was jealous I wasn't on the freeway, on my way to work, living life as usual. It didn't seem fair. I wanted to see Derian more than I wanted to feel sorry for myself, so I quickly brushed my hair, put on a hat, and threw on some sweats. It was hard to feel glamorous this early in the morning being seven months pregnant.

Robb and I left the room at the same time, hoping we could catch rounds and hear the latest report on Derian. As we rounded the corner, we saw the three nurses trying to weigh Derian. He weighed all of 15 pounds, but you'd think he weighed a ton by the way he was being weighed. A crane-like machine with a wide sling dangled from it. One of the nurses moved the sling close to the bed, while the other two gently picked up Derian's upper body just enough to slide the sling underneath and slide it down to the middle of his body. Once he was supported, the crane slowly lifted Derian a few inches off the bed; a nurse got the weight and lowered Derian back onto the bed. By monitoring Derian's weight and the input and output of fluids, the doctors were able to monitor what was going on inside Derian. That information would determine the drugs and dosages he needed.

That morning's rounds were going to be later than usual. Since Robb had to get to work, I would call him with the report. The hospital does not conform to the hours and minutes the rest of the world lives by. *A little while* could mean eight hours, *a few minutes* could be two to three hours. To ward off frustration, we adapted to living in the moment rather than by the clock.

Derian's body was still swollen; all tubes from the day before were still in place. Derian's nurse put fresh ointment on his lips and his eyes. *Poor Derian, I wish you didn't have to have all this done.* I spent most of the day reading stories to my precious eleven-month-old. The rest of the day, I touched him and loved him up. Rounds finally came. The staff was pleased with Derian's progress—he had peed the right amount, his saturation numbers were right on, and his heart was beating fine. I guess all was going as planned. I phoned Robb with the news and he updated the rest of the family. My brothers and sister were stopping in that afternoon with their significant others; our parents were stopping by that evening.

The process of recovery had begun. With each passing hour, new challenges were set for Derian's body. He was slowly weaned from the ventilator and challenged to breathe on his own. They expected Derian to be on the ventilator for four days. His nurses encouraged me to rest during those four days. "Once Derian wakes up, he will need you."

The morning of the fourth day the nurses asked if I would leave the area while they extubated Derian. I figured this must be a really ugly procedure if they asked me to leave. I trusted they were probably right, so I went to the cafeteria. A half an hour later I returned to the unit. It was wonderful to see Derian's little boy face again. His thin body shook each time he inhaled. It was obvious that he wasn't ready to be off the vent. I asked the doctor to observe his breathing; she agreed with my observation and intubated Derian again. This was a disappointing second setback, but I knew it was the right thing to do. Derian just needed a few more days to rest. I phoned Robb with an update. To this day, I have no idea how Robb was able to work while Derian was in the hospital. I would have gone crazy if I could not have been in the hospital talking to the doctors and nurses.

It had been six days since the surgery and Derian was still on the vent. We were frustrated things were going slower than planned. We had a wedding to go to that Saturday and were hopeful Derian would be further along in his recovery. I wanted to go, but how could I leave Derian in this fragile state? My family was adamant I get out of the hospital for a day. Since they knew I wouldn't leave Derian unattended, they collectively organized their schedules so Robb and I could attend the wedding of my college roommate.

I was glad for a day off. The church was about an hour away, so we took the pager and gave the numbers of the places we would be. Robb pulled me out of the hospital, reassuring me things would be fine. We held hands as we walked to our car. Our rule for the day: no talking about Derian or the hospital. That day was about us having fun and celebrating a new marriage. On our way to the church, we laughed, sang songs on the radio, and talked about the arrival of the new baby. I felt more connected to Robb in that one hour than I had in the last few days. It was wonderful to escape; I welcomed the feeling of "normal."

The tiny white church sat on top of a country hill. It was the perfect place for Janice to be married. Janice was a country girl who prided herself on simplicity. Her white satin dress had clean lines; it was simple and stunning. She looked radiant as she walked down the aisle, bursting with joy.

I became jealous as I witnessed the freshness of her life unfold. Our lives were about as different as two people's lives could be. I felt weathered as I watched her. My worry was harbored in my smile these days and the careless joy I used to feel was dead. How I wished I could go back in time just for a little break. I longed to be carefree once again. My thoughts were interrupted as the woman in front of us laid a soft blanket on her pew and carefully placed her baby on it. As I watched her baby rest, I became lonesome for Derian. I wanted to yell and shout to the crowd, "I have a baby, I have a baby too." My life felt more hollow and empty as I watched the newborn lying in the pew, listened to a young bride take her vows, and heard the words of a wedding hymn. We shouldn't have come to this place.

Robb tuned into my feelings, kissed my forehead and softly whispered, "We have a baby; we will have two babies soon." I was lucky to have my Robb and lucky to be blessed with a happy marriage.

I gave Janice a hug in the receiving line and wished her the best. It was difficult to be around all these happy people when our reality was so tough. I put on a mask that day laughing when everyone else did and going through the motions of having a good time. Once we left the reception, I felt free again. I didn't know what was more difficult—pretending everything was fine, or going back to the reality that was waiting for us. There was no escape.

I was anxious to get back to the hospital. Since we had not been paged or called, we were confident all was going well. When we got to Derian's bedside, we discovered that he was no longer on the ventilator! Robb and I were thrilled to see Derian's little face again—the vent took up so much of it. He was sleeping when we arrived. I couldn't wait to see him awake! I was giddy as I sat at his bedside waiting for him to wake up. The doctor let us know that if all would continue to go as planned, Derian could have dinner and would then move to the PICU. He was going to eat a meal again! It must be my German background and my own love for food that made eating a good sign.

I wondered how active Derian would be once he woke up. His previous surgeries all took place when he was a newborn and couldn't do much. Now that he was older and more active, I was anxious about how we were going to manage a toddler and the remaining tubes. Most of the big tubes were gone, but an IV tube was still in his neck and another in his arm. "What might we expect when Derian wakes up?" I asked the nurse.

"He will be very thirsty, and his throat will be scratchy."

"Will I be able to give him a bottle?"

"Patsy, his tummy is completely empty, so we will start him off on few ice chips for the first hour. Once he proves he can hold something down, he can have two ounces of apple juice."

When Derian woke up, he did it in a big way. He flailed his body around and tried to sit up while coughing as if he'd smoked ten packs of cigarettes a day the last 80 years. It hurt to hear his vocal chords grate across his chest. He reached his arms up to me and wanted to be held. I asked the nurse if she could help me get him out of the crib. Maybe holding him would help him relax. As excited as I was to have him coherent again, watching him struggle like this was harder than having him drugged.

He shook his head uncontrollably as I placed the ice chip in his mouth. As soon as it melted, he looked up to me and begged for more with his eyes. The nurse gave me strict orders not to give him much. I was torn between orders and motherhood. Derian looked so weak and frail. It seemed cruel not to give him what he wanted. I stroked my fingers through his hair and rubbed his chubby little feet as I watch the minute hand go around the clock. We had to wait one hour before he could have anything else.

Holding him made me feel like a mother again. This part of motherhood was as natural as can be. I loved rocking Derian. "Derian, you can have a bottle in fifteen minutes." Derian looked as if he understood what I said. Robb walked into the unit. A nurse passed Derian from my arms and placed him into Robb's. Derian was still pale and shaky, but he seemed more peaceful with Robb. His sternum bone was wired together underneath his stitched-up chest. He was going to be sore for a while. To ensure proper healing, it was imperative that he not be picked up underneath his arms for at least six weeks.

Derian gulped down two ounces of apple juice. He was starving! As soon as he finished he wanted more. Robb asked the nurse for more juice. Although the nurse was excited Derian was hungry, she wanted to wait thirty more minutes before giving Derian another bottle. This seemed a little unreasonable! He drank the first one and did just fine and ate ice chips. Obviously he was ready to eat! Thirty minutes later he downed his next bottle. We were given strict orders after that not to give him anything else until dinner. I could deal with this; at least I knew he had something in his tummy.

Derian stretched his body. He was ready to lie in his bed again. We carefully transferred him off the pillow and into the crib. Once he was settled, we entertained him with bubbles and stories, without any response from him. Maybe we were expecting too much from Derian. In our excitement, we forgot he was hurting.

When the dinner menu arrived, I studied it and picked out Derian's favorite baby foods: squash, potatoes, and apple dessert. Maybe after dinner he would bounce back to his regular self. Derian's hands continued to shake like an old man's. His skin was pasty white and he would whimper a muffled sounding cry after each painful cough. His full tummy did nothing to stop this.

Chapter 16

After dinner, we wheeled Derian to the other wing. This would be the first time we had been on this side of the hospital. We were shown to our room and told that a nurse would be stopping by. The room was a little larger than a college dorm and had a big window that overlooked the hospital parking lot. It was a bright, shiny day and the chrome on the cars sparkled in the sun's rays. It was almost too bright to look outside. A TV hung from the ceiling in one corner of the room and a bench served as a couch in the other corner. There was a tiny closet in the center of the room and a bathroom that was to be shared with the people in the next room.

Derian's crib took up the center of the room. On the wall closest to his bed were outlets, oxygen machines, heart monitors, and different-shaped outlets. Derian didn't bother to look around; he just stared at the ceiling. He seemed depressed. I was getting nervous about this move. Perhaps Derian still needed one-on-one care.

We waited for 45 minutes before a nurse finally popped in. I couldn't believe it! Derian had never gone 45 minutes without a doctor or nurse's attention. It became clear to us that non-intensive care was much different than ICU. This would be a whole new experience. The nurse introduced herself and asked if we were planning to stay for the evening. Robb and I looked at each other and said together, "Yes, we will be staying with him. One of us will be here each night." She left the room and put a request in for a rollaway bed that night. When she returned, she invited me on a tour of the unit. Still slighted from the wait, I wasn't especially friendly to her.

Our tour included the bathroom, shower rooms and the lounge. I noticed a free phone on the table under the TV in the lounge. The lounge looked like a great place from which to make a private call. There was an ice machine, a snack drawer, and a refrigerator filled with juices at the main nurses' station.

I was a little friendlier when I returned to our room. It was obvious that parents were expected to play an active role in their child's care in this wing. If we had questions, we could ask a nurse for help, but we would need to provide Derian's recreation. Our room felt like a small house; it was nice we could be in the same room. Robb had to be at work early the next morning, so he decided he would spend the night at home. Since Derian was out of the ICU, Robb was more comfortable about leaving for the evening.

As homey as our room was, there wasn't much privacy. Its door had a large window that faced the nurses' station. A thin curtain could be drawn to separate the small space between Derian's crib and the couch. Before I left the bathroom, I made sure I unlocked my neighbor's side of the bathroom door, set my basket of toiletries down, and peeked in on Derian. He lay in the dark with his eyes wide open, staring at the ceiling. His hands continued to shake as he raised his arms and rotated his palms back and forth, over and over. What he was thinking?

I was hopeful that after a few more bottles, another meal, and a good night's rest, we'd catch a glimpse of our Derian. I put on some pretty piano music, kissed Derian good night, and crawled onto the rollaway bed.

Since our room was across from the nurses' station, the bright lights spilled into our room. I could hear the nurses talking and the man next door couldn't carry on a conversation unless he was shouting. I lay in the partial darkness on the bumpy rollaway, trying to find a comfortable spot that would coax me to sleep in this crazy place.

No sooner had I fallen asleep than a high-pitched beep from Derian's IV went off. The nurse soon came in with another bag of fluid, threaded it through the IV machine, and reset it. The beeping stopped. I went back to sleep. About an hour later, Derian awoke, his body thrashing around as he emitted a hoarse cry. His knees were drawn to his chest and he trembled violently. He was so pale he almost glowed in the dark.

Oh my God—what now? What is happening? I grabbed my robe and went out to the nurses' station. "Help, something's wrong with Derian." Two nurses ran into the room with me. "What is wrong? What is happening to him?"

The nurses looked at the readings on each of Derian's machines trying to figure out what was wrong.

Heart rate: Normal

Pulse: Normal

IV fluid: Full

IV: Not leaking

"What? What is wrong?" There were no clues. "What is happening? What should we do?"

While they tried to piece this puzzle together, the nurses asked me what he ate for dinner. When I mentioned he had squash, both nurses nodded their heads. "Derian has gas. Squash is a gassy food to begin with. Combine that with the drugs trying to get out of his system, and you have the perfect combination for a bad tummy ache." Knowing I had done this to him made me sick. I never thought about gas when I ordered his food. I felt horrible. The last thing I would ever do was hurt Derian. His painful whimpers continued as his body quivered from gas pain and withdrawals from the drugs he was on. No medicine could make this better; Derian would pay the price for my mistake. Why didn't someone check what I ordered? If they knew squash could be a problem for him after surgery, why didn't anyone change his order or advise me differently?

Derian was out of his mind with pain for hours. I begged the nurses to give him something. He had heart surgery just five days earlier. The nurses agreed. Written in the orders was a prescription for Nubian. I wasn't excited about adding more drugs to his system, but he needed something—his body needed rest. The nurse injected a syringe into his IV. That was the one advantage about having an IV—Derian could get an injection without getting stuck. I stood over Derian most of the night, smoothing his hair, and putting warm washcloths on his tummy. That seemed to relax him in between his cramps. Watching him reminded me of being in labor. I would never make a mistake like this again!

The sun was just beginning to rise when Derian finally went to sleep. Pink hues touched the floor of the room as the sun hit the curtain. I was weak from standing, exhausted, and starving. What a bad combination!

If I didn't get enough sleep, I was guaranteed to have morning sickness. I had to rest.

I collapsed onto the rollaway for about five minutes until I was sick. I ran to the bathroom, but the door was locked—my neighbor forgot to unlock my side. In sheer desperation, I threw up in the sink in our room. I threw up so hard I wet my pants. How would I get through this day? I had to get something to eat or this would get worse.

My sweat pants were soaking wet, I had to change before I could even run across the hall and grab a treat. I rummaged through my clothes-basket for something else to wear. I had a few minutes before I would throw up again. Once I was dressed I bolted out of my room and made a mad dash to the snack drawer, grabbed a package of cookies, ripped it open, shoved a cookie into my mouth, and chewed as fast as I could. At least five nurses witnessed my savage eating habits, not to mention my lovely appearance. My hair was a mess; my pink shirt was wrinkled and buttoned wrong, hanging over my red sweats. We looked at each other and started to laugh. Luckily, these nurses were all moms and knew the "joys" of morning sickness. Once my stomach was satisfied, I sat down with the nurses who worked the night shift. We all compared pregnancy tales. I felt comfortable with them. It's amazing how humor and embarrassment can connect people. Once we had finished our stories, our conversation turned to Derian. A feeling of victory was shared as I announced he was sleeping.

Wanting to catch a few more winks, I excused myself and went back to my room. I lay still, hoping to calm my stomach down. As I rested my hands on my belly, I could feel Connor kick. Each time he kicked, I moved my hand to another spot. Connor followed my lead as we played in-utero tag. I slept for about a half an hour before the next shift of nurses arrived. Their schedule was rigid—all children must be weighed by 7:30 a.m., regardless of whether they were up all night and just got to sleep.

The morning nurse had a job and she was hell-bent on doing it. She whipped opened the door to our room with such authority, I almost expected her to pull out a bugle and greet us with a hearty, "Rise and shine, up and at 'em." I glared at her. Did she have a clue as to how hard I worked to get Derian to sleep? I wasn't ready to begin the day. She woke Derian as she stripped him from his pjs and threw his diaper off. Since there was no negotiating, I surrendered the idea of getting rest in order to rescue Derian from the drill sergeant.

I picked up his tired, shivering body and lowered him onto the scale. Derian began to cry as I laid him on the towel on the scale. The nurse got his weight and charted it. While I wrapped him in a warm blanket, the nurse ran a small plastic pink tub of warm water for his morning bath. Poor Derian! What a way to begin the morning—yanked out of bed, stripped down, placed on a scale, and now bathed. He must have been annoyed with this whole routine! I placed a washcloth on his back and one on his chest, and then poured a cup of water on his body. Even though he was warm, he cried his hoarse cry through the entire ordeal. There was no comforting him.

Taking him out of the tub was tricky, since he couldn't be lifted from under his arms. I reached into the tub water, placed his behind into my hand, moved my arms close together, and lifted out his wet, slippery body. The nurse had prepared several towels on the bed and as soon as I lay Derian down, his arms sprung into a spread-eagle position. I took a heated towel and tucked it underneath him to make him warm and cozy. Even though our faces were inches apart, Derian's eyes wouldn't connect to mine—he was in his own far away world.

Determined to make him mine again, I dressed him in one of his own outfits. While planning clothes to bring to hospital, I needed to made sure they fulfilled the following requirements:

1. Easy to get over the head.

2. Plenty of room in the sleeve to pull over the IV board.

3. Be relatively warm.

I found an outfit that fit all the requirements: a striped short-sleeved shirt, teddy bear pants, a white jacket with a teddy bear on it, and teddy bear shoes. Derian was somber as I dressed him. I turned on Barney, expecting that to breathe some life into him. He stared at the TV for a while and then turned his head away. *Barney always excited Derian. What was going on?* Each time I asked a nurse or doctor about Derian's behavior, I would get the same response: "It takes a while to get drugs out of the body's system. Give him a few days—he's been though a lot!"

One of the boys who was in the ICU unit next to Derian had heart surgery the day before Derian. That little boy was almost back to normal. In fact, he was going home the next day. It didn't seem fair—why were they ready to go home when we weren't. I was impatient with recovery.

There was no magic formula or timetable; it was an individual, minute-by-minute, hour-by-hour thing.

As I fed Derian, he stared into space and automatically opened his mouth when I placed the spoon to his lips. His large eyes looked like empty saucers rather than the shiny, wise, communicative eyes they usually were. His sparkle was gone. After breakfast, I decided to get Derian out of our room. A walk might be just what he needed. The nurse suggested I put him in a wooden L-shaped contraption that would support Derian's trunk and allow his legs to stretch out. I padded it with blankets so Derian would be comfortable, and grabbed a bottle of juice for the road.

Derian didn't even acknowledge me when I wheeled into the room. He was flat on his back, staring at the ceiling. Determined that sunshine would do Derian some good, I sized up the situation. I needed to figure out which side of the crib I should be on to get Derian out without tangling his IV tubes. Once I got that figured out, I lifted Derian's bottom up, cradled him and the tubes in my arms, and slowly lowered him into the cart. I padded a few more blankets around him for extra support before I buckled him in. All I needed now was the IV pole. Once I got a grip on it and a feel for how I would maneuver everything, I pushed both contraptions out the door. As I moved down the hall, the nurses stopped and made a fuss over Derian. No reaction. I was crushed. This was the kind of attention he thrived on.

My somber young child and I went outside on the balcony of the hospital to get some sun. I breathed a big breath of the morning heat. Derian swung his head back to move his eyes out of the bright sunlight. He was not enjoying this! We ditched this plan and resorted to Plan B: walking up and down the hospital halls. Derian attracted plenty of attention, but none of it could break the spell he was under. We went back to the room, defeated. I pulled out the rollaway and decided to take a nap with him. I moved Derian from the cart and onto the bed and closed the curtains. I loved to feel Derian's face next to mine, even if he was stiff and lifeless. How long before he would be himself again? It had been eight days—eight long days since I'd gotten any reaction from him.

Chapter 17

We slept for about two and one-half hours before there was a knock on our door. Someone from the lab wanted to take blood from Derian. Since this blood was going to be used for a culture, she needed to draw it from his arm rather than the IV. I asked her to come by later when Derian was awake. I wasn't about to allow Derian to be awakened in such a terrible way. He deserved to have a few minutes to be snuggled and feel safe after his nap. An intrusive procedure might produce nightmares. I could accept the fact that Derian's life was going to include many unpleasant procedures, but I was NOT going to allow sleep to be one of them.

Derian woke up about a half an hour later. His listless eyes gazed at the ceiling. The day was nearly over, and he wasn't making any progress. *What else should I be doing? What could snap him out of this fog?* After dinner, the social life person stopped by and asked if we would like to check out some toys and a play mat. Great idea! Perhaps this would do the trick. She left our room and returned with a colorful floor mat and lots of toys and books. I was excited to have something new to entertain Derian. I played peek-a-boo with some of the stuff animals. No reaction. He looked blankly at me as if he didn't remember playing this game. I was crushed. Had Derian's brain been damaged while he was on the pump?

Later that evening, another person from the lab stopped by. I couldn't buy Derian any more time. I picked him up and lay him in the crib. The tech flipped on the bright light, a light that was only used for painful procedures requiring concentration. I wondered if the brightness signaled anything to Derian. She tied the rubber tie around his arm, found a good vein, then untied the rubber band and prepared his right arm for the stick. Derian stared at the wall as she elevated his bed. He had a look of despair in his eyes, almost as if he were saying, "Is this all I can expect from life? Am I good for anything else other than being poked? The lab tech opened the package with the needle and placed a vial on the bed. Derian slowly turned his head to look at her. Instead of screaming Derian lifted his arm and offered it to her. She poked the needle in without any reaction from Derian. He was still as he stared at the wall, but a tear rolled down his cheek.

I watched in disbelief. Derian was accustomed to this life; he knew how it all worked. Why in God's name should a child need to accept this? I wondered what Derian thought about me, watching as these tests were taken? Did he wonder why his mom allowed strangers to hurt him so often? I knew Derian was giving up—there was no fight left in him. The edges of my heart curled. Despair had left its mark on both of us.

The lab tech was as saddened by Derian's reaction as I. She left the room shaking her head and saying, "Poor little guy." She gave me a depressed smile and closed the door. I wanted to isolate myself too. I didn't want to see or talk to anyone. The steel crib bars felt cold against my forehead. I studied the pasty white color of Derian's skin, the redness in his lips, and the shadows that gave his dark eyes a hazy look. The gleam I depended on seeing was gone. Derian lay listlessly in his crib, his hand moving upward on its own. He still didn't have control over his body. Where was my spirited little boy? Will he ever come back to me? As those questions ran through my mind, my worry turned to tears. I needed this child.

I began to sob; my cry was cut short when there was a quiet knock at the door and a resident doctor walked into the room and over to the crib. There was no faking—it was obvious that I'd been crying. But the resident wasn't scared off. She looked at my puffy red eyes and gently said, "This must be really difficult." Recognizing she understood, I continued to cry empty despaired tears. I had no shame about crying in front of this woman. She stood next to me as she examined Derian. After a few minutes she asked what concerned me. It didn't take long to answer. "Look at him. This is not the little boy I brought to you eight days ago. He doesn't smile, he doesn't laugh, and he doesn't look at me or even call me 'Mommy'. I want to know where my son is. I want to know what happened during his surgery. Something must have gone wrong." She jotted my concerns down and told me she would speak to the head doctor. Before she left she squeezed my hand and in a caring voice she said, "Hang in there, Mom."

My soul ached with loneliness even though friends and family supported me. Every one else's life was moving forward; they still had places to be and places to go. I was alone in the hospital with a child who was a stranger. My world stopped. I had no control of my life or Derian's. No matter what I had pulled off in the past, I could do nothing to help our situation now.

Robb was saddened by Derian's reaction to the lab tech and as concerned as I. He would come to the hospital as soon as he finished work and he'd plan to spend the night. I longed for one of his hugs and was interested in hearing his observations. Maybe I was wrong; maybe Robb would look at this situation differently.

When Robb arrived he did his best to make Derian laugh: making weird faces, blowing bubbles, reading stories, watching crazy kid movies. Nothing worked. Derian's reaction was a big zero. We went to bed fearful of the next challenge we would face with this child.

I was in a deep sleep when Derian's machines exploded with sound. These machines got excited about everything, and often needed resetting. I knew the nurse would come in, so I just lay there and waited for her. The nurse pushed a few buttons and we had instant quiet. A few minutes later, the scene replayed itself. This time the nurse noticed Derian's heart rate was beating at different rates. She called in another nurse. I sat up. They decided to set the alarm at a slower rate. The alarm continued to go off. Robb and I got up. Something was wrong. The nurses added paper to the machine so Dr. Hesslein would have something to look at when he arrived for work that morning. Derian slept right through the beeps and lights, undaunted by the commotion.

Robb and I were nervous and waited impatiently for Dr. Hesslein. Each time the machine went off, the tension grew. What did all this mean? What would happen now? Our internal frustration spilled into anger toward each other. We snarled thoughts back and forth while we waited. Fear was evident. Our plate was plenty full. There was no more room for disaster—we had another baby coming.

Dr. Hesslein was a welcomed sight! He greeted us with his usual cheer, grinned a funny grin, and said, "So, it sounds like you had a rough night. How's the little guy doing this morning?"

"We don't know. We're scared!" I said. He pursed his lips, pondering his explanation.

"It looks like Derian's heart has slipped into a different rhythm—I'm not exactly sure why. Perhaps his heart is irritated with the felt patch we gave him. Sometimes this is just a temporary setback and it corrects itself. I will study the tape and figure out what Derian's heart is telling us. Then I'll be able to tell you what our plan of action will be."

My thoughts raced ahead wildly, "Surgery?"

Dr. Hesslein calmly addressed my fear. "Sometimes we can control this thing with medication. The worst we might have to do is put in a pacemaker, but we would do this during the big repair of this heart. This would not be a surgery by itself. Let me see what's going on. I'll stop by later. Get a nap today!"

Dr. Hesslein shook Derian's hand as he left. We were so relieved Derian wasn't in any immediate danger that we completely forgot to ask about his behavior. It never fails: When you have the doctor's undivided attention, you forget to ask the questions you have, and new ones pop up once they leave the room.

When Robb left for work, our hospital routine began with a call from my mom, the breakfast cart, Barney, a bottle, blood pressure, and a weight check. Everything went on as usual, except for Derian's spirit and his heart. Dr. Hesslein returned that evening. He had read the tape and wasn't too concerned. Apparently, Derian's heart had slipped into a Bradycardia rhythm, which was common for an elderly person. He was sure Derian's heart would go back into its regular rhythm within a few days but wanted to monitor this for a few days in the hospital, and for 24 hours at home.

"Home." That was always a great word to hear in the hospital. "Home! When do you think we could be going home?"

He smiled a smile that offered good news: "Tomorrow." As great as that sounded, I had to refuse. There were too many questions unanswered, and I wasn't confidant Derian was okay. "Dr. Hesslein, I don't want to take Derian home yet. Not like this. He's not the same little boy I brought in. Look at him, he doesn't usually act like this."

Derian was sitting in his crib staring at the wall. I told Dr. Hesslein about Derian listlessly offering his arm to the lab tech. He listened and then took out his little penlight. He shined it into Derian's eyes, moving it back and forth. Derian's eyes followed the light. Then Dr. Hesslein turned the lights on and off and measured the responses of Derian's pupils. When he finished his exam he said in a serious voice, "Patsy, it is possible that Derian could have had a mild stroke while he was on the pump during surgery. Sometimes it takes awhile for the effects to show themselves. Let's wait a few more days; I think Derian's body is still trying to recover from the drugs."

I was numb with that possibility. Not his brain! For as many problems as Derian had, I was always grateful his brain was fine. I couldn't handle brain problems on top of everything else. The bottom of our world was falling out. We were being swallowed whole into the merciless jaws of despair. I looked at Derian and felt nothing. We were pulling away from each other. How would I ever be able to love this child if he couldn't communicate with me? How could that part of him be taken away? I tried to be brave as I listened to Dr. Hesslein. The last thing he said was he couldn't release Derian until I was comfortable bringing him home. He said he would keep Derian a few more days for observation. I felt so listened to. Dr. Hesslein never questioned my maternal instinct.

A surge of fight and defiance interrupted my thinking. I needed to know what someone felt like after surgery. Who did I know who'd had surgery? David and his wife! David was a man I had worked with for years. He and his wife were in a serious car accident a few years ago. In desperation, I called him, hoping he would be able to tell me how long it took him to bounce back after his surgeries. His calm spirit and objectivity eased the unsettled frenzy I felt.

He reassured me that it was weeks before he felt the drug fog lift from his body. As he described feelings of disorientation and delayed reactions, I watched Derian. Talking to David gave me hope again. He had to be right! Derian's body just needed more time. This would be the diagnosis I would choose to believe until something medical would prove differently. I called Robb after I spoke with David. I had to be careful about how I presented news to Robb. If I had called him before calling David, I would have shaken him for the entire day. That wouldn't have been fair.

I spent the entire day looking for some sign of Derian to appear. Nothing happened. Another day passed. The days slowly blended into each other: Monday, Tuesday, and Wednesday. The days of the week meant nothing to me. Time was measured with the rising and setting of the sun and the black "X" on the calendar at the end of each day.

Two more days. Two more "Xs." Nothing. No changes.

Chapter 18

Day 13

I woke up to the sound of the meal cart rumbling through the halls. I sat up in bed and looked to see if Derian was awake. He was sitting in his bed, looking at me. Looking at ME, not the wall! I got out of bed and rubbed my eyes. *Is it really him? Is he back?* "Good morning Derian, how are you? I missed you."

Derian had been examining his body. He held his chest and said, "Owie Momma, owie Momma." Tears filled my eyes. He remembered me; he said "Momma." The door on my heart opened and a welcoming feeling began to melt the frozen part of my soul. Everything felt better.

I grabbed his tray off the cart outside our room. "Derian, how would you like some French toast this morning?"

Derian clapped his hands when he saw his breakfast. I couldn't wait to call David and tell him he was right! I called Robb while Derian watched Barney. Derian laughed from his belly just like before and a crooked smile soon followed. Robb was elated. He couldn't believe the sounds Derian was making. This was a great way to begin the day—to end the emotional roller coaster we'd been on.

I couldn't wait for Dr. Hesslein to see Derian. I spent the day enjoying my son, rejoicing in our reunion. Each time I saw Derian smile, reach for a toy, or wave at someone, a feeling of victory rumbled in my gut. Being connected to such a fighter unleashed a fury of pride within me. I felt braver than I ever felt, like a pioneer, a warrior, a revolutionary. This feeling inspired me to do and be more than I was the day before. I was infected with Derian's triumphant spirit.

Dr. Hesslein was as surprised as I was over Derian's progress. It was a great day! Before Dr. Hesslein left he said, "If Derian keeps up like this, we could be thinking of going home very soon. I just want to keep my eye on him a little longer."

I was in complete agreement with that!

On Day 15, Derian was discharged from the hospital. Robb had been having trouble with his wisdom teeth and had them taken out the day before. He was pretty much out of commission, so I would be the one moving us out of the hospital. I had horrible morning sickness the morning we left and ended up throwing up in between each load. I was exhausted by the time all four loads were in the car. Bringing Derian out to the car was my favorite load. Once he was placed safely in the car seat, I knew he was mine again. What a blessed feeling to be outside with my little hero. I was so warm with feeling I threw up one more time; it was going to be a long day. Fortunately Robb was feeling okay and could take care of Derian while I slept. This was a less climatic homecoming than I expected.

Happy Birthday to you... ♪ ♩ ♪

Derian's first birthday was a monumental day! So many times throughout the year, we wondered if we would ever be able to celebrate the

Grandma Neary and Derian

Grandpa and Grandma Keech, Joe, Colleen, Grandma Neary, Robb.

day. We always imagined having a huge Hawaiian luau to mark August 2nd; but since Derian had only been home for a week, only our families and a few friends helped us celebrate.

Derian became stronger with each passing day. His Birth-Through-Three teachers were working to strengthen his body and recondition his muscles, while being respectful of his healing. I was lucky to have such wise women around me. They were my teachers as well as Derian's.

Becky was Derian's primary teacher; she and I became especially close. It was a privilege to see another woman so in love with my son. She was Derian's biggest cheerleader, and Derian adored her. Derian would crawl over to her and wave wildly when she walked into our house. He loved to show off for her, and she loved to challenge him. She went to great pains to plan out lessons that Derian would enjoy. I often thought about my first reaction when it was suggested that I sign Derian up for the program. Funny how time and experience change things. Birth-Through-Three was one of our favorite parts of the day.

Chapter 19

Our time of being a family of three was running out. Making the transition to four would be tricky. How would we welcome the new baby without making Derian feel left out? What would we do if the baby came in the middle of the night? Where would Derian stay while I was in the hospital? We had a lot of plans to organize before it was time to race off to the hospital. I was adamant about having Derian stay in the hospital the second night with us. He would not be pushed aside for the new baby.

But before I could deliver this child I had many fears to face. I wasn't a rookie any more. Labor was all too fresh in my mind! Besides the physical pain, I had to get a grip on the "what ifs." There were no guarantees that Connor was going to be healthy. Needless to say, I had no birth plan for this baby. Gail and Dr. Matt knew this was going to be a tough delivery for me. I wasn't opening myself up to allow this baby to enter the world. I thought that maybe writing would help me face my fears and give me some peace.

It was two weeks past my due date. I was hot, uncomfortable and sick of people calling and saying, "Haven't you had that baby yet?" I called Dr. Matt on September 12 and asked if I could be induced. I went into the hospital and was given a gel that was supposed to start labor. I stayed for a few hours. Nothing was happening. I went back to the car, hopeful that things would pick up that night. Nothing. The next day I tried this same routine. Still nothing. Dr. Matt and I decided that if the gel didn't work she would hook me up to Pitocin the next day. Even though I swore I would never take Pitocin again, the thought of being pregnant one more day was all the coaxing I needed. I spoke to my sister that night and told her about the plan. She asked me if I was excited about the next day. I replied, "Colleen, how excited do you think Jesus was the night before he was crucified?"

I woke up that morning to the kicking of my sweet unborn child. Soon I would be able to see the way he moved. Knowing these would be the last few hours we would be together like this, I wrote a letter to him.

To my soon-to-be-born baby boy,

I feel like there is something I need to talk to you about before you're born. As you look through your baby book, I'm sure you're going to compare it to Derian's. One obvious difference is that his is much larger and more detailed than yours.

This does not mean I wasn't excited about you or that I love you any less. The truth is…

I was just plain scared.

Your brother surprised us all with his health problems. We were so incredibly excited about having a baby; it never dawned on us that something might be wrong. It was a huge, scary shock! The excitement was quickly mixed with fear. Shortly, after we started to be a normal family, we found out about you. You were definitely a surprise! I wasn't quite ready for a new baby right away. I needed a little more time to forget the trauma that followed Derian's birth and rejoice a little longer in his being home with us.

As you were growing, you might have felt some of the emotions I was carrying. I was afraid of what was going to happen next. Was your birth going to follow the same pattern? Could more heartbreak be lurking ahead? I've prayed for you—I've felt you move and seen you grow. I know you are going to do wonderful things in my life and bring more joy than I can imagine. It's time for you to come out of hiding and present yourself to the world. So many people are anxious to meet you! I can't wait to hold and kiss your tiny little hands, feet, and face.

We're about to begin a journey—you and I. We're going to have to be strong and work together. I hope God guides us on our way and prepares us for whatever lies ahead.

I am anxious to meet you, and I love you already, Connor Robert Keech.

Love,

Your mom

Robb woke up when I had finished my letter to Connor, gave me a hug and asked how I was doing. He knew I was nervous about labor. We talked until we heard Derian's "good morning" yelp, beckoning us to let him out of his crib. When I entered his room, he was standing in his crib. This would be the last night he would spend in his room alone. I picked him up and squeezed his body close to mine. His big brown eyes searched my eyes for a reason for such sentimentality. I found his doll and told him in an excited voice, "Baby will come today." He picked up on the excitement in my voice and began crawling in circles.

I was moving in slow motion, since I didn't have to be at the hospital at any set time. I was going to enjoy these last few hours of being pregnant. Robb was going to drop Derian off at his parents' house and meet me in the hospital later. Since I was twelve days overdue and not having any signs of labor, we knew nothing was going to happen for hours. We were very relaxed this time around. I grabbed my bags, kissed Derian good-bye, and gave Robb a ton of last-minute instructions. As I walked out to the car Robb yelled out "I hope you're pushing by the time I get there." We both laughed. I hoped things would go quickly!

I thoroughly enjoyed my drive to the hospital; I listened to the radio and tried to get psyched up for labor. Since I knew it was going to be a rough day, I decided to treat myself to a nice, leisurely breakfast. While I ate, I asked that God would help me through the day and that Connor would be healthy. I also asked for help in making this transition a smooth one for Derian. I finished my breakfast and headed for the hospital.

I passed by a parking place close to the ramp door, so I backed up, only to hit the car that was behind me. Both of us got out of the car to see if there were any damages. This was not a good way to start labor. Luckily, there was nothing. The man was so nervous about me going into labor in the parking ramp that he just wished me good luck and drove off.

This time, I brought in my bags into the Birth Center, set them down, and told the staff I wasn't leaving without a baby. We all laughed. Once I was moved into the room, the nurse asked if I wanted a few movies to watch. Hey, this was a different type of delivery already! The nurse hooked me up to the Pitocin, put a heart monitor on my belly for the baby, and put A Few Good Men in the VCR. Robb poked his head in the door and asked in a hopeful voice, "Do you need to push yet?"

"I wish—I haven't had one contraction, and I've been hooked up to this thing for two hours. I think I'm going to be pregnant forever." I began asking him a million questions. "How did Derian do this morning? Did you remember to bring the "I'm a big brother" T-shirt I made for Derian to wear to the hospital?"

He laughed at my reminders. "Yes, yes, I got it all. Everything is under control—you just need to have this baby." We watched another movie. About 5 p.m., things really started to pick up. I was having contractions every minute lasting a full minute. By 9 p.m., Dr. Matt decided I had

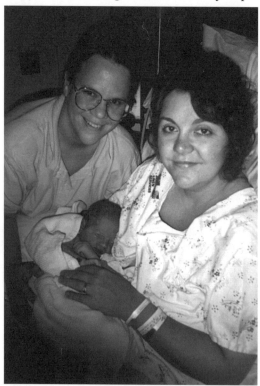

been on the Pitocin too long and needed a good night's sleep. We would try for a birthday the next morning. I was relieved and disappointed at the same time. My body had another birth plan. Robb called Gail around 11 p.m. The two of them were up all night with me, trying to make me more comfortable. The next morning I was dilated to three. I began to cry—all that work for nothing. I wasn't any closer to having this baby than I was the night before. My disappointment was obvious to Robb, who was also

Gail and Patsy

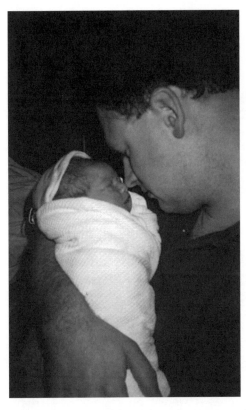

dealing with his own disappointment. He too, was anxious for all this to be over.

Dr. Matt came in around 6 a.m. to see how I was doing. She could tell I was irritable and depressed at the same time. She said in an upbeat, confident voice, "Let's have a baby. This has been going on way too long." Of course, I was in favor of her decision. She hooked me back up to the Pitocin, and we began again. I must have gotten a huge dose of it, because by 9:10 that morning, Connor came shooting out.

I watched as Robb cut the umbilical cord and witnessed the tears that he shed as he looked at his new son for the first time. His eyes were filled with pride as he presented Connor to me. The three of us looked at each other; our bare skins touched and Robb sweetly said, "You did good, Patsy—thanks for another beautiful son."

It was a wonderful moment, but too short. I was starving! If I didn't get something to eat, I was going to get sick. "Robb, I need something to eat—NOW!" After not knowing what to do for me during labor, he responded immediately and returned with a meal. Gail stroked my hair and commented on how strong Connor was. It was nice to have both Robb and Gail with me.

That evening, our parents and families came to the Birth Center—a much happier part of the hospital. Grandparents Bob and Lois brought Derian into our room. He looked so cute wearing the "I'm a big brother" shirt I made for him. They carried him to my bed so he could meet his little brother. I was curious how he would respond. Instead of being mesmerized by the baby, he was much more concerned about the IV in my arm. He kept pointing to it, saying, "Owie Momma, owie." His

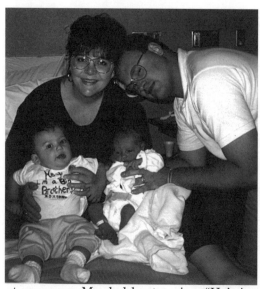

brown eyes filled with empathy. He wanted to take care of me. The only way I got him to acknowledge Connor was to wrap up the IV.

Everyone else in the room made up for Derian's lack of enthusiasm. Our family members took turns passing Connor around and commenting on his toes, hands, face, and how alert he was. Connor looked around the room at everyone. My dad kept saying, "He's just so glad to meet his people." Derian went home with my parents and would visit the next day. He gave me a sweet little kiss and cried as he left his "Momma" behind.

The next day was filled with calls, visitors, and congratulations. I was relishing this second day. In the back of my head, I kept thinking, "If we can just make it through the night, we will be home free." Derian's pediatrician knew I needed reassurance about Connor's health. He personally came up to exam him. That evening, Derian came to see us. He entered the room with a robust smile and hearty enthusiasm. Derian was so happy to be wherever he was. Robb unfolded the playpen and we made a big deal about Derian being the big

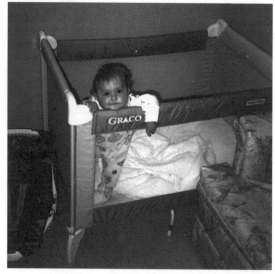

brother. Derian must have known this was special because he puffed out his chest a bit and showed us his muscles each time we talked about it.

The four of us spent the night together in our room in the Birth Center. We prayed that our last night in the hospital would be different than it was with Derian. Relief washed over me as the morning sun's brightness filled our room. We'd made it through the night. We would have a new beginning with this child. Thank you, Lord.

Movement Three—

Roam Not Far From Me...

Chapter 20

Robb had been planning to build a small deck onto the front of our house all summer. It just so happened that the arrangements had all been made prior to Connor's homecoming. I have no idea why I went along with this plan. Robb left the hospital early that morning and headed off for home. As I heard the door shut, panic washed over me. Two boys—how was I going to do this?

An hour later, Derian abruptly sat up and pulled the covers off. He was up and ready for the day. I put him in his walker and he began exploring everything within his reach, banging into the furniture.

Connor woke up and expected to be fed immediately! Breast-feeding was a breeze with him. While I was nursing Connor, Derian decided we needed to snuggle right then and tried to push Connor away from me. We talked about baby Connor and why Mommy needed to hold Connor to feed him, just like Mommy did when Derian was a baby. I followed that up with a concept older siblings hate—"sharing."

While things were still somewhat calm, I decided to take a bath. Connor was sleeping in his infant seat and Derian was in the bathroom with me. I closed my eyes, breathed deeply, and prepared for the day. Suddenly, a mad cry came from the infant seat. Derian scooted from the bathroom. He checked out Connor. Connor's irritated cry let me know he was upset about the lack of supervision. He cried furiously. Derian, startled by Connor's response, began to cry himself. What should I do? Help, I need help! I picked up the phone, "Mom, Robb left to build the deck and I'm alone with both boys in the hospital. Could you come as soon as possible?" I felt relieved knowing help was on the way.

By the time my mom and Aunt Ellen arrived, I was frazzled. The two of them pitched right in, packed up our things, entertained Derian and held Connor while I made arrangements to have him circumcised. How would I have managed without them! Ellen and my mom were relaxed and enjoyed the kids. We checked out four hours later.

A hot, sweaty, and hungry deck crew greeted us. Without even thinking of my new responsibilities or my freshly labored body, I volunteered to get lunch for everyone.

Ellen loved babies, so she took care of Connor in between feedings. Robb's mom supervised the deck building and my mom helped with Derian. I played the role of hostess and new mom. My parents insisted I sit down, relax, or take a nap. A nap would be tough with all the pounding going on, but sitting down was a nice break. Once I sat down I never got up. The guys worked till dinner.

The crew was coming over the next day and working until the job was done. At this point I was having a problem with this plan! Two of the five days Robb had taken off for the new baby were shot. That night I made Robb promise not do one more thing on the deck after the crew left. His last three days were ours! Robb was also starting to feel a little disappointed with our homecoming. He wasn't getting to know Connor, play with Derian, or talk with me.

In a guilty voice, Robb asked, "Patsy, you're not going to leave me, are you?"

"Why?" I asked coldly.

"Well, I think if I had just had a baby and was thrown into everyday life, I'd probably be a little upset."

"I am, and if I only had one baby, I might consider leaving; but two babies are too much work to do by myself," I said teasingly. We were terrible planners. We always take on too much. Thankfully, the next three days were quiet, cozy, and intimate. It was great to be four! We rested, played, and got to get to know each other. Things didn't seem nearly as chaotic when Robb was around.

The doll we had bought earlier must have worked because—Derian was careful with how he treated Connor. Derian's job was to rub powder on Connor's tummy after his bath. He took this job seriously and made sure all the power was smoothed out. He would smile and flash a look that said, "See what a good big brother I am."

Our experiences with Connor were much different than those with Derian. We were like first-time parents, taking care of his umbilical cord, being able to rock him at home, walk in his room, and see him anytime we wanted. Normal was okay, even if it felt strange. Everything we did was a new experience. We didn't take anything for granted.

Our family time gave way to reality. We had budgeted carefully so I could take the first trimester of school for maternity leave. I would be a stay-at-home mom until November 27. I was excited about staying at home with my boys. But, no matter how good my motherhood intentions were, letting Robb go that first morning was difficult. I remember kissing him good-bye and then looking into the faces of the boys. My head rang with disaster:

- *What if they both start crying at the same time?*
- *How do I go anywhere with two babies?*
- *What if I'm an awful mom?*
- *I don't think I can do this—I'm sure I can't do this!*
- *I'm in way over my head!*

"Robb, come back," I yelled. I could tell these two were really going to break me in.

By the time Robb had pulled out of the driveway, I had to confront my fears. Both boys started to cry. I pushed the fears aside and just "did."

I worked harder those weeks off than I had ever worked in my life. But, I got the hang of it. Within a few weeks I could nurse Connor, feed Derian, and talk on the phone all at the same time. Amazing! It was at this point that I realized motherhood was not given nearly enough praise. I contemplated contacting Mr. Hallmark and proposing mothers have two holidays. One day a year was not nearly enough to thank a mom for all she does.

As the days passed, I realized going to work would be a vacation. I wouldn't work nearly as hard at school as I did at home. The boys kept me so busy with diaper changes, making bottles, walks, clothing changes, and laundry. Watching our little boys interact was my greatest joy. Throughout the day, Derian would pull his face up to Connor's and gently pat his baby cheeks. Connor watched with wide, excited eyes when Derian scooted his body around, eventually learning to crawl.

However, Derian had a few kinks to work out before he mastered this skill! He kept his head down when he crawled so he ended up with major rug burns on his forehead. Connor watched Derian so intensely that I knew it was just a matter of time before he would be trying Derian's tricks himself.

By the time Connor was three months he was crawling like it was nobody's business. The two boys crawled in unison up and down the hallway. Connor was in such a hurry to be a little boy; he did everything early. Since Derian was a little behind, they evolved into "twins," accomplishing many of their milestones at the same time. Connor was a great motivator for Derian.

They made a great team, sharing a room, toys, clothes, and talents. Each evening they would sing or talk to each other to sleep. There were pros and cons to having the two in the same room though. Many evenings one would wake up crying and wake up the other one. Then all hell broke loose. Of course this usually happened around two in the morning. Despite that, I loved doing things in twos; two car seats took over our back seat, two coats to put on, two sets of shoes, two bags of diapers, etc. We were settling into this new life just fine!

Chapter 21

November 17, 1994—18 days before returning to work.

Derian was scheduled for a routine heart catheter. Since Connor's god-parents were in town, they volunteered to watch Connor for the day. We checked into the hospital at 6 a.m. and were prepared for a long day. By the time we turned Derian over to the team, we were exhausted and breathed an "off duty" sigh of relief. Luckily, Derian didn't put up much of a fight about going with the strangers; however, I knew some day he would be wise to all this. These were easy days, compared to the ones coming. How would we explain all this to him, or what would it be like to hear him explain it all to us?

Once Derian was in the heart lab, we would wait for updates from a cardiac nurse. Depending on what Dr. Hesslein did in the lab would determine if Derian would come home that evening. If he ballooned open an artery, Derian would need to stay overnight. Dr. Hesslein knew we would need to make plans for Connor, so he was conscientious about keeping us abreast of what was going on. He always finished his report to the nurses with something like, "Derian's being a good boy." The small cardiac staff was becoming a big part of our parental team; they were key people in our lives.

Heart catheters had become routine. We weren't worried, but instead were confident we would get a positive report. Robb and I passed the time reading, eating and talking, something we had little time to do these days. Around 4 p.m., the procedure was complete and Dr. Hesslein came to tell us what he discovered.

Dr. Hesslein was usually optimistic and offered hope, even in the face of trouble. However, today he was very serious. Something was up. A fear tornado began winding up my spine. I moved to the edge of my chair. Dr. Hesslein didn't have good news for us.

"The pressures in Derian's heart have increased since his surgery. His heart is working too hard forcing blood through his tiny arteries. We need to expand these accesses to the heart. We have no choice but to do this through a surgical procedure."

"Surgery again! He is just healed up from the last one." I asked. "Is this because of the valve that was cut or the rhythm his heart went into?"

"No, I'm sorry. I know you all have been through a lot and I wouldn't suggest surgery if there was another option."

"Can he just get a new heart?" Robb asked. "Maybe that would be the best thing—how can he keep going through all these surgeries?"

"Robb, I know this is frustrating, but a new heart is not a walk in the park either. There are many things involved with that."

We were back to the same place we were four months ago. It wasn't fair—it just wasn't! Why should Derian have to go through this again? My head was so heavy; it felt like it was going to roll off my shoulders. Dr. Hesslein realized this news was a blow to us, but he couldn't do anything to lighten things up.

"When?"

Dr. Hesslein took a deep breath and said, "Soon. Derian will have to have this done before school is out, within the next month or so."

How, how, how are we going to make it through this time? We have another baby. How will we take care of two babies during this stay? Recovery. I don't know if I can handle that again. The only thing that pulled me through last time was thinking Derian wouldn't have to have surgery again for a long time. I can't believe this is happening. Please, someone just take it away. I can't take this anymore.

Work—I was just supposed to start back. What are we going to do for money? We used our entire savings. I'm not leaving Derian in this place alone.

Robb finished the conversation. "We'll call tomorrow and schedule surgery." Once Dr. Hesslein left us we phoned our parents and some friends. Everyone was disappointed with the results. Another surgery was unimaginable.

My feet felt heavy as I paced the cold hospital tile floor. *How come in another lifetime, I was a stranger to hospital life and now I can't get away from it? Why? Why Derian again?*

The nurse brought Derian into our room and placed him in my arms. I held him until his drugged sleep wore off. I went through the motions of being coherent but found I couldn't process anything past the moment. Robb pulled me into the future as he began thinking out loud. The most logical solution was to schedule the surgery for the following month. I already had a sub that knew my students. It would be easiest if she continued on with my students. I would take another month off and stay in the hospital with Derian. But what about Connor? How were we going to care for both boys at the same time? First things first. I needed to call Arletta and ask if she could continue subbing for me. Poor Arletta never really had a choice. How could she say no after hearing what was going on and listening to me cry?

Connor's godparents brought Connor back home and stayed for dinner. Seeing Connor's spirit had the same effect on me that lightning has on dark sky. He was quick, bright, and immediately lit up the darkness. We tried to carry on a conversation with Bobby and Rosie, but our hearts were too heavy.

The next day I didn't even bother to get dressed. Why should I? I wasn't going anywhere—ever again. Our life was a mess, and death was hanging over our house. This was going to be a big surgery. What if Derian didn't make it? I pulled the kids into a tight hug; it felt so good to hang on to them! They must have sensed my need as they pressed their cheeks into mine and then quickly slipped out of my arms and over to the toy box. The room quickly filled with a color mess as they dismantled the toy box. Amidst their laughter and play, I withdrew. The "what ifs" were too damn scary.

Chapter 22

Figuring out our finances

As I rubbed my foundation in the next morning, I saw the woman in the mirror asking me how was I going to take a leave. My checks covered the mortgage. If I could find some way to pay our mortgage, we would be okay.

Derian had Birth-Through-Three school that day. Becky came to the door with her bag of stuff and a big smile for Derian. Derian and Connor greeted her and excitedly pulled out the toys in her bag. She handed the bag to the boys and asked in a chipper voice, "How did the test go yesterday?"

"Derian needs surgery again."

"No! Why? I thought the surgery he just had was supposed to be his last." She sat next to me. "I am so sorry; what can I do to help, Patsy?"

I had given a lot of thought to this question. What could anyone do? "If I can figure out a way to get my mortgage paid, then taking another month off wouldn't be quite so devastating. I called my mortgage company, told them our situation and asked if we could skip a payment until I could go back to work. The person was clueless. He had a simple solution. 'You can skip two or three payments if you want to, but at the end of three months, we will expect the entire lump sum.' Let's think about that: Unpaid Leave + no money = three months of payments."

By the time I finished explaining my conversation with the mortgage company, Becky had an idea. From the living room, I could hear her explaining the situation to someone over the phone. I had no idea what she was thinking or whom she was talking to. She hung up the phone and walked into the living room like she had solved the problem. "Patsy, I spoke to the people at Neighbors Inc., a non-profit in the area that helps people in the your region of the county with a variety of services. I told them about your situation and asked if they would pay your next month's mortgage. They said yes!"

I couldn't believe it! This was too easy; I didn't want to get excited until the money was in my hands. We were up to our eyeballs in the paperwork required for TEFRA—a state program that assists with the medical bills of disabled children living at home. This seventy-two-page form had to be filled out every three months. There had to be a catch, a huge form, something.

Becky promised that if any paper work were required, she would do it in addition to making meals, running errands, and watching Connor. Derian's school time that day was spent on helping Mom cope. Thank God Becky came over!

I called Robb after she left to tell him about this possibility. He, too, thought it would be great if it worked out, but wasn't going to hold his breath. His lack of enthusiasm frustrated me. We couldn't process these moments the same way because his work separated him from life in the trenches. We weren't mad at one another; we just couldn't look at each other's pain yet.

It was going to be tough to get through the holidays knowing Derian was going into surgery on January 10. But we tried to get into the Christmas mood for the kids. We bought a real Christmas tree and the challenge was to make it kid proof. I tied raffia bows to the branches and put a few lights on, then we went to see Santa.

Even though we were doing all the things that were supposed to get us into the Christmas spirit, there was just no "Merry" in Christmas that year. This was tough on Robb and me. Holidays were always an important part of our lives.

When Robb was invited to a Christmas party after work, he jumped at the chance, if only to feel some sense of "normalcy" once again. I was glad he was going, as I hoped he could be free from worry for just a little while. I got the boys down to sleep relatively easy that night and was just preparing for bed when Robb came home. He was unusually pale and was trembling. I was almost afraid to hear what had happened.

In a deep, serious tone, he said, "Patsy, a strange thing happened to me on the way home. As I was driving, I was talking to God." I held my breath. Robb and I had never spoken to each other about God like this before. I never even knew he had conversations with Him. The air between us felt still and reverent. I listened intently.

"Patsy, I told God if he needed to take someone from our family, it should be me rather then Derian." Tears began to pool in his eyes. "Then I felt the deep heat of a hand resting on my shoulder and heard a soft, quiet whisper of an angel say, 'Derian is going to be okay. Don't worry.'"

I was stunned by what he was saying. For a moment I just stared at him, and then we fell into a peace-filled embrace. This was the most powerful moment in our marriage. His willingness to share his spiritual encounter with me was the most intimate experience we had ever had. He allowed me to walk in his soul. The depth of his love for our son moved me in a profound way.

The next few weeks flew by, along with the fear of what was ahead. We were given a promise and greeted January 10 with confidence, peace, and a stronger union together with God.

As we prepared for this surgery, not only did we have to pack for ourselves but for a baby as well: clothes, diapers, bottles, baby wipes, formula, toys, etc. In addition to the packing, I made a rough schedule for where Connor would stay each night. All I really cared about was that I would be able to see Connor in the evenings, and that he was being loved when I couldn't be with him. Since all four grandparents were crazy about having him, there was no shortage of love.

Chapter 23

Tuesday, January 10, 1995

We moved into the morning of that surgery with confidence. The staff was both amazed and saddened at our carefree attitude surrounding this surgery. I remember hearing comments like, "It's sad to think that you are so conditioned to this lifestyle." We never shared the message Robb's angel gave to us; perhaps then they would have understood our lack of fear. We had been given a promise from God himself that Derian would live. Why should we fear anything? All would be well. Since Derian's heart rate was still beating in Bradycardia rhythm, Dr. Hesslein decided they would put in a pacemaker during surgery in order to eliminate another surgery later.

Derian was kept drugged for a few days after surgery. Once the drugs wore off and most of the tubes were gone, I debated about whether I should bring Connor, who was four months old, to the hospital. I didn't want to scare him, but since the hospital would be a part of our lives he would need to understand where Mom, Dad, and Derian would go sometimes.

I laid Connor in the crib next to Derian. Even in his early stages of recovery Derian seemed glad to see his little brother. Connor was so happy to be with his big brother that he placed Derian's bare heel into his mouth and began sucking it.

Connor was our reminder of the outside world. Part of our life belonged to him and would revolve around the world of a healthy child. This was the beginning of another challenge we would struggle with. How should we parent and encourage one child without holding the other one back?

The recovery from this surgery was much smoother than the last one. Like I said, there was "no fear." We took one day at a time. The one thing I do remember about this recovery was the day the surgeon came into our room to remove the pacemaker wires that poked out of Derian's stomach. The four wires were in the shape of a square, and a wire from each corner poked through his skin and was coiled into glass tubes. I couldn't imagine how these would be removed. The pacemaker was placed under his ribcage, making him look like he had swallowed a Walkman. What did it feel like to have such a big thing bulging out? Would it hurt if he fell on it?

The surgeon was in good spirits and assured me that the removal of these wires was simple and painless. Simple I could buy. It would have to be easier then heart surgery. But painless? I wasn't sure if I believed that. "Are you going to give Derian anything for pain?"

"Nope. If everything goes as planned, he will barely feel this." I hoped he was right.

As soon as the bright lights over the crib were turned on, Derian stiffened his body. Dr. Nichols approached and spoke to him like a grandparent would. It seemed like a trick to get him to relax. I held Derian's hand.

The first wire came out quickly. Derian cringed but didn't cry. Maybe Dr. Nichols was right. One down. Three left. The next one was stuck. He pulled but the wire didn't let go. Derian cringed in pain. Letting out a battle cry, he looked as if an arrow was being pulled from his body. I couldn't watch. Derian screamed begging me to make it stop. I could do nothing, except hold his hand. *Why can't you give him anything? Obviously this is not going as planned.* Even the surgeon was uncomfortable with Derian's "coherent" reaction. He was torturing my child. If the next wire didn't come out easy I was going to insist Derian get something for pain. Thank God they did!

Derian was shaken by this procedure. As soon as it was over, he sat up and waved bye-bye to Dr. Nichols. Derian was ever so glad to see him leave. I hated being stuck between a doctor's work and my son. I wondered what kind of a mother Derian thought I was. The rest of the day I held him, hoping to repair his sense of security and trust.

Two days later we signed the release papers and took Derian home. How wonderful to have all four of us home again. A huge stack of welcome home letters from the students I hadn't even met was placed in our front door. I scattered them on the floor and showed Derian. As smooth as the last surgery went, I sensed Derian was feeling rushed back into reality. His voice was still hoarse from the vent tube—so hoarse we couldn't hear his cries. It broke my heart to think of Derian crying and no one hearing him.

It was amazing the magic the word "home" had in the hospital. But now that we were home, I was going crazy. Connor was determined to be independent. He held his own bottle and refused to cooperate for a diaper change. Derian was depressed and unable to communicate without his voice. I was clueless as to how to mother them. I never felt like I was doing a good job. Maybe God should not have entrusted me with them. I wasn't able to make them happy.

Derian's voice came back about a month later. We were reconnected. I was back in school and working diligently so I wouldn't have to bring work home in the evening. I had no time at home to do anything except watch my boys. Derian's heart was stabilized and he was 100 percent recovered!

Derian was 22 months old and crawling. His teachers were working hard to strengthen his leg muscles so he could walk. Our goal was to have him walking before he was two. Robb and I sat on opposite sides of a room and tried to get him to walk back and forth. Walking practice took place everywhere we went. Some days this was a fun adventure and some days it was just plain hard work. Derian was not all that interested in walking, but Connor was. At nine months he decided to give it a try. 48 hours later he mastered it. Connor's accomplishment was a blow to Derian's ego. In fact, he quit trying to walk altogether. Every time we mentioned walking or tried to play our walking game, Derian retreated. I felt sad for him; he was discovering that he had a different body than Connor's. He took this walking business as a personal failure. How was I going to help him through this problem? This was probably the beginning of many skills that Connor would master quickly and Derian would struggle with. How do I encourage Derian without holding Connor back?

I searched my heart for the best thing to do for Derian, and came up empty. Derian was the only one who could make it happen. We would just have to be patient until he was ready to do it. After a few days of sulking, Derian decided to be a walker after all. He woke up one morning determined to walk. He bumped his head 10,000 times, and fell even more, but by the end of the day he was walking all by himself. We all slept well that night, not only from exhaustion, but with pride. Connor was thrilled for Derian. We were now a walking family!

Walking gave Derian a new sense of independence. He maneuvered himself up and down the sidewalk or walked to and from the sandbox. How proud I was of his success! His curiosity and newfound mobility made each day more exciting. Holding a balloon, blowing bubbles, and sliding down the slide were all adventures too exciting not to be noticed. The boys rejoiced over these simple wonders in what we referred to as the "happy dance." With hands in the air, they'd stomp their feet and twirl in circles.

Their energy infected onlookers who couldn't help but smile. These toddlers shared their spirit of joy not only of life, but also of life together in a unique way.

Even though Neighbors, Inc. paid our mortgage in January, as we added up our bills, it was obvious that the aftermath of my extended leave was beginning to show. The mortgage help was wonderful and something we were truly grateful for; but the expenses we incurred while in the hospital (meals, parking, and $500.00 to keep our insurance going) left little for groceries, formula, and other necessities. We were in trouble financially, and there was no way around it. We hadn't even gotten the bills for Derian's last surgery. We were responsible for twenty percent of the total bill.

Derian's teachers had often told us about programs that Derian could qualify for. We were convinced that we could pull our own weight—we would provide for our children. We were college graduates and not the type of people that got assistance. But we looked at our budget, and the amount of money coming in versus going out, we realized that we had to change our philosophy. As great as it was to be proud, we had two children who were counting on us to make good decisions for them.

My dad helped me accept assistance. "Patsy, get all the help you can. Sign up for every program that you qualify for. Take as much as you can." I couldn't believe this was coming from my dad, and in the same token I was glad it was. He gave me permission to ask and the respect for doing it.

It was early May before Robb and I sought help. We had done the best we could for as long as we could. I had heard about the WIC program (a program to assist new mothers and their children with vouchers for milk, cheese, cereal, beans, and juice) and made an appointment.

The morning of my appointment I felt incredibly nervous. The kids and I changed clothes at least three times. *What do we wear so we don't look too well off but not poor either?* I knew our situation would be evaluated as well as my mothering ability: not too firm, look in control, confident, and hope the boys cooperate. Exposing our situation was like going under a magnifying glass. What would they see?

It was a long walk with four toddler legs. Once we got into the building, the boys took off running in different directions. Teasing their mom was their primary source of entertainment. I felt like a bowling ball in between opposite pins. I grabbed Derian first and then we chased Connor. I worked up a full-blown sweat by the time we got in and out of an elevator and into the office. Luckily, there was a kid's toy area toward which the boys gravitated. WHEW! I had a few moments to regain my composure.

I signed in and then sat in a cushioned chair. It felt cool under my steamy body. As I looked around the room at the other people who all had stories and situations of their own, I felt ashamed of myself. Any stupid and ignorant thing I had ever said about the "poor" was now about me. It was my turn to be poor. I didn't like it, didn't deserve it, and couldn't handle it. I was tempted to leave and forget the whole thing. But as I searched the bright eyes of my children, I knew I had to stay.

For the first time in my life, I understood why the homeless people I used to serve at Loaves and Fishes were not especially thankful for what I was doing. This was a terrible place to be. Who wants to be this down and out? I clenched my teeth as my name was called. I would be utterly humiliated if someone recognized my name and knew I was asking for public assistance. In my "loser state of mind," I picked up both boys and quickly escaped into the room the worker showed us. I was relieved when they closed the door. I filled out several forms while the boys played with the toys in the room.

I realized that our case was far more medically complex than these people were familiar with. It would be insulting to have them tell *me* Derian was underweight. *Duh, I know he's below the fifth percentile; you're not telling me anything new.* They had no idea about the entourage of doctors and professionals that work with Derian. He was a first-class operation! (Literally.)

As the caseworker talked, I kept my mouth shut and nodded as if I was paying attention. I did become interested when she started talking about the vouchers. This was what I needed. No lectures, just WIC coupons. The three-hour appointment was taking its toll on the boys. They were tired, crabby, and made it clear they had had enough. I hoped their behavior would hurry things along. We left with several folders on nutrition, wellness, and the most important information: how to get WIC coupons. Having help with two different types of formula alone would ease up our money situation. The boys were ready for naps so leaving was much easier. They fell asleep on the way home.

It was a nice spring day, so I took advantage of the boys' naptime and sat in the car in with them as I read the information on WIC. I knew everything I needed to know by the time the boys woke up. I was confident I could do this the "right way."

When Robb came home that evening we calculated what we would save with WIC. With this help we could get back on our feet. But on the way to the grocery store, I felt my stomach tighten up. I asked Robb if he was uncomfortable about using these coupons. His answer was simple. "We need the help, and I'm not afraid of it." This response gave me enough courage to go through our first WIC shopping experience.

When the groceries were in the cart, the next challenge would be handing the coupons to the cashier and having her look at me. Robb and I looked for a cashier who appeared friendly. When we were confident we'd picked out the "right" person, we got into line. We emptied one cart and paid for the groceries and then took the items from the WIC cart. I covered each item with its coupon so it would be easy for her. With trembling hands I handed her the first one. She had a confused look on her face as she examined the coupon. Without saying a word to us she got on her microphone and announced, "I have a WIC transaction on lane three."

Robb and I looked at each other in complete disbelief. My heart sank to my knees. I was sure everyone in the store was looking at the "poor" people in lane three and angry that we were getting help and they weren't. Thank God, she only yelled in the microphone once. After pushing several buttons, all the groceries were accounted for. The automatic doors barely opened before both Robb and I took a big gulp of air and started laughing. We were so embarrassed. Laughter was the only thing that could shake out the stress and humility. The kicker was— we chose that cashier. I will never forget that evening. To this day, I refuse to listen when people complain about "the system" or the people who use it.

In addition to the WIC program, we also utilized the personal care attendant (PCA) services that Derian qualified for. This service is based on the child's condition and mastery of skills. The state determines how many hours a family should receive for respite. Derian qualified for 12 hours a week. We were lucky to find two college women who fit in with our family and adored our boys.

Chapter 24

We made an appointment with an audiologist that spring. The office had a mural of primary-colored animals and a room filled with toys. Derian was pulled into the excitement. This was great. I could complete the forms while he entertained himself. A few minutes later Derian's name was called and the audiologist led us to a small room. I filled her in on his elaborate medical history while a nurse gave Derian some medicine that would put him to sleep for the test. Derian was moved to a table in another room, tiny microphones were placed in his ears, and a few sticky monitors were attached to his head. The audiologist and I watched the screen in the other room for the reactions of his brainwaves. We were looking for waving movements; a lack of them would mean the brain was not picking up the pitches. Wavy lines began to move across the screen. *That other doctor was wrong. Look, Derian is hearing.* When the pitch changed, the wavy lines stopped quivering. They were flat. I gulped back tears.

"Derian's speech has been delayed because of his hearing loss. You do sign in your home, don't you?"

"No."

"With a hearing loss this significant you need to be signing to him. Why haven't you been?" she asked accusingly.

"We never really got a clear answer on his hearing capability. His hearing took a back seat to his heart problems."

"Well, you need to start signing immediately. I will give you a list of places you can take classes. It is important you start this now so he can still catch up." Once again, we were failures as parents. Yet, Derian responded to Connor's cries, doors shutting, dogs barking, etc. How could he hear all these things if he were deaf?

"The bones in Derian's ears are fused together, making it impossible for sound to pass through."

"Can this be corrected with surgery—the bones be un-fused?" I asked

"I'm not sure. I'd like to have you see Dr. Levie, who is one of the best ENTs around. I'd like him to examine Derian and decide if he could do anything surgically for him."

I left the office with a groggy toddler, a heavy heart, and Dr. Levie's number. I called for an appointment with Dr. Levie. It would be a month before we could see him. When the date for the appointment arrived, Robb and I met the highly regarded Dr. Levie. A tall, older man with volumes of gray hair and a thick beard, he exuded experience and confidence, keeping his comments short and to the point. He called in a nurse and asked her to prepare Derian for a scope procedure. A few minutes later she brought in an apparatus that looked like a straight jacket. It was a long board with several dangling blue straps.

"Derian will need to be strapped to this papoose while I insert this tube-like microscope into his nostril," said Dr. Levie.

This scope was about a foot long and had a light on the end of it. This procedure sounded horrible. Derian was going to hate this.

Dr. Levie picked up Derian and placed him onto the board. Derian must have sensed trouble; his fighter instincts kicked in. As the nurse strapped his arms and legs into the apparatus, sweat formed on Derian's face. A husky wail scraped across his vocal chords. God, I hated watching Derian go through all this. I stroked his hair. As Dr. Levie sprayed a nasal spray into Derian's nose, he let out a growl. A few seconds later, Dr. Levie inserted the scope. Derian's sounds grew fiercer; his face turned a deep shade of red and his hair curled from his sweat. Dr. Levie peered through the glass eye of the tube and shouted out terms the nurse quickly jotted down. He then pulled out the long tube and reinserted it into the other nostril. He couldn't get it though. We had warned him about this. He tried again, realized it was not going to work, then pulled the tube out. After the nurse and I quickly unwrapped Derian, he jumped into my arms. While Robb and I consoled Derian, Dr. Levie examined the x-rays taken when Derian was a newborn. As he held them up, he traced his finger on the nasal passage on the left side to the right side. The right side was filled with bone.

"This should have been chiseled out and reshaped at birth. I can correct this, but I am not willing to do anything with his ears. He will at least be able to hear out of one ear with a hearing aid. Doing surgery could jeopardize him hearing at all."

"What all would be involved in the surgery on his nose?" Robb asked.

"It's a simple, same-day surgery. However, given Derian's complex history, I'd feel more comfortable if Derian stayed overnight in the hospital. The surgery takes a few hours. To keep the passages open, I will sew stints in his nose. These will need to remain in for a few weeks to keep the passages open."

The procedures seemed manageable and the best thing for Derian. We left his office relieved that the surgery would be easy and helpful for Derian. By the time we arrived home, we'd accepted the idea, but we decided to tell our families closer to the day of the surgery.

That night arrived. Robb was working late, so the boys and I invited my parents over for dinner. After dinner, I told my parents about our visit to the ENT. They were disappointed about the results of the hearing tests and were surprised this problem couldn't be fixed. I did my best to drop only one bomb at a time on my family, but it seemed the perfect time to tell them about the upcoming surgery. I explained the procedure and the benefits of this surgery as routine and as matter-of-fact as possible. My dad flinched and sighed his heavy, "Oh my God" sigh. My mom turned a shade of white and lashed out words meant to protect Derian.

I was being attacked for thinking breathing out of two nostrils was a necessity. It felt as if my parents thought I had developed a taste for blood or something. My mom was very upset. There were accusations, hurt feelings, and doubts about what was best for Derian. I knew this surgery wasn't going to be a picnic, but in the long run, it would be beneficial for Derian to breathe out of two nostrils. My parents thought we were expecting Derian to go through too much. "He just had open-heart surgery a few months ago," they pointed out. We were at a standoff.

Chapter 25

Memorial Day Weekend, 1995

We purposefully scheduled the surgery over Memorial Day so I would miss only two days of school. We had gone through so many surgeries by this time; we pretty much knew what to expect. Derian would be weighed in, measured, we'd answer lots of questions, wait, meet the anesthesiologist and wait. Then we'd hand Derian to a team of doctors who would do the procedure, we'd go get something to eat, come back and wait, wonder and wait. And just when we were sure things were taking way too long, the surgeon would show up and let us know how the surgery went. And that's pretty much how it all happened.

When Dr. Levie had completed the surgery, he escorted us out of the waiting room to a conference room. He drew pictures of what he'd done during the surgery on the white board.

"In order to open up Derian's nasal passage, I went through his nostrils and chiseled about a quarter size of bone from his skull. I've sewed stints the size of McDonald's straws into his nose to keep the new passages open and prevent scar tissue from building up. The stints stick out about one inch on both sides and will need to be suctioned every four hours, round the clock for two weeks."

What? I knew every detail about this surgery except that last part. I didn't know they would need to be suctioned, and every four hours. How was I going to be able to do that and teach the next two weeks? If we had known this part of the deal, we would have scheduled the surgery for another time. I felt like a stubborn child "I can't do that, I won't do that! Reverse this. Put the bone back, make it like it was before."

Derian was about to wake up in the recovery room. We had a good idea of what to expect: the stints, a heart monitor, an IV, and a crabby child waking from anesthesia. I didn't think I would see anything that I hadn't seen before. I was completely caught off guard with what I saw: BLOOD! Gallons of it spewing from the tubes in Derian's nose. Derian thrashed around in his crib, crying drunkenly from anesthesia. The more frustrated he would get, the more blood exploded from his nose. I had dealt with many scary things as a parent, but seeing my child bleed like this was beyond what I could handle. I felt so sorry and frightened for him. To make it worse, we had chosen this for him. I couldn't stand to look at my mistake. I had to leave for a few minutes to pull myself together.

When I was able to put my own fear aside, I returned to Derian's bedside and picked him up. I held him and tried to calm him down. He was wild with pain. I was terrified that he'd hit those stints and hurt himself even more. That was afternoon was the longest of my life! I would just get him settled down, and a nurse would stick a tube inside the bloody stint and suction blood from it. This pain would send Derian into a tailspin, and the entire process would start over. Several hours had passed and there was no sign of the bleeding slowing down. I could tell Derian was getting weak. To make things more worrisome, the nurses couldn't reassure me that this was a normal part of recovery. None of them had cared for a child after this surgery before. We were all rookies.

I tried to be a good mom. I knew that suctioning was important to help Derian heal so I helped the nurses hold Derian down while they did it. I thought it would comfort him to know I was with him. By 7 p.m. I couldn't take it anymore. I asked the nurse to find someone else to help her suction. When she found an assistant, I left and made a few calls in the lobby. I was gone for about 15 minutes. As I rounded the corner into our room, I stopped in disbelief. Five doctors and nurses were hovered over Derian. They held a black oxygen mask over his face and were pumping oxygen into him. My legs couldn't carry me into the room. I ran down the hall, horrified and confused, wondering what was going on. Robb was on his way to pick up Connor, so I was on my own. I felt like the astronauts on Apollo 13 must have felt, when their mission went out of control. Feelings of dread and guilt permeated my being. *Why did we choose this surgery for Derian? He could have lived just fine breathing with one nostril. This was a huge mistake. How could we have done this to our little boy?* I hollered out to God, "Please God, make him live. Let him be a fighter. He's got to live—we can't lose him now. God help him!"

I stayed away for as long as I could stand it. I had to know what was going on. I sheepishly peeked in the room. Derian was hooked up to the ventilator. *This was never in the plan. Things were out of control!*

I found the doctor and asked what had happened. Apparently, Derian had been intubated three times within a half an hour period. It took that long to find the right size tube. That meant a team of people held down Derian, while someone forced a thin tube between his vocal chords into his lungs three times. This made me want to vomit. To prevent him from aspirating and getting blood into his lungs, he was placed on the vent.

When I felt like things were under control, I went to the lobby to phone Robb. While I was on the phone, a nurse entered, frantic. Her voice trembled as she said, "Derian is in trouble again. We've given him two blood transfusions and his bleeding isn't slowing down. Dr. Levie is on his way to the hospital and will take Derian into emergency surgery."

I gasped and ran into the room. My poor, poor Derian. We were tricked into thinking this would be easy. I was a failure as a mother. How could we have ever thought this would be a good for Derian? Would Derian ever forgive me?

Guilty tears had dampened my T-shirt by the time Dr. Levie arrived. He was honest and told me he had never taken a child back to surgery before. He had no idea what he would find. I couldn't deal with the awful, stupid, horrible, cruel decision we'd made, and felt numb when I signed the surgery permit. I handed it back to the nurse and angrily said, "I thought this was supposed to be an easy operation." Just as I was ready to collapse, I felt a familiar hand on my shoulder. It was Robb. I was no longer alone.

Our family members were on their way to the hospital. Robb and I kissed Derian good-bye and placed him into the arms of the surgeon.

In restless silence,

we waited…

and prayed…

I couldn't bear to look at my parents. Thankfully, they never reminded me of their objections and just continually supported me. An hour later, Dr. Levie reported that he'd cauterized the bleeding and it had stopped.

Derian was now resting comfortably. Needless to say, the overnight plan had fallen by the wayside. We were now looking at a minimum of three days. Derian was on a paralyzing medicine and the vent. He really needed those days to rest.

The next two days were thankfully boring. Derian slept and regained his strength.

Chapter 26

Hard Lesson Learned...

The afternoon of the third day, Derian started to wake up. I couldn't wait to hold my little hero. I expected him to reach out his arms and give me a great big smile. I couldn't believe it when he made it clear he wanted nothing to do with me. He wouldn't look at me, touch me, let me hold him, or even feed him. I was stunned by this reaction. The only emotion Derian ever expressed was unconditional love or agony. I was on his "ISH" list in a major way! He must have felt betrayed by me.

I learned something very valuable that day. In order to keep a good relationship with Derian, I was going to have to be the hero in his life, not the villain. Therefore, I would need to change my role as a hospital mom. I would leave the room whenever something unpleasant was going on, so he wouldn't hold me responsible for it. I would only play the role of Mommy from now on, showering him with hugs and kisses when the procedure was over. I decided to take the back seat that day and let Robb be Derian's #1 parent until Derian was ready to give me a try again. He shunned me the entire day. I was desperate to change the role I played.

Unfortunately, it would have to wait. Before Robb and I could take Derian home, we needed to learn how to care for him. That meant we needed to become more involved in his care at the hospital so we would know what to do once we got home. We were given a crash course in how to suction Derian's stints. This needed to be done every four hours around the clock for a minimum of twelve days. So much for my retreating from the role of nurse.

We dreaded suctioning the stints. It required a sterile procedure: gloves, saline solution, a suction catheter tube, and a machine. I was clumsy doing this; my hand would always touch something, and I would have to begin the whole process over. The nurses were patient and coached me repeatedly. Getting past Derian's re-trusting eyes was the hardest part of the whole thing. I just couldn't look him in the eye. Surely he would think I was betraying him once again.

With as much courage as I could muster, I peeled the folded gloves out of the package and pulled them on. I successfully got the glove on, dipped the suction catheter into the small sterile fold-up box, and then into an envelope of KY Jelly. Once the catheter was moist, it was ready to be inserted. I approached Derian, who was crying and kicking while Robb and a nurse held him down. I held the stint of one nostril and carefully inserted the suction tube into the hole of the other. Once it was in place, I pushed in the nine-inch tube. The fighter in Derian came out and his cry turned into a growl.

Once the tube was completely in, I closed the hole on the tube and suctioned the secretions, pulled the tube out, dipped it in the sterile water and re-entered the same side of the nostril again. This needed to be done twice per side. Derian was covered with sweat and almost blue from crying by the time the suctioning was completed.

I couldn't believe we were going to have to do this every four hours for two weeks. *How were we going to do this in the middle of the night? What a great way for Derian to wake up out of a deep sleep. Talk about creating night tremors!* I got quicker each time.

Now we had to figure out how to do this every four hours while I was teaching…and how to manage two boys plus the stints. I was not going to attempt to be a hero mom on this one. I needed help with suctioning and with Connor. Since Robb's mom was at home, she said she would watch Derian during the day, providing a nurse could do the suctioning. That would solve one problem, but what were we going to do with Connor? It would be impossible for one person to watch both boys.

Pastor George stopped by to visit. He was so good about supporting us during each crisis. Perhaps he might be able to help us out with this dilemma. As soon as I mentioned we needed help with Connor, he calmly held his hand up. "Patsy, I can take care of this. Plan on this problem being solved." What a relief; I had total confidence in George.

He called me later that evening and told me he made an announcement at church that we needed help with Connor the last two weeks of school. A woman named Ann had come forward with her family, offering to help. I was depressed to think I was so desperate I would entrust my nine-month-old to a complete stranger. George sensed the despair and apprehension in my voice.

Reassuringly he said, "Patsy, if I needed someone to take care of one of my grandkids, I would choose this woman."

Chapter 27

Robb, Derian, and I arrived home from the hospital to a messy, cookie-faced Connor. It was wonderful to pick up his little body and give him a squeeze. I hadn't seen him for five days. Connor let out a squeal when he saw Derian and wiggled himself out of my arms to walk to his brother. To think that we had to separate these two another two weeks seemed cruel. Connor pointed to the stints in Derian's nose. He seemed to understand this was an "owie" and not something to be touched. Maybe they would do just fine together, but should Connor ever forget, Derian would pay a high price. We decided Connor could stay over at my parents' the nights Robb worked late. We could handle the boys the other nights. A home health care unit dropped off the suction machine and the supplies we needed for the next two weeks. Derian would be suctioned the next two weeks at the following times: 9 a.m., 1 p.m., 5 p.m., 9 p.m., 1 a.m., and 5 a.m. It was going to be a long two weeks.

It was difficult to return to the classroom the next day after experiencing such a traumatic event. Grade books, assignments, tardy slips, and hall passes didn't seem to be all that important after our experience. My entire life was changing; all the things that used to be important weren't any longer.

George's directions to Ann's house led me to a brown house that overlooked a pond. A large weeping willow swayed in the gentle wind as I took Connor out of his car seat. Ann came out to greet us; her smile was as warm as the spring sun. Connor and I liked her instantly. She had a peppy spirit and was dressed in play clothes. We introduced ourselves and Ann helped me bring Connor's things inside. She gave me a quick tour of her home while I shared information about Connor and his schedule. Connor acquainted himself with his new surroundings. Within minutes, he discovered the cupboard with pots and pans and began pulling them out. Ann delighted in Connor's curiosity and reacted in the same way I would in this situation—relaxed and mellowly. I left her home knowing Connor was in good hands. Thank God Connor was a flexible child. How would we have made it if he didn't have this quality? I was confident both boys were going to be fine. Derian was with Grandma and a nurse, and Connor was with Ann.

I began to feel sorry for myself once I was at school. Everyone else was involved in everyday activities, something I didn't have anymore. I didn't know anyone that dropped his or her child off with a complete stranger before coming to school that morning. Life just seemed so crazy and mixed up; I felt bulldozed. My friend Maggie listened to my plight that morning and reminded me this was a bump in the road of life. There would be plenty of time for Connor later. He was a resilient child and surrounded by grandparents that loved him. I had to concentrate on what needed to be done.

Connor challenged my motherhood as the week went on. If I were insecure at all, I probably wouldn't have appreciated the great job Ann was doing for me. Connor crawled out of his car seat as soon as I unbuckled him and ran into Ann's outstretched hands. The two of them sent me on my way with an eager good-bye wave. Ann was a godsend.

Chapter 28

I was sitting at my desk planning a lesson for my sub when several teachers surrounded my desk. I felt nervous. My friend Barb said, "Patsy, we know this has been a hard time for you and your family, so the staff decided to lend a hand. Eunice and I took up a little collection for you. We hope it will help." She handed me a huge card, which read…

As far as friends go—you're one in a million!

The inside of the card was filled notes and the signatures of my co-workers. It screamed 'we support you'. The stress I had carried the past week was cut in half when I saw all the people that shared it with me.

Barb went on to say, "Patsy, I've never seen anything like it. People just emptied their pockets and were happy about doing it. We collected $875."

That pushed me over the edge. I sobbed uncontrollably. At that moment, I felt like George Bailey from *It's a Wonderful Life*. I walked around school the rest of the day feeling like the luckiest person in the world. I hit the jackpot working at Valley Middle School. How often in our world today do we run across so many good people in the workplace? I learned two things that day I shall never forget: miracles really do happen, and angels walk this earth in different shapes and sizes. Robb wept when I told him what my co-workers did for us. It was amazing the power this gesture had. The money was incredibly helpful, but the idea that we were cared for by so many during this time was even more awesome. No, we were not alone; we were not forgotten.

Derian's second nose surgery was scheduled for the last day of school. He had a 50/50 chance of having the stints removed. If not, we were looking at another two weeks. I was able to be with Derian that morning, thanks to my co-workers. Derian got his first break that day. He beat the odds; the stints were removed! No more suctioning every four hours! We were free, done with this whole thing. Victory was at our door!

It was wonderful to see Derian's nose, and Eskimo kisses never felt so good. Connor came home and the four of us had a victory dinner that evening. It was great to look at the clock and thumb our noses at 5 p.m. No suctioning tonight. We celebrated the freedom from each hour that had once owned us, and we were on the verge of "normal" again.

I went back to school the following day for the end-of-the-year staff breakfast. I couldn't wait to tell people our "good news." My principal asked me if I wanted to speak to the staff. I was honored for the chance to thank them personally.

> I am very excited today to be able to stand in front of you and look each and every one of you in the eye to say "thank you"
>
> *You know, before Derian was born I knew two things about the heart:*
>
> *1. Everybody needs one.*
>
> *2. Hallmark sells a lot of cards with hearts on them for Valentine's Day.*
>
> *As far as I was concerned that's all I would need to know about this organ.*
>
> *However, in the last 22 months I've learned a great deal about the heart, about defects, repairs that can be made with felt and pig intestines, heart monitors, different heart rhythms, echocardiograms, and heart catheters. Unfortunately, learning about this high-tech heart stuff has not been an interesting hobby, but rather a way of life for us.*

It wasn't until I received your gift, that I was reminded of a simpler heart, a heart that is even more fascinating then this technical one.

When Barb, Maggie, Chuck, Sue, Darlene, Dave and Holly gathered around me to give me your incredible gift, I was simply amazed at how the giving spirit of the heart can do more healing then any surgery or medicine could hope to do.

When I opened this card and saw all your names, I instantly felt the gap in my heart close. But, it wasn't from a surgery or a miracle drug. It was from honest support and encouragement. It was so comforting to feel as though we were all a part of this struggle, that it was not one I was carrying by myself.

I am going to keep this card forever and, whenever I feel alone in this battle again, I 'm going to open it up and feel your cheers over the next hurdle we face.

You gave a tremendous gift to us. Not only did you give us security and support, but you put the "heart" back into the "heart" for Robb and me.

I thank you with all my heart.

Chapter 29

My brother Tim was getting married in two weeks, so life got busy once again. Yet, in the course of the preparations, the memories of Derian's nose surgery consumed my thoughts. I was haunted, wondering if the surgery was a good thing to have done.

Robb and I made plans to bring the boys to the church for pictures the morning of the wedding. Shortly after arriving, I found myself chasing the boys around the church in my long dress. As the soloist rehearsed, I picked up Derian and walked over to Robb and Connor. Derian shifted his weight on my hip. I assumed he was trying to wiggle out of my arms; instead he leaned over my shoulder and smelled the corsage I was wearing. As he inhaled, he let out the most magical "MMMM" I had ever heard.

Robb and I looked at each other with tears in our eyes. He had never smelled anything so intensely before. From that moment on I never again doubted whether the nose surgery was the right thing to do. All the pain and misery he had gone through was transformed into a fragrant rainbow that would be his forever.

We told Dr. Levie about Derian's reaction to my corsage at our follow-up visit. We asked if Derian was able to smell prior to that surgery. He explained that with the nasal blockage Derian had, he would not have been able to take a deep-enough breath to enjoy aroma or even taste much of anything.

What a gift that horrible surgery turned out to be. How Derian loved his gift of smell. He dramatically "MMMMed" everything he smelled—even the silk flowers at Michael's craft store. Derian taught and re-taught us that summer, that no matter how much of a hurry you are in, there is always time to stop and smell the flowers.

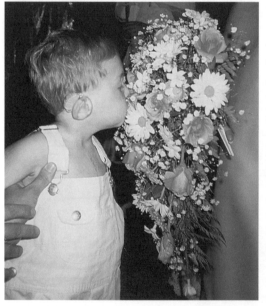

Robb and I decided to celebrate our victory with a weeklong family vacation. After a great deal of research Robb, found a cabin up north. It sounded perfect: an outdoor swimming pool, sandy beach, and a playground for the kids. We packed extras of everything—just in case. Robb insisted we bring the TV. I was irritated by this suggestion. We were leaving home for a break from everything, including TV. But he insisted, reminding me the boys begin their morning routine with Barney. He was convinced if Barney were not part of our vacation, all hell would break loose. So the TV and Barney joined us.

Our getaway cabin was affordable, and took us away from home. There was a hole in the screen door, so the flies lived with us. The slope in the floor made for a great slide for the kids, and the refrigerator was broken. Despite our efforts to prepare for all possibilities, we had to buy a cooler and another high chair. One chair was not an option!

The next few days were a hell of a lot of work. By the end of the weekend, Robb and I needed our own vacation! The kids were everywhere: on top of the picnic tables, jumping on the beds, sneaking out of the cabin, and forever running towards the pool. Connor jumped in the pool twice with his clothes on with no life jacket. When Connor dumped the entire bag of Doritos Robb had been savoring under the picnic table, I grabbed Connor and Derian, and we made a run for it!

Though the boys kept us busy chasing them around, Derian was healthy and doing remarkably well. This time together was a gift!

Chapter 30

One step forward, two steps back

Derian's eyes began to cross that summer. The treatment included patching one eye full-time for three weeks. Derian would cry such a sad cry as I pasted the patch over his eye each morning. In addition to putting it on, I had to scold him when he tried to take it off. He looked to see if Connor was wearing one, pointed to the patch and then to Connor saying, "Onnor, Onnor?" I bet he wondered why I singled him out all the time. He didn't understand, but like everything else it was "best for Derian." If we didn't patch the eye, he would have to have surgery, so this was a better option. Gradually Derian became more accepting of the procedure. We did it just long enough to strengthen his eyes and avoid the surgery.

While the eye patching was a drag, it was nothing compared to heart problems. The pause in Derian's medical crisis allowed some issues unrelated to Derian's body to surface. I was up to my eyeballs in mothering and somewhere underneath all of it, I longed to be a woman. I wanted someone to take care of me for once—not my mom or my family, but the man in my life. Our marital relationship was suffering. In hindsight, I see there were two things going on. I expected Robb to fill my emotional needs and I was at the end of my "acceptance" rope. Derian was draining me. Who could I tell that to? I could barely face it myself. What kind of a mother was I? How could I feel resentment toward my child?

It was easier to transfer the "acceptable" feelings of dismay about our life to my husband than it was our child. Robb knew something was wrong. When he would ask me, all I could do was tell him I was unhappy. I thought about what the nurse told me the first week of Derian's life: 75 percent of all marriages fail with a special-needs child. I knew our marriage was not expected to make it, and yet I didn't have the energy or desire to go through a divorce. I wanted Robb to make me feel better. Why wasn't he doing it?

A few more empty weeks passed before I laid it out for Robb, "We either go to a marriage counselor, or a Marriage Encounter weekend, or we're not going to make it."

Robb's face turned white; he seemed lost and confused by what I was saying. I loved Robb and didn't want to hurt him, but I was stuck between denial and blame, unsure of how to sort it all out. Thank God, Robb is the man he is. Even in his confusion he responded, "If our marriage is in such turmoil, I most definitely want to fix it." I was grateful for his proactive approach; he confirmed that my feelings were important.

While Robb initially was motivated to work on our marriage, the scheduled Marriage Encounter weekend conflicted with a big football game Robb was interested in. He had thought things had gotten better on their own and he was frustrated about giving up the weekend to participate in something he didn't understand. I was mad at him for his negative attitude. As with a lot of people, when forced to go somewhere, Robb made his dissatisfaction known.

After we checked in, Robb flopped on the bed and said something like, "This will be the dumbest thing I've ever been to."

With out-of-control rage, I grabbed my unopened suitcase, flung the door open, and shouted, "Have a great stupid weekend alone! I'm not going to listen to you moan and complain the entire weekend. You can walk home!" My deliberate steps echoed as I stomped down the tile hallway. Neither one of us had ever seen me that angry. I couldn't believe I was acting that way.

Luckily I didn't get more then ten fiery steps away before Robb peered out of our room and sheepishly yelled, "Patsy, come back, I promise I'll try." The volunteers registering couples witnessed all of this. I'm sure we were thought of as a "red-flag" couple. I went back into the room much quieter than I'd left. We decided we better make a few ground rules:

1. No unreasonable expectations.

2. No complaining.

3. No controlling what the other person gets out of the weekend.

Twenty-five couples shared the weekend with us. After introductions and housekeeping expectations, the weekend format was explained. Each session included personal testimonies from the couples leading the weekend about the ups and downs of their marriage. After each presentation we would complete an assignment, first by ourselves, and then with our partners. I knew Robb was going to hate this, but he rose to the occasion and became the leader in our discussions. I was impressed with how seriously he took the assignments. The activities made us think and the sharing taught us more about each other. One of the Marriage Encounter rules is to be honest. It was through this honesty that we discovered some weaknesses in our relationship, and came up with some solutions to our problems. As we uncovered this information, we laughed and cried, agreed and disagreed, and listened to each other's needs. We became a unit again.

Toward the end of the weekend, I was going crazy. I couldn't stand any more focused talks. I needed to play or do something bad, like not show up for the next session. My skin was beginning to crawl and my heart was following it. Robb was shocked by my behavior, and in a serious voice, told me he had signed us up for another retreat the following weekend. I threatened to tie the bed sheets together and escape through the window.

One of the last assignments was to write a letter to each other. Robb wrote me a poem instead of a letter. This amazed me. No one had ever written a poem to me before. I was thrilled and flattered by this act of romance, and hearing him read it to me was the best of all.

That Tuesday I first saw you I knew,
That we could have something so true.
But two friends we would have to be.
Maybe a year or two - I couldn't go out with you till three.

I asked you out—you seemed weary
A pig farmer's wife to you seemed all too dreary,

I promised you a life of fun.
A continuous time in the sun.

You became my wife.
And you changed my life.
It does get better all the time.

A few gray clouds have come, then strayed
And I love you more and more each day.

I want to be with you and the boys
Till we can give them away.

To start their own lives of sun-filled days.

I love you a ton—Robb

The last session allowed us the opportunity to take our marriage vows again. We could write our own or copies of the traditional vows would be provided. I never really realized how powerful those vows were until I witnessed several couples say theirs. Even in my giddiness, I was moved to tears as the promises of this commitment were restated. I pondered on the reverence in this moment and came to the conclusion that these brides and grooms were in the process of "for better or worse, in sickness and health, and in good and bad times."

Robb jumped up, so I followed his lead. He held my hand as he read the vows from the sheet. He looked at me at the end of each sentence, almost to emphasize how much he loved me, even if our life wasn't perfect. To hear him say he would do it all again—and choose me—profoundly moved me. It was my turn. I looked at the sheet for a long time. Thick tears filled my eyes; I couldn't even begin to make out the words. My throat was so tight I couldn't speak. All I could do was stare at Robb. He nervously shook his leg. I knew he thought, "She's not going to do it, she's going to leave me at the altar." I couldn't pull it together. God, I had to say something, and yet I couldn't read a word. My heart took the lead; I set the paper down and made my own promises to Robb.

Five years ago I took these vows, not really knowing what they meant.

Part of me said them, but the other part thought, "Well, we will just see how it goes."

Today I stand before you, knowing what these promises mean as I speak them.

I Patsy, take you Robb to be my husband.

I promise to walk up and down all the hills that stand in our way together.

I want you and will need you all the days of my life.

I love you more each day the sun rises and sets.

We have made two little boys.

I know I made the right choice five years ago when I said, "I do"

Each time I hear our boys call you "Daddy."

How proud I would be if each of our boys could grow up to be a man like you.

I love you, and I love being your wife.

I choked back the tears as the words fled from my soul. I was a bride committed to move though any part of life with my husband. Robb gave me a kiss in front of everyone. We had a great wedding that day.

Movement Four—

Can You Cast the Pain Away?

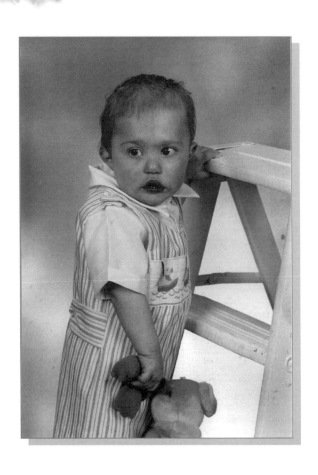

Chapter 31

Once we were stronger as a couple, we were able to face Derian's hearing problems. Becky, Derian's teacher, had been teaching a little sign language with each of her lessons. Robb and I were still uncomfortable about this until one day Derian signed, "More." That was it—the turning point. Derian signed what he wanted. We made an all-out effort to learn sign language.

Becky invited Mary Dee, the Deaf and Hard of Hearing teacher on board. She came to our house each week for sign language class. She made flash cards of items found in the kitchen, bathroom, bedrooms, etc. We posted these cards next to the specific items in each room, so that we were constantly reminded to use the sign when we spoke it. It was amazing how quickly signing was incorporated into our life. Within a few weeks all four of us could sign over 72 words. The boys were very good at it.

Christmas 1995

The boys were growing up so fast; Derian was now 28 months old and Connor 15 months. I believed we were finally getting a taste of normal. We still had several doctor appointments, but overall, Derian was doing great, even though—despite the patching—he ended up having eye surgery. Since things were settling down, I volunteered to direct the Christmas pageant at church.

The entire country gears up for Christmas after Halloween. Our pageant committee was no different. We moved at full-force, making church announcements looking for kids to play parts, planning schedules, writing the script and finding volunteers to help us pull it off. I had no doubt the pageant would turn out great! The show was scheduled for Sunday, December 17. We were running out of rehearsal time and, as always, in the drama of creating drama, there was drama. Some of the volunteers dropped out and several lead characters weren't showing up for rehearsals. Each time we rehearsed, someone new was playing a new part. It was nuts! Yet, my soul danced in the creative chaos. I felt alive!

The morning of our dress rehearsal, Derian woke up with a puffy-looking face. I thought he might have a sinus infection on top of a cold, so I plugged in the steamer and laid him down for a morning nap. When he woke up, his face was even puffier, his breathing labored, and he was extremely crabby. I phoned the doctor on call and explained Derian's symptoms. He asked me to hold the phone to Derian so he could listen to him breathe. After listening he urged me to bring him to Urgent Care telling me "this could be serious." Since this was not one of our regular doctors or a doctor that knew Derian, I was not overly alarmed by his phone diagnosis.

I called Robb and told him I was bringing Derian in. This always brought up a moment of contention. "Why are you bringing him in?"

"His face is puffy and he is breathing really weird."

"That's because he has a sinus infection, Patsy. I think you're overreacting, but if you think you should, go ahead."

By the time I got off the phone, I was a little more anxious about getting Derian to the doctor. I called my mom and told her calmly that I was bringing Derian to see the doctor. I knew whatever I said would make her panic, so I tried to be brief. I asked her to watch Connor until I got home. As I scurried around the house to get the boys and myself ready, Derian lay motionless on the floor with his blanket around him. His head was hot to the touch. I had to get him in, NOW! I couldn't wait the twenty minutes it would take my mom to get to our house.

In desperation, I phoned a neighbor who had a teenage daughter. I explained I was on my way to Urgent Care with Derian and that my mom was on her way to pick up Connor. I only needed about 20 minutes of help. You can imagine my surprise when this woman coldly replied, "No, it's Saturday morning and I want Sarah to sleep in today."

Did she listen to me? I wished my child could sleep in and that all was won-derful in my corner of life. Thankfully the rest of the neighborhood was more helpful. I phoned another neighbor who renewed my faith in humanity. She said she would be right over.

I wrapped up Derian in a blanket as soon as she arrived, kissed Connor good-bye, and hurried to the car. My heart was pounding from the intu-itive "hurry-up feeling" I had.

On the way to the hospital I began to think about what Robb had said. Maybe I was overreacting; maybe his face wasn't puffy. Was his breath-ing really different? But when I looked at how pale he was as he slumped to the side of the car seat, I knew he needed help. I had to trust myself. I would rather bring him in and look stupid than be sorry. Since it was still early, I figured I would be able to get Derian seen, get a pre-scription filled, and have enough time to get to church for our one o'clock rehearsal.

In the emergency parking spot, I threw a blanket over Derian to protect him from the 10 below wind-chill. Derian was weak and frail-looking. He didn't show any interest in the toys in the waiting area. I held him close to me, stroked his hair and rubbed his feet through the blanket. All of a sudden it hit me: he had all the signs of heart failure, his heart was failing. I couldn't sit in the waiting room for our name to be called if he was going into heart failure—I needed help NOW! I told the check-in nurse what my diagnosis was. Since the staff was familiar with us, she trusted me. She brought us to a room, promising to send in a doctor within a few minutes. I hoped the doctor would be someone we knew. Derian's medical information was the size of two encyclopedias. Someone new would not be able to absorb all that information within a few minutes.

The doctor—a stranger—entered our room. Before she even sat down, I firmly asserted my diagnosis. "Derian is going into heart failure!"

She smiled a tight smile and asked, "Does Derian have any history of going into heart failure?"

"Yes; he had a full cardiac arrest when he was one-week old." She immediately ordered a chest x-ray.

Derian was so weak he didn't cry as the x-ray was taken. We returned to our room and waited. The doctor shared her findings with me. "The x-ray shows that Derian's chest is filled with fluid. As you know, this is the first indication of heart failure. Before I decide that's what this is, I want to pump some IV fluids into him and get some blood work done. I'm admitting Derian." *Oh my God! This is the first time Derian is hospitalized for sickness.*

I left the room while the nurses drew blood and hooked him up to the IV. I called one of the other pageant directors and told her what was going on. I felt terrible about leaving them in such a jam, but what could I do? I leaned up against the wall and called Robb. He couldn't believe the news.

"Patsy, I will never doubt you again. I'm glad you didn't listen to me," he said apologetically.

"Yeah," I replied, "It was a tough morning!" I had longed for the feeling of "normalcy", and now that I had a taste of it, I didn't want to let it go. "I'm going to miss my rehearsal. Heck, I don't know if I'll even be able to sneak out and go to the final performance tomorrow night."

Tenderly, Robb replied, "People will understand."

"I'm just so sick of never being able to plan anything."

I went back to the room. I could hear Derian's screams through the closed door. *God, I hate this!* The door opened and a nurse came out. They were unsuccessful in placing the IV so someone from anesthesia was coming to give it a try. That meant Derian had already been stuck several times. *God, couldn't you have at least given him big veins? Poor, poor baby.*

I pushed against the wall and lowered myself to the cold floor. The anesthesia nurse entered the room. God, please help her get it in right away. More screams. A few minutes later the door opened. She'd gotten the IV in on the first try. I wrote down her name so I could have her paged the next time Derian needed blood work or IVs. As soon as the nurses had things wrapped up I could come back into the room. I couldn't decide which was worse, waiting outside or being inside watching. I knew Derian would be scared, hurt, and sick. How much longer would this child be tortured back to health, I wondered? I wished I could just take the pain from him.

When I was able to enter the room, I found Derian laying on a hospital cot with an IV pole towering over him. His needle-pricked arm was mounted, wrapped, and taped to a thin plastic board that secured the tubing which led to the IV pump. Derian tearfully held his arm up to show me the damage that had been done to him. As I wiped away the leftover tears on his cheeks, he looked up and said, "Owie, Momma." He began pulling at the towel the IV was buried in. His brown eyes begged me to free him as he signed "off." It broke my heart not to be able to help him the way he wanted. Calmly, I reassured him the medicine in his IV was going to make him feel better, saying this was a "good thing." For some reason, Derian seemed to stop fighting and surrendered to the situation. How I wished he could teach me how to do that.

Chapter 32

I turned off the light and snuggled with Derian. Before my head was on the pillow, Derian had his hand under my neck. In the midst of his own pain he took care of his mom.

Wet? Why am I getting wet? I could feel the front of my shirt getting wet. I shifted my weight until I could sit up and sneak out of bed without Derian noticing. I pulled the damp part of my shirt to my nose and smelled it; Blood! My shirt was covered in blood. I ran out to the nurses' station. "Help me! Derian needs help. Something is wrong!" The staff hurried into our room, flipped on the lights, and rapidly quizzed me. They were not happy when I told them I was lying next to Derian. They thought I must have pulled the IV out. The dampness on my shirt was a mixture of both blood and IV fluid. The IV needed to be replaced. *God, can he get a break? Why did you make me Derian's mom? I can't believe he needs to go through all this again because of me. Derian, I am so, so sorry.*

When the nurse left the room she said in a disgusted tone, "He really didn't need to lose any blood, he was weak enough. He may need a blood transfusion now." *God, why did you make me so stupid? Derian needs a good mom, one who doesn't hurt him.*

After what seemed like an eternity, the doctor came in with the blood test results. "We can rule out heart failure. The blood work shows a significant elevation in his white blood cells, which means he has an infection going on. His chest x-ray shows some cloudiness in his lungs, which indicates that he has severe pneumonia. I've ordered a few blood cultures. I want to see what will grow in these in the next few days. There could be two infections going on at the same time." *Pneumonia, I can't believe it. It came on overnight. Pneumonia! Thank God it is only pneumonia and not his heart.*

I phoned Robb with the results. He was as shocked as I was. We were bummed to be back in the hospital again, but how much time could pneumonia require? Certainly we would be out within a few days and still have a week to prepare for Christmas. This was just a little setback.

The hospital was filled, so we had to wait for a room to open up. We were expected to get the first available room on third floor. I wasn't expected at play rehearsal, so I had nothing to hurry off to. We were back on hospital time. From this point on, time was measured by Derian's progress.

As I waited in stilled silence, my mind was working on answering the how-do-we-hold-things-together question. I wanted to make sure we would come up with a plan that kept Connor's schedule as "normal" as possible. Since I only had six sick days left, Robb and I would have to figure out a way we could rotate days in the hospital until Derian came home. I was sure I could leave Derian and go to work this time. I had to space these days out.

Around 4 p.m., a room opened up and a nurse helped me transport Derian to the 3200 unit. We had stayed in this unit before; usually this unit represented the homeward stretch of recovery. It was strange that we were here without a surgery. Derian had never been *just* sick before.

As the elevator doors opened, I noticed the holiday decorations on the room doors and the Christmas tree next to the nurses' station. It was decorated with tinsel, homemade ornaments, and paper chains. I was grateful we were only going to be in the hospital for a few days. I felt sad for the people who would have to spend the holidays there. The nurse led us to a room overlooking the parking lot in the corner right across from the nurses' station. The roof was thick with snow and the sun's brightness cast a glimmer throughout the room. It felt safe and inviting. The nurse placed the bag of Derian's belongings in the corner and left.

I took the soft, white cotton blanket from the foot of the crib and wrapped Derian in it. He panicked anytime I wasn't holding him. So I sat up, holding him, staying in that position for four hours imprisoned by a little boy who needed me. But I had needs too—I was starving, and my bladder had reached full capacity. My arm was wet with Derian's sweat and no matter how I shifted I couldn't get comfortable. I needed to get up and walk, but relief was nowhere in sight. Robb wouldn't be showing up for at least three hours.

Another hour went by, and I couldn't stand it anymore. I buzzed a nurse, even though they were really busy. When the nurse arrived, I told her of my predicament. She admitted she was swamped but would hold Derian long enough for me to use the bathroom. I passed Derian into her arms, but he awoke and sobbed uncontrollably. I know nursing babies are dependent on their mom for food, but Derian was dependent for every realm of his world. As soon as I reopened the bathroom door, his little arms reached out to me. I was trapped in my son's world. Once we were re-situated, the same nurse stopped by with juice and a few treats. We were back in business.

My arms ached. I had rocked Derian for six hours. I couldn't help but think back to my early days of teaching. Each time a co-worker called absent due to their child's illness, I had envisioned the relaxing day they must have had as their child slept the day away. Brother...was I wrong!

Around 5 p.m., a volunteer from the hospital knocked on my room door. He noticed that Derian was sleeping, so he quietly pushed the door open and whispered, "I heard you need a break in here. I'm Patrick from the volunteer program. I would be happy to stay with your son if you want to go to the cafeteria." Those words sounded so wonderful that I almost asked him to say it again. Time was crucial. If Derian woke up before I left, I would miss my chance. Patrick carefully dropped the crib side, and with complete grace I transferred Derian into the crib and ever so quietly, pulled the side up. I thanked Patrick as I grabbed my purse and bolted toward the door. "I'll be back in 20 minutes," I whispered.

I closed the door and inhaled. What to do? Eat? Make a call? Now that I had freedom, I really didn't know what to do with it. I called Judy to see how dress rehearsal went and gave her an update on Derian. Poor Judy. Apparently rehearsal was pretty wild, but overall it had gone okay. I hoped to sneak out and watch the final performance, but I knew better than to make plans. As I hung up the phone, disappointment showed its ugly head. This was terrible. I had worked for six weeks preparing for that show. I was crushed not to be a part of the grand finale! Nothing in my life could be planned. Would "normal" ever find me again?

I grabbed a sandwich from the cafeteria and wolfed it down on my way back to the room. My allotted time for freedom was nearly over. I wandered back into my cave, refreshed and grateful to Patrick. Thankfully, Derian slept the entire time. Patrick graciously accepted my thanks and went on his way to help out the next crazed parent.

About an hour later, Robb entered the room. I was never so glad to see him! He picked Derian up and rocked him while I told him about our day. Since we were still waiting for test results, we spent the rest of the evening mulling over different scenarios. We were sure we wouldn't be looking at any more than three days. The practical thing to do would be for me to continue working so I could postpone using up my sick leave. Robb would care for Derian during the day and work in the evenings.

My head and my heart were having a serious disagreement. I knew finishing up the week would be the smartest thing to do financially but I had always been at the hospital. I knew how things went. I wasn't sure I could leave Derian, even with Robb.

Chapter 33

Our parents came to visit the next morning and brought Connor along with them. His face was a welcomed sight! As sick as Derian was, he found enough strength to wave and blow a kiss to everyone. He was especially glad to see Connor, who managed to put a spark into his glazed eyes. Connor was good medicine for all of us. Derian kept an eye on how much attention Connor was getting from Mom. He wanted me for himself: I was HIS mom! Derian would break into tears if I hugged or picked up Connor. To work around this insecurity, I put both sets of grandparents in charge of entertaining Derian so I could sneak out and snuggle with Connor.

Later that day, a resident doctor stopped by to tell us that one of Derian's blood cultures was growing something. It would take at least three days to identify the bacteria. Amazingly enough, we were not concerned. Sickness seemed so mild compared to other things Derian had faced. There was always the chance that the first culture was contaminated, so they would see if anything grew on the other five cultures that were taken as well. That conversation ended with my usual question, "How long do you think it will be until we can go home?" The resident told us we needed to stay until three cultures were negative. That would be at least four days. *Monday, Tuesday, Wednesday, and Thursday—that gives us at least a week to be home before Christmas. We can handle this.*

Pastor George stopped by to bring us communion that afternoon. He had heard from the pageant staff what was going on and must have known I'd have some crazy notion to get to the pageant. He insisted I stay with Derian. "He needs you more than the pageant does." Apparently, he made an announcement in church that morning about

Derian and the short-handed status of the pageant staff. "Patsy, several people volunteered to help. You are not responsible for the show anymore. Other people are taking care of it."

Now I could really concentrate on Derian, but my spirit slipped out for a few hours and sat in the audience.

Throughout the day, Derian's fever persisted. He couldn't get comfortable with the IV board in his arm and cried most of the day. I decided that if he didn't improve overnight, I wasn't going to work on Monday, no matter what we had decided previously. Since we operated on the "what is best for Derian" mode, I was sure Robb would agree to this change in plans.

Derian made little if any progress throughout the day, so I called in for a sub. I put some lesson plans together and called a few of my co-workers to let them know what was going on. They were always supportive and understanding. "Patsy, we've got it covered. I'll take care of your classes. Don't even worry about school." Honestly, if it weren't for the caring teachers in my department, I know I would have lost my job, simply because I was incapable of doing it. How does one come up with lesson plans when one's mind is consumed with a child's health?

Around noon that Monday, the medicine took effect and Derian was back to his kiss-blowing self. By the end of the day the fever was gone. Since all was going well, I decided to go back to work the next day.

Later that evening the resident doctor returned to our room and told us another culture came back positive; the same bacteria was growing. Something else was going on, but what? We would need to add another day to our stay. Since Derian was bouncing around, we couldn't imagine what could be going on. The staff was as baffled as we were. Within the next twenty hours they would be able to identify the mysterious bacteria.

I went to school Tuesday morning. While I was busy teaching, Derian kept Robb busy chasing him up and down the halls pushing his IV pole, playing in the playroom, and participating in all the hospital activities: bingo, transplanting plants and socializing.

Wednesday afternoon, I called Robb from work to see how things were going. "Okay, I guess, but some guy from Infectious Disease Control was up here."

"From where?"

"Infectious Disease Control."

I was alarmed by his cavalier attitude. "What did they say?"

"Nothing really—they're going to stop by later tonight."

In all the time that I had spent in the hospital with Derian, I had never heard of that unit. The rest of the day, my stomach was a knotted mess. I picked Connor up after school and we headed to the hospital. We barely got our coats hung up before the Infectious Disease Control doctor came into our room. He was somber and yet gentle. He explained that all of Derian's cultures had come back positive. Just as he was about to explain what that meant, the boys began whooping it up. The doctor adjusted his volume as he said, "Derian has a bacteria infection called enterococcus. This bacterium lives in the intestines but somehow it has gotten loose and entered Derian's blood stream. Enterococcus likes to attack the heart." My hands began to shake.

"The only way to treat this bacteria is through six weeks of intravenous antibiotics, all of which need to be done here in the hospital."

Surely I had heard this wrong. "Excuse me, what did you just say?"

"The treatment is six weeks of intravenous antibiotics."

"You mean we have to stay here for six weeks? How can this be? Look at him, he looks healthy."

"I know this is really bad news, and I'm sorry to have to deliver it so close to the holidays."

As Derian and Connor watched Barney in the rocking chair, the IV pole hovered over them. Things would be like this for six weeks. Six weeks. That meant we would spend Christmas in the hospital, the boys would be split up, and another financial nightmare loomed over our heads. The doctor reassured us this treatment would get Derian back on his feet.

I found Robb's arms as soon as the doctor left. His body shook in a rhythm similar to mine. We were crushed. The boys heard the sounds of our cries and knew something was wrong. They climbed out of the chair and wrapped their arms around our knees. We were overwhelmed by responsibility. There was no place to run form the sinkhole we were stuck in.

Chapter 34

"I'm taking another leave from work. I'm calling Penny." I just had to have a few minutes by myself. I went into the lounge, turned off the TV and closed the door. I opened my address book and called my assistant principal.

"Penny, this is Patsy." I couldn't hide the sadness and choked out each word. Penny was like my fairy godmother at school. She had often helped me out of tricky situations. "Derian is really sick; he'll be in the hospital for six weeks. I need to take another leave."

Without a moment of hesitation she answered, "Take all the time you need. Do what is best for your family. We will work things out at school." Penny could give me the time I needed, but Robb and I had to live the problem. No one could take that away.

My mom was standing in the middle of the room when I returned. Her eyes were red and she was full of questions. Thankfully, she didn't ask all of them and just gave me a hug. This was so different. Sickness had never touched this child. I never even thought of Derian as "sick" before; he was always fixable! We were going into uncharted waters, unsure of what to expect. My mom decided to join us for the holiday program. I still needed time to myself, so I made up an excuse, left the room, and went back to the lounge. I grabbed a pen and paper and wrote what I felt.

Lost, ripped out of life again,

Connor—Help

Fear

Anger

Anxious

Fed-up

Confused

Dismal

When will it end?

Helpless

Why?

Please save my baby!

I could hear the boys' squeals from the lounge. As sad as we were, it was impossible to dwell on it. We had two toddlers going to see Santa! Their energy and excitement electrified the room. We walked down the hall, lost in our grownup worries, accompanied by an IV pole and two children galvanized by Santa's magic.

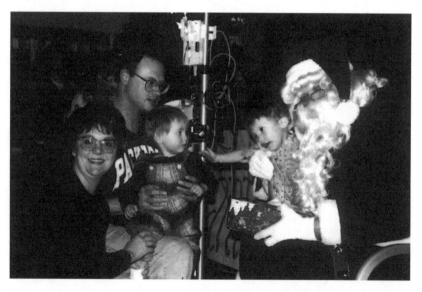

The elevator doors opened up and the boys ran down the hall following the music. We ran to catch up. Entering the cafeteria was like stepping into a winter wonderland. Beautiful Christmas trees lined the entrance, paper snowflakes hung from the ceiling, and colorful lights twinkled in the dim cafeteria. The National Guard representatives were dressed in uniform and smiled as they directed us to the buffet. The long buffet table was covered with a red cloth. Silver platters proudly displayed the beautiful assortment of hors d' oeuvres and goodies. We were their invited guests. We were touched by their Martha Stewart efforts, their warm and welcoming hospitality; they made us feel as if we were doing them a favor by allowing them to serve us. The atmosphere they created enchanted me. Sadness was not allowed in this room. Even though the hosts and hostess were aware of our pain, they went to great lengths to give the gift of joy. I couldn't feel sorry for myself in this environment.

We sat in front of a makeshift stage and listened to a man and woman lead the group in singing. Derian couldn't sit and sing at the same time. He stood next to his IV pole clapping his hands and dancing to each song. He was my inspiration that evening! The IV couldn't keep him down. He didn't even consider it an obstacle. At one point he turned around and encouraged others to sing and applaud after each song. He slapped his hands together near his chin and roared a hearty, drawn-out "Heh." His spirit was like a sponge, absorbing the positive feelings and squeezing out anything that would poison life's magic. Derian and Connor danced their little hearts out that night.

Watching them giggle, squeal, and react to each other gave Robb and I the courage to accept what we needed to face. We returned to our room feeling lighter than we did when we left. Derian was a fearless leader. With him setting the pace, we knew we had to find the joy he managed to find in this place. We accepted this challenge.

Maggie and her husband Jim arrived after my mom left. Having the support of friends, in addition to family, made us feel less alone. As Maggie and I visited, Jim watched the boys play together. Maggie easily coaxed the boys into performing the Christmas poem they learned. Thrilled to have an audience they stood up and signed "Barney's Christmas" poem in unison. When they finished, they applauded themselves loudly and encouraged everyone to do the same. Jim and Maggie applauded wildly. Their response delighted the boys so they began doing their happy dance. It seemed odd that Derian was as sick as they said and he was still energetic and happy. I let Maggie know I wasn't going to school the following day. She understood and offered to come up with a lesson for my sub.

As the evening wore on, several doctors and nurses stopped by and let us know how disappointed they were to hear our news. The staff had become another extension of our family. With such support, it didn't feel as though we were carrying the entire load by ourselves. Everyone carried a small piece.

Chapter 35

The next day while I was at the hospital watching Derian, Maggie made an announcement informing the student body about Derian's newest crisis. Many of the students knew Derian or at least knew of him. I had shared Derian with my students through stories that lent themselves to the topic we were studying. I often reminded them how lucky they were to be healthy and challenged them to defend that gift, no matter how much pressure they received to try drugs or alcohol. My students were an important part of my life and, in turn, Derian became important in theirs.

Friday before Christmas break

I was nervous as I got ready for school that morning. I was going to say goodbye to my students. It would be hard to be in an environment where everyone was excited. I was jealous I wasn't going to have a Christmas this year. It was difficult to take a leave of absence from the part of my life that was going smoothly. I arrived at school later than usual, dragging my feet. The halls were buzzing with activity, with students dressed in red and green clothes, and glitter covering the lockers. I made my way through the cheerful crowd focusing on getting to my area. When I passed the last row of lockers, I noticed several students standing by my desk. They saw me and began shouting, "Mrs. Keech, you're late. We have some things for you." I took my coat off and greeted my receiving line. Each student presented me with a gift they felt would offer comfort to Derian and Connor. One by one they presented me with beautiful stuffed teddy bears, bubbles, plates of home-made goodies, cards, and hugs. Lots of wonderful kid hugs. Starting my day like that melted all those rotten feelings I had as I drove to school that morning. I was drenched with a Christmas miracle!

I cried as I said good-bye to my classes. We had a special bond; they were worried about who would replace me, yet they all understood that Derian needed to come first. One student raised his hand and said, "Mrs. Keech, I think being with Derian is the most important place for you to be. I want everyone who agrees with me to raise your hand and promise Mrs. Keech you will be good for the sub." Thirty-four hands shot into the air. I promised I would keep them in touch with Derian's progress and would make a movie for them so they understood all that was involved in Derian's care.

One student asked me, "Mrs. Keech, can you rent Barney?"

"I would guess so."

"Well, I got a hundred dollars from my aunt and I would like to rent Barney for Derian." I reached out and gave him a big hug. He hugged me back so tight he lifted me off the ground. Such selflessness touched my heart. I was afraid to leave the safety and warmth I had in school and push off into the unknown. Teaching and my students anchored me into the mainstream of life.

By the end of the day I had acquired 14 teddy bears, hundreds of cards, two jars of bubbles, three bags of diapers, five toys, three bags of candy treats, banners for our hospital room, and several plates of homemade goodies. As I packed up our newly acquired treasures, a group of teachers gathered around me. Carol, one of the assistant principals, had a big smile on her face as she said, "Patsy, this came from the students. After Maggie's announcement yesterday, a group of students came into my office and wanted to have a fundraiser for your family. They called it 'Dollars for Derian.' The staff joined in with the students and we are proud to present this envelope to you. Patsy, they raised over $1,600 in twenty-four hours for you to be with Derian." I sobbed.

I took a leap of faith, unsure of how we were going to get through this financially. I was prepared to sell the house, whatever it took to help Derian though this. Thankfully, God placed me into the arms of people who cared and took care of the money piece of this puzzle. I left school that day feeling like the luckiest person in the world! Robb and I had a school community helping us raise Derian.

One of my students who had helped on several other occasions offered to help me bring everything to the hospital and to hang Christmas lights in our room. Her mom would pick her up when she was done. I was grateful for her help! We brought in three wagonloads of stuff for our room. Robb and I read the cards for the boys and hung each one of them up next to the banners. The boys rolled back and forth in the stuffed animals while we snacked on the holiday treats. By the end of the evening, our room was the finest decorated room on the floor. Dr. Hesslein made the comment as he stopped by, "I hate to sound mean, but it sort of looks like Santa puked in this room." Valley Middle School brought pizzazz to the hospital. Robb was overwhelmed with the kindness we received. We thanked God over and over for the people who gave us a miracle.

Chapter 36

Facing Christmas Day...

Despite the incredible experience at school, facing Christmas morning was tough. As much as I tried to focus on the "real" spirit of Christmas, that morning by myself in the hospital with Derian was one of the hardest mornings of my life. I peered out the large hospital window and watched as people entered the hospital with gifts, returned to their car empty-handed, and slowly drove away.

That morning, Derian and I left our floor for a change of scenery and walked the halls on the first floor. As Derian pushed his IV pole down the hall, a well-dressed man passed and cheerfully said, "Merry Christmas." Feeling as left out of this holiday as I did, his words added salt to a fresh, deep wound. *Did those words automatically slip from his lips? Was he blind to the IV pole? Did he realize we were in the hospital on Christmas? Keep your Merry Christmas, buddy. I want nothing to do with it. Christmas was stolen from my husband, our two boys, and me. There is no tree at our house, no gifts, and all we have is a pass, which will buy us four short little hours from this place.* Pity pooled around my soul.

As we continued our walk, I heard the jingle of bells ahead of us. Great, another holiday geek! Derian heard the jingles through his hearing aid. He looked up at me. Curiosity and wonder shone vividly in his brown eyes. His short little legs began moving faster. As we made it to the intersection of the hallway, what to our wondering eyes should appear but Santa Claus! Derian signed, "Santa, Santa!" He confidently approached Santa. Santa welcomed Derian into his space, knelt down on one knee, and extended his arms. Derian was awestruck. He had Santa all to himself and was lost in the greatness of the man wearing a red suit with white gloves. Nestled into the cove of Santa's body, Derian looked up at his great white beard and touched it. Charmed by his bravery, Santa offered his sleigh bells. Derian shook them proudly and the magic of the bells' ring echoed through the empty hospital hallway.

In that instant, I learned Derian's experiences with Christmas were different than mine. As sad as I was not to have a tree with presents under it, to eat a holiday feast, or to go to a Christmas service with my two boys, my boys hardly knew of those things. Santa was what made the season magical for them, whether it was in a mall, a Santa breakfast, or in the hospital. They weren't being cheated because they weren't missing anything.

Stillness wrapped around the moment as Santa gave Derian a hug and stood up. Then, ever so slowly, he reached out his white satin glove, placed it under my chin, and pulled it toward him. He looked into my eyes with the same gentleness he used with my child. He said, "Hang in there, Mom!" *He knew. He knew* exactly what to give me that Christmas morn. His words of understanding and empathy were not wrapped up under a tree. They came from his heart and were carefully placed into the crack in mine. He yelled out a "Ho, Ho, Ho", and went on his way down the hallway. Derian signed, "Bye-bye Santa," and the two of us stood in awe, watching the ball on his hat prance until he faded out of sight.

Pastor George was waiting for us when we returned to our room. Derian was still on a Santa high and was glad to share his story with someone new. George relished Derian's joy. In the middle of our conversation, I heard a huge racket in the hallway, followed by a loud knock at our door. I opened our room door and saw three familiar faces: our neighbors, Julie, Don and Dan Johnson. They had a huge box filled with food, presents, and a beautiful Christmas centerpiece. When twenty-year-old Dan heard Derian would be in the hospital for the holidays, he went door-to-door informing the neighbors and asked if they wanted to contribute to a Christmas care package for us. Derian wasted no time digging into the box and soon had everything pulled out and on the floor. We all laughed at his eagerness. Julie filled the champagne glasses she brought with her grasshopper mix. We gathered in a circle and she made a toast to good health and happier days in the New Year. I was touched that people would take time out of their own holiday to visit us. Derian waved and blew kisses as our visitors left.

It was time to get Derian dressed in his holiday outfit and get to Robb's parent's house. We had just four hours to celebrate—Derian was thrilled to put on his coat. I was glad he would get in on a few holiday traditions. Just as we were getting ready to leave, Derian's teacher, Becky, and her son Brian stopped by to visit and drop off a few gifts. Derian jumped up and down and squealed when he saw Becky. The two of them joined hands and did a little dance together. Since we were on our way out they helped carry some things to our car.

The elevator brought us to the lower floor of the parking ramp. Even though we were underground, I could feel the coolness of winter. Derian blew the cold smoke of his breath out in front of him. He welcomed the freshness of the winter air. Once the car was loaded, we said our good-byes and drove to the Keechs' for Christmas dinner. It was wonderful to have Derian back in his car seat, to listen to his car jabber. He kept saying "Onnor, Onnor." The closer we got to White Bear Lake, the more excited both of us were to walk in and see Connor. I hadn't seen him for a few days and was anxious to hold him.

When we pulled into the driveway, Robb's parents and Aunt Jean came out to greet us. This was the welcome one would expect for a hero. Derian was everyone's hero! They each gave Derian a big hug and grabbed a bag of stuff from the car. Connor was peering out the window. I walked into the house and excitedly called out, "Connor, where is my little Connor?" Connor took one look at me and ran away screaming. He stood next to the Christmas tree and hit it as he cried. Grandma Lois was surprised by his reaction and said, "He has never even touched the tree until now!" I walked toward him and he ran away again. This cold greeting baffled Derian. I was completely caught off guard. Connor had always bounced back and forth. What was going on? Suddenly it registered. Connor was growing up. He knew what the routine was supposed to be like, who mom and dad were, and who his favorite playmate was. He must have been angry that he was left behind. We were trying so hard to be good parents for Derian that we overlooked Connor.

I was not going to let this little kid lay a guilt trip on me and I didn't have the time to let him warm up to me. Robb's parents went into the kitchen as I swept Connor up and brought him upstairs. He kicked and wiggled so I couldn't hold him. I held tighter and pretended not to notice he wanted nothing to do with me. I asked him, "Where do you sleep when you're at Grandma and Grandpa's house?" I was not going to lose him! Once Connor looked at me, his put-out exterior began to melt. It started with a tickle, then a laugh and then, "Mom loves you very much," and kisses all over his face. Once we were friends again, I picked him up and carried him over to the stairs. From the top of the stairway, I was able to see into the kitchen. A sweet pride kissed upon my heart as I saw Grandma, Grandpa, and Aunt Jean circled around Derian, dancing to a Christmas song. I knew Christmas was to celebrate the birthday of baby Jesus, but somehow that night I felt Derian was the one we were celebrating. He upstaged baby Jesus that year.

I was curious to see how Connor would interact with Derian. I hoped he would be excited to see him. Connor was Derian's thrust for life. The last thing Derian needed was to be snubbed by his little brother. Once Derian finished his dance, everyone cheered for him. He walked out of the circle, reached out his hand attached to the IV and said, "Onnor, Onnor." Connor accepted his hand, but was puzzled by it. He spotted a tiny amount of blood peeking out of the tube and with great concern said, "Doo-doo has owie." He convinced me that, at fifteen months, he understood what was going on.

Robb had to work until 5 p.m. to accommodate all the last minute shoppers. He arrived at the same time the Keechs' neighbors, the Jacksons, arrived. The Jacksons always spent Christmas Eve with the Keechs. It was good to see everyone, even though I didn't have much energy to socialize. I couldn't shake the sadness. I did my best to get excited for the boys, but felt nothing. I was a holiday castaway. Even though Christmas decorations, traditions, and family surrounded me, I was lost. How could I participate in all of it the way I once did when everything was so different? The homey feeling of past Christmases was a memory. I didn't like feeling like a bystander but I was. I could see Christmas through the boys' eyes but not mine.

The hours passed with conversation, laughter, food, and gifts. The clock chimed seven times; it was time to leave. Robb and I knew we would not be spending this Christmas Eve together. For some reason, he was upbeat and didn't seem to feel any of what I was. He was coping so much better than I was. Was it because he was out and about working? Was it that his life didn't stop? I was irritated by his Merry Christmas attitude. Was I turning into Scrooge?

Robb decided he would spend the night in the hospital with Derian so Connor and I could repair our relationship. Once Derian's coat was on, Robb took him back into the dining room to say good-bye.

I didn't have to go anywhere, but I couldn't stay without Robb. I was on the verge of spilling out all the emotion I shoved to the side to get through dinner. I really needed to cry but I didn't want an audience. Robb's mom helped me pack up Connor and his things. She put her arms around me and told me to hang in there. I totally lost it. I cried as I muttered, "Thanks for making a nice Christmas for us." Saying that made me realize that I felt sorry that I was not able to make my own Christmas for our boys. I cried hot, sad tears, and admitted out loud, "This is so hard." She hugged me a little tighter. I didn't care how loud I cried or if anyone else could hear me. Life was overwhelming!

In the background, I could hear one of the guests say, "These are hard times." I knew he was talking about us, and that made it even harder. Maybe I could have shared all the feelings I had inside and they would have understood…but there was no looking back. I had to go.

My face was chapped by the time I had the car loaded. Tears and below zero weather were a bad combination. I said good-bye to every-one and left.

Chapter 37

The freeway was empty, only a handful of cars and me. The ride home was another reminder of how alone I was. What kind of loser is out on Christmas Eve without their family? Connor was too little to have a conversation, so I turned on the radio and we listened to Christmas music.

We drove up to the only dark house on the block. I got out of the car and heard some of my neighbors' company leaving, laughing, and saying what a great time they had. "See you next year." *Wow, what could next year possibly bring that could top this? Was there anything for us to look forward to? Would next year possibly bring a magical cure for Derian? Would we be able to celebrate a holiday without being in the hospital, or having a surgery follow it?*

Connor hated the cold and snuggled his little nose into the collar of my coat. I put my arms around him and held him tight, hoping I would be able to repair the rejection he felt. God, how could I give anything to Connor? I had nothing left. Derian took everything from me.

I turned the lights on and took our coats off. He knew this was a familiar place, but he didn't seem to know this was home.

How many days had it been since he was home? He looked hesitantly around the house, as if he were entering a past life, taking in all the sights and smells. I sat on a bench and reached out to him, hoping he would accept my hands and come to me. I couldn't stand one more jab of loneliness. Connor accepted the touch and I gave him a full-body hug. We were strangers to each other, our house, and this life. I lit a few candles, turned down the lights, and tuned in the radio station that played all-night Christmas music. I wondered why I was torturing myself. This was the only thing I still knew of Christmas and I had to do this, even if it hurt more. I rocked Connor to the music for a long while before I carried him into our room. I was not going to sleep by myself. Connor was a good snuggler and it had been a long time since I had felt him next to me. I wanted to hear the sounds of his toddler snores and hold on to his soft little hands. I needed to look at him and remind myself he was mine, a part of my life—even if it was a life that was unpredictable

The weight of the darkness closed in on me. I was caught in a web of solitude, unable to talk to anyone. It was Christmas Eve and I would not ruin anyone else's holiday. Desperate, I called Robb, hoping we could connect. What a mistake! Robb was back at the hospital where the lights were bright, people were coming and going, and the spirit of Christmas was alive and well. When I explained how lonely I felt, he insensitively responded, "You're not going to commit suicide, are you?" It's a good thing Robb is not a counselor!

Feeling completely unfulfilled after that conversation, I returned to the quiet and watched the moon slowly change shapes throughout the night. That was the dark night of my soul. I visited the well of loneliness, the place where desperation can hurt no more. I felt nervous being in this spot. I had no desire to fight anymore. As I lay in this tomb of solitude, I could feel my mind drifting from this world. If I allowed myself to disappear in the darkness, I would never return with a full mind or spirit.

Chapter 38

The first light of day beckoned me to break my silence. I couldn't be silent one minute longer. I called Robb's sister, Heather. I knew little Madeline was sure to have awakened her. Heather must have been overwhelmed by my call. No doubt she heard the desperation and panic in my voice. I spoke with pent-up energy, grateful to hear the sound of another voice. I read her the letter to the editor I was submitting. We both cried. Slowly the layers of ice that had rested on my soul melted. I was up, moving, and I would never enter the tomb of no return.

I called my mom after speaking to Heather. We had another four-hour pass and planned on spending Christmas Day at my parents' house. My mom arranged for an extended family member to come over and play Santa for the boys'. She could hardly wait to see the boy's reaction when Santa came walking in.

Connor and I dressed and met Robb and Derian at the hospital. Derian was waiting outside the elevator when we arrived. He was so excited about going to a party! We got the kids bundled up and left for Grandma and Grandpa Nearys' house. My parents ran out and welcomed us as we pulled into the driveway, clapping and cheering as the boys got out of the car. The warmth of spiced apple cider hung in the air while snacks and goodies awaited little boy hands.

My mom knew we had limited time and budgeted in dinner, present-opening, and visiting with Santa. After we opened the presents, there was a loud knock at the door. The door opened and a gust of cold winter wind followed a loud "HO, HO, HO." In walked Santa and Mrs. Claus. The boys' eyes grew as big as saucers, tracking each move the

▢ letters

12/95

Family gives thanks to those at Valley Middle School who brightened their holiday spirits

To the editor:

Political correctness has spread through this country like wild fire. As far as I'm concerned, it has destroyed many traditions in its path and has become America's new phobia — a fear to offend.

People now struggle with the politically correct thing to do and put their humanness in the back seat. Let me tell you a story about a special place on Gardenview Drive where people took a risk, let humanness take priority over political correctness and the affect it has had on me and my family.

I am the mother of two small sons — Derian, 2, and Connor, 1. I am a teacher at Valley Middle School which is located on Gardenview Drive.

The past two years my family has experienced many trials. Derian has Charge Syndrome, a birth defect that affects the eyes, ears, nose, heart and development.

During the past two years, Derian has had four heart surgeries, choanal atresia, eye surgery, was fitted for hearing aids and is beginning to learn sign language. Needless to say, these years have been challenging but things were looking up. I was sure we were in a medical pause when something new cropped up.

On Dec. 16, I took Derian into the emergency room for what I thought was a severe sinus infection. Well, it turned out to be a severe pneumonia. He was admitted to the hospital and hooked up to intravenous antibiotics immediately. The pneumonia would be wiped out in a few days and we would be home soon — so we thought.

Unfortunately, a new bacteria showed up — enterococcal bacterium. This bacterium is a nasty one, especially for someone with the heart history of Derian, and requires four to six weeks of intravenous antibiotics.

We received this news on Wednesday, Dec. 20, so I called the assistant principal and asked her about taking another leave of absence. Her response was, "Take all the time you need. We'll work it out." I took off Thursday just to cope with this "snafu," organize bags, clothes, and schedules for my little Connor.

Things were going to be hard and even harder over Christmas. That day at school a friend announced over our PA system what was going on with Derian and my family. Twenty-four hours later, I returned to school to say good-bye to my students, my friends, and to get things in order for my substitute.

Much to my surprise, there were boxes, packages, cards, and letters piled on my desk, hugs from the people I work with and dozens of students who hand-delivered their cards and gifts. The day was filled with bittersweet tears as I said good-bye, for awhile, to each one of my classes. Colleagues gave me smiles, ears of concern, words of encouragement, and generous gifts of financial support.

The students also organized their own little fund-raiser, "Dollars for Derian." Inside their envelope were rolls of bills, and lots of pennies, nickels, and dimes.

As the day went on, banners were delivered. I was given countless, supportive and meaningful hugs from students — one student hugged me so hard he picked me up. One student gave me his blessing, "Mrs. Keech, I think it's important for you to be with your son during this time." There was a list of students willing to do free baby-sitting for Connor and another student, a seventh grader, who wanted to rent "Barney" for my son with the hundred dollars he had gotten

for Christmas. If that doesn't pull at your heart strings, I don't know what will. Other students told me they were praying for us and others said they had put us on their church's prayer chains.

I suppose all of these precious moments, people, and hugs were politically incorrect, but you know, I wasn't offended. I was given enough strength and courage in that one day to make it through spending Christmas in the hospital.

It's still hard, but there is a great deal of power in humanness. It is that humanness that will get us through the days ahead.

To all my miracle makers, I want you to know that every word is remembered, each card and letter has been read and is hanging in our room, each stuffed animal has been snuggled often and is watching over Derian. All the toys, books, and bubbles are being played with, the decorations and banners are hung, each cent has been placed in a reserve fund, the diapers are being used, the prayers are felt, and the breads, treats, and goodies are being gobbled up.

Thanks to all of you for giving us the best gift we could ask for this Christmas — your love and support. If Derian ever has self-esteem problems, I will pull out your cards and letters and tell him the story of our miracle on Gardenview Drive. Your kindness has touched our hearts.

PATSY KEECH and family
South St. Paul

(Editor's note: Keech is a seventh grade communications teacher at Valley Middle School in Apple Valley.)

Reprinted by permission of Sun Current Newspaper

two of them made. They weren't as confident as I would have expected them to be. They didn't really seem to know what to do, run or move closer. Santa and Mrs. Claus sat down in a chair near them and began speaking in gentle voices. After a few minutes the boys became brave enough to go over to Santa's green sack and see what was in it. Derian bravely dug right in while Connor stood back and watched. Santa stood up to help Derian retrieve the presents in the bottom of the bag. He leaned over Connor, who reached up his hand and ever so gently touched the white fur lining the bottom of his coat. We all laughed. When the sack was completely empty Santa and Mrs. Claus announced that they needed to get back to the North Pole. Both boys were braver when Santa was out the door "Ho, Ho, Ho–ing." The boys were utterly amazed by Santa's visit and they kept imitating what had happened. Robb coaxed them into signing their Barney poem. Everyone let out a cheer when they were done. The boys had a special day. Thank goodness for grandparents. I was grateful they gave the boys the Christmas I could not.

Robb slept at home with Connor that night and I stayed in the hospital with Derian. When the lights turned out that night, I was relieved Christmas was over and wouldn't bother us for a while. Perhaps next year there would be more to celebrate.

Chapter 39

I crossed the eleventh day off the calendar; only thirty-some days left to go.

Derian had a new nurse that day. As she changed Derian's IV bag, she mentioned that there was a mom across the hall whose little boy was going through the same treatment Derian was. She left the woman's name and room number with me. I was anxious to meet someone else who was in the same boat we were and decided to visit her after Derian's nap.

Derian's medicine was super-charging him. Overall he was a relatively mellow kid, but this high-speed power-driven force he was operating on was a change for him and us. With Derian on the move, it didn't take long to do a few laps around the floor. This was a sight. Derian, all of two and one-half feet tall, hooked up to an 8-ft. steel IV pole. An elaborate set up, but not for Derian. He quickly figured out how to maneuver it and could even push it with his board hand while waving with the other. He joyfully made his way through the halls and socialized with everyone.

After a few more laps, we looked up Caroline, the mother the nurse told me about. She was a young mom, in her mid twenties, tall, with a long blonde ponytail that hung over her shoulders. She seemed to be in deep thought as she answered the door. Derian and I introduced ourselves and explained that the nurse suggested we talk. Derian pushed himself and IV pole into the room and pointed to the crib. He began signing, "Baby, baby." Caroline seemed charmed and taken aback at the same time watching Derian. Derian continued to sign, "Baby, baby." I asked if Derian could look at her baby. She agreed, but she was nervous to have toddler hands close to her fragile Scottie. He had an IV and something else stuck in his head. Caroline explained this was the end of a shunt that was placed in his brain a few weeks earlier. Derian pointed to it, "Owie." Caroline relaxed when Derian said that. It was clear to both of us that Derian understood what an "owie" was and wouldn't touch or hurt the baby. Before I could put him down, he insisted on giving the baby a kiss. We were both conscious of germs and decided in unison Derian could kiss Scottie's hand. That seemed agreeable.

Once Derian met Scottie, he started looking at his room. Their room was different than ours; it looked homey, like an apartment. There was a bulletin board with charts of information, baskets of folded clothes, boxes with shoes, a cordless phone, and signs that were written to Scottie's nurses about how to care for him. One of the signs read something like this: *Scottie's body needs to be respected. Please talk through the procedure with him as you're doing it.* Another sign detailed Scottie's likes, dislikes, and his schedule. Caroline and I decided on a late dinner when the kids were down for the evening. I was positively giddy about having a friend in the hospital and anxious for Derian to get to sleep so I could go out that night.

Derian was never able to get himself to sleep in his crib; he needed major bedtime snuggling. Each night, the two of us began our bedtime ritual lying on a bumpy rollaway snuggling until he would fall asleep. His gurgling snore let me know he was out for the night. The tricky part was getting him from the bed into the crib. Once I moved the IV pole closer to the crib, I picked him up and carefully lowered him to the crib mattress and laid him down. At that point I'd hold my breath, hoping he wouldn't roll over and notice I wasn't there. If that happened we'd have to start the whole process over and I wouldn't be able to meet Caroline. I tucked one blanket around him and another one under his chin and crossed my fingers that the jolt of the crib bar going up wouldn't disturb him.

Hooray, it latched! Derian snored away—the coast was clear. I tiptoed over to Caroline's room. The light was out—a good sign. I knocked on the door with my fingertips and waited for a few minutes. She cracked opened the door and whispered, "I can't find my purse. Hang on just a second." She continued to pat around the floor until she found it. She opened it and discovered her husband had taken the checkbook. "I can't go. I don't have any money."

"I'll buy tonight, you buy another night." I promptly replied.

She agreed. We decided to go to a restaurant within walking distance from the hospital. We looked up the phone number, gave it to the nurse at the front desk, grabbed a pager, and off we went.

Excitement twirled in my gut as the two of us walked out of the hospital. I had never had the chance to develop a friendship with another mother in the hospital. Even though it was 20 below zero, we decided to walk the three blocks to the restaurant. We thought the fresh air might be a nice treat to the stale hospital air. Our teeth chattered the entire way there, and mid-block I began to think we should have driven.

We arrived at the restaurant with red cheeks and frozen eyelashes. As cold as I was, realizing this woman knew of my experiences first hand warmed me up. The hostess quickly found us a table in the center of the restaurant. The place was busy, but we didn't mind. We were in our own world. That evening was unforgettable. In the three hours we sat in the restaurant, we poured out the pieces of our lives no one else understood. It seemed like the universe stopped to allow for our meeting. We shared our experiences of labor, birth, near-death experiences, hospital life, and our anticipation for the future. I felt safe and reassured of my own feelings as I listened to Caroline speak of hers. It seemed as though we were twins meeting each other for the first time, comparing pasts and futures. We marveled at the intricate understanding we shared.

When we returned to the floor, one of the nurses smiled and said, "It looks like both of you found a friend. Perhaps the two of you should leave this place more often. You look alive." Caroline and I smiled at each other. The nurse was right. When I called Robb, I could almost see his smile through his voice as I shared the details of my evening. He was pleased I would have some company during the days and was very interested in getting together with Caroline and her husband. It would be so nice to have another couple to do things with, another couple who wore the same shoes we did.

Robb was lonesome for Derian, so we decided to switch boys and places the following evening. We were committed to keep Connor's schedule as "normal" as possible: going to Mary's (his day care mom) house during the day, eating dinner at the hospital, and spending evenings at home.

"Robb, give Connor a kiss for me."

"If you give one to Derian for me."

"Goodnight sweetie, I'll see you tomorrow." As rich as the evening was, I was disappointed Robb and I were not together. But the few hours I had with Caroline allowed me to escape from the loneliness of being separated from Robb, Connor, home, work, and life.

Chapter 40

The next morning, Robb and Connor surprised us with a breakfast visit. The boys hugged each other and twirled about. After a few minutes, they both were at the door ready to go to the playroom. I dreaded being in the playroom with both of them. Connor had no concept of Derian's equipment, or how far Derian could move without pulling the IV out. Derian probably didn't either. Two toddlers scooting around fearlessly beneath an IV pole were a dangerous combination.

The highlight of the playroom was a wooden refrigerator that opened up. The two of them would pull out the plastic food, put it up to their mouth say "yummy." and throw it on the floor. Once they emptied it, they would gather everything up and stick it all back in the refrigerator, only to do it all over again. It was a crazy game, one I never understood, but it was fun watching. When Robb and I decided we were pushing our luck, we steered the boys in a different direction: the coloring table. Derian was familiar with where everything was in the playroom and got some drawing paper for them. Derian reached in the bucket of crayons and picked out his favorite color, brown. Derian began signing and talking to Connor almost as if he were explaining how to begin coloring. Connor listened for a few seconds and then did his own thing. Connor began all his drawings with a green crayon.

Robb and I managed to get a few sentences in between the interruptions from the kids. "Did we get any mail?" "How was work yesterday?" "Did Connor sleep well last night?" "What's the latest on Derian?" After we got that important discussion out of the way, we finalized our plans. I would pick up Connor once my mom arrived at the hospital, she would stay with Derian until Robb got off work, and Robb's parents would come that evening to see Derian. It was almost like having two worlds, one that revolved around hospital life, machines, IV poles, and a supposedly "sick" child and the other revolving around the needs of a healthy child, home maintenance, laundry, mail, and bills to pay. Rotating evenings at home was a way to keep some sort of balance.

If I wanted a shower that morning, I had to squeeze it in before Robb left. I hustled back to the room, grabbed my shower supplies, and headed down the hall. By the time I got back to our room, Robb had his coat on and was ready to leave for work. He seemed relieved to be getting on his way. The intense watching of the two boys and the IV pole was enough to zap anyone. We all kissed him good-bye and I marked another day off the calendar. It had been twelve days so far, four weeks left. Crazy as it sounds, this was the most fun we had ever had in the hospital. Because Derian wasn't hurting, he was able to participate in the activities the Child-Life staff had organized. Bingo was on the schedule for the afternoon.

I was solo with wet hair, no make up, and two wild boys to contend with. Luckily, Barney was on, so they sat in the oversized rocking chair doing whatever Barney asked them to do. While they were watching TV, I got ready. I needed to get Connor to Mary's house and zip back to the hospital. I made arrangements with Derian's nurse to keep Derian with her until I returned. Because I was running behind schedule, I hurriedly grabbed Connor's coat, tucked his arms into the sleeves, and zipped it up. As I was zipping up my own coat, I noticed Derian pulling at Connor, saying, "Onner stay, Onner stay."

I knelt next to him. "Derian, Mommy has to bring Connor to Mary's house. Mommy will be right back." Derian frantically began searching for his coat. He wanted to come with us. I was caught off guard by his reaction. How left out he must have felt! He continued pulling desperately on Connor. Connor sensed something was out of control. He began to cry. Then Derian. Then me. The three of us, two with coats on and one without sat, on the cold hospital floor and cried. This was a terrible way to live. Another four weeks of living like this was unimaginable.

The nurse stopped by as we were regaining our composure. "Having a bad day?" She stood in the doorway for a few minutes and then excused herself. A few minutes later she came back with a small package of cookies for each of us. She reassured me Derian would be fine and she would keep him with her until I came back. She had three other patients assigned to her so I would have to hustle up. Connor and I gave

Derian a kiss before briskly walking down the hall. The nurse kept him distracted. I was thankful he wasn't crying.

The first breath during a Minnesota winter morning is always a welcoming thrill. It felt clean and fresh and reminded me that another world existed outside the hospital. On the way to Mary's, Connor and I sang "Itsy Bitsy Spider" and wiggled our chilled fingers inside our mittens. As intuitive as Connor is, I have no doubt he knew I was faking having fun with him. Inside a hailstorm of emotion was on the verge of exploding. As soon as I dropped Connor off, I decided to treat myself to a good cry.

As I pulled into Mary's driveway, I was confident she was the person who needed to be with Connor that morning. How lucky we were to have found her! I was confident in Mary's gift with children and admired her spiritually. She was kind, sensitive, and considered caring for children her ministry; she genuinely loved each child. She greeted us at the door with her usual cheerful smile. Connor immediately jumped from my arms into hers and then down to the floor to join the kids that gathered around him, beckoning him to join their fun. While Connor was quickly swept away, Mary asked how Derian was. I gave her the "Derian Daily." Mary gave me a hug and I rushed back to the hospital.

When I parked at the hospital, my new home, I grabbed the steering wheel and leaned my head against it; it felt cool on my face. I decided not to rush back. I was going to sit out in the cold until I was ready to go back to my prison. I inhaled and exhaled deep, heavy sighs before forcing myself to get out of the car. In a robotic state, I walked to the elevator and pushed the button for the third floor. As I watched the numbers in the elevator light up floor-by-floor, my heart began to pump faster, my head throbbed, and my stomach knotted up. The voices of the people around me seemed so loud, the lights so bright, and the pictures on the wall too familiar. I hated this place!

As I walked down the hallway, Derian clapped his hands and welcomed me back. He challenged me with his joy and love for life. How could he feel so happy living like this? He put me to shame.

Derian played his first game of Bingo that afternoon. I would point to the number called while he would carefully pinch his fingers together to pick up a token to cover the space. When B12 was called, he had a bingo. Excitedly I told him, "Raise your hand, you have bingo!" Even though he had no idea what that meant, he picked up on my enthusiasm and began waving his arms in the air. Once his win was confirmed, he was pointed in the direction of the prizes. There were all sorts of items for a variety of age groups lined up against the wall. Derian picked out a pink Baby Bop sweatshirt. He proudly held it up and everyone cheered for him. Enthused by this wonderful game, we continued to play. He won again and picked out another pink Baby Bop sweatshirt. He held it up saying "Onnor, Onnor." Feeling extremely proud of his winning, we sat down and played another game. For once this kid was on a lucky streak—he won again. The little boy sitting at our table was disappointed that he wasn't winning anything. I asked Derian if he could pick out a prize and give it to him. He cheerfully obliged and presented him with a puzzle. The little boy smiled and thanked him. Derian was proud to share his good fortune. Having made three consecutive wins, he now thought this was how the game was played. "BINGO" was called and Derian went to pick out a prize. Someone else had won, but he did not understand why he wasn't able to pick out the prize. It was time to move on to the next activity. As we were making our way out the door one of the nurses stood in the doorway, held up an IV bag and asked, "Is anyone missing an IV bag? I found this lying in the hallway." Every adult sitting in the room looked up to the top of their IV pole to see if their child's bag was missing. How many times have you seen an IV bag in lost and found? So much for hospital humor.

Caroline worked during the days, the two of us planned on hanging out in the evenings with the kids.

Chapter 41

News Year's Eve

Accepting the challenges of hospital life was difficult enough, but rolling with the punches really was a challenge on day 16. A new Infectious Disease Control doctor came on board and told us we could go home. He had to be joking, or he hadn't read Derian's chart to know that we still had 26 days in the joint. But this doctor was serious. He decided Derian didn't need to spend the remainder of his time in the hospital and could go home with a Hickman (an IV line surgically threaded into a large vein in the chest that would last the duration of his treatment). A home care health nurse would come to our home and train us on giving Derian his medications. Wow, how come this wasn't explained to us before? Things wouldn't have seemed nearly as bad had we known this.

This half-hour surgical procedure was scheduled for that afternoon. I met with the discharge nurse who arranged for home health care training and ordered the supplies needed to complete Derian's treatment at home. We went home, jubilant.

Yet, I was confused by this rapid change. It seemed odd that the first doctor was adamant about parents not administering this treatment at home and now they were expecting this from us. But at least Robb, the boys, and I could be together. That evening Robb came home with a steak and all the fixings for a great meal. "Robb, why don't we save that for New Year's Eve?"

Puzzled by my response, he said, "Patsy, tonight is New Year's Eve." I didn't believe it—the whole world was about to move into the next year and I was a day behind. I would have missed it.

The home health nurse arrived just in time for Derian's evening dose of medicine. She showed us how to use the infuser machine, cap the Hickman, and plug the drugs into the machine. As the medicine was entering Derian's body, his shirt became wet. The nurse smelled it and discovered the medicine was leaking. She examined both Derian's chest and the Hickman and determined that the Hickman was leaking. There was a hole in it! She called the hospital and made arrangements for Derian to have a new one placed that night. I was furious. After spending 16 days in the hospital, adjusting to the change in plans, and becoming settled at home, we had to return to the hospital for another surgery—all because someone working on the assembly line didn't check that product. I never felt like suing anyone until that moment. Why should Derian pay the price for people not doing their job? Why didn't they check it out before inserting it?

I had nothing good to say to anyone that evening. It was a good thing I was in a confrontational mood because the lead doctor was determined to release Derian that night. "Look," I said, "we were in here for 16 days; we packed up today and went home. Once we were settled in, this problem was discovered. It is 11 p.m. and I am not alert enough to learn how to care for my son tonight. I need a nurse to administer Derian's medicine tonight so I can sleep. Tomorrow I will be ready to care for him."

Thank goodness he changed his mind and let us stay overnight. We returned home the next morning. As much as we longed to be home when we were in the hospital, life kicked in high gear once we were home, with two toddlers, a Hickman, an infusing machine attached to Derian's chest, and six syringes of medicine every 4 to 6 hours. After a few days of living like this, I was ready to check myself into the hospital. It seemed too large a task to ask parents to do this treatment at home. The first doctor really knew what he was talking about. Derian was on two drugs; one needed to be infused every six hours, the other every four hours around the clock. The entire process took around 45 minutes. Because I promised to keep my students posted on Derian's progress, I made a videotape that explained Derian's treatment and showed the boys interacting. Our life was insane.

A friend from church stopped by one day while I was giving Derian his medicine. She gasped when she watched me for 45 minutes running behind a super-charged Derian with the machine hooked up to his chest. It was like walking a dog on a leash through a dangerous obstacle course. After witnessing the craziness first-hand, she went to church and contacted a group of women who filled our freezer with oven-ready meals. For the first time in our lives we were homebound. These women's dishes gave our life some normalcy—at least at mealtime.

The boys were wrestling a week before Derian's treatment was to be completed when Derian's Hickman came out. We raced back to the emergency room. This time surgery was not the answer. Instead, they decided to hook Derian up to an IV and have him finish this treatment in the hospital. I've never been so glad to be back in the hospital! I knocked on Caroline's door on our way to our new room. She was glad to see us. I got more sleep that last week then I had gotten the entire time we were home. On day 42, Derian's blood cultures were clear— the enterococcus bacterium was blown out of Derian's system. He was home free—we all were.

Chapter 42

March 7, 1996

Derian went in for an echocardiogram on March 7. Thankfully, we received good news. The pressures in his heart were normal and all was going well. We really needed a report like that after our Christmas experience.

It took us two months to get back to normal. Normalcy was such a lost concept; I wondered what normal even meant. My definition would be no hospital, no Hickman, no surgery, and no recovery. It meant being healthy.

A few weeks after feeling "normal", Derian went into the hospital again. He had a high temperature, was breathing oddly, and looked extremely pale. The same doctor who admitted him before Christmas ordered the same tests for the same symptoms. She was worried he may have had a relapse and we would need to repeat the same six weeks over. Not again! I would go crazy if I had to relive the Hickman, the medicine, and the treatment.

The doctor admitted us and we returned to the third floor. As kind as the nurses were, they were disappointed to see us again. It wasn't fair! We had just been put through hell a few months ago, why again? Derian was feeling the same way. I could see the disappointment disguised in his smile.

The results of the cultures came back three days later. Thankfully, they were all clear. Before the doctor would release Derian, she wanted an echocardiogram. The echo revealed the pressures in Derian's heart had increased. This was alarming, especially since the pressures were nor-mal two weeks ago. Something was going on. Something was horribly wrong. Dr. Hesslein would be notified of the echo results prior to Derian's scheduled heart catheter procedure.

Echocardiograms and heart catheters had become a somewhat normal event in our lives, but something about this upcoming heart catheter felt worrisome. I remember the secretary calling to schedule the appoint-ment. Initially, I scheduled a date that was impossible for Robb to attend, so I called to change the date and time. The secretary seemed irritated. After going through great effort, Derian's heart catheter pro-cedure was scheduled for April 11.

I hated waiting so many days in between the scheduling and the actual procedure. I couldn't really get into Easter, egg hunts, or bas-ket stuff. I was consumed with fear. What if Derian needed another surgery? Would this be our last Easter with him? What was going to happen? The waiting before the procedure was worse than the pro-cedure itself.

A few days before Easter, one of our family friends died. During his funeral I took mental notes about the beauty of the service. My head filled with thoughts of Derian's funeral. I listened to the beautiful eulo-gies and wondered what people would say about Derian. This was crazy, yet I couldn't get those thoughts to flush from my mind. My heart began pounding like I had been told something terrible. A cold, clammy film covered my skin as the thoughts continued. It can't be true. It can't be true. God can't take him away from me. Not now! The feelings and thoughts grew stronger with each passing day. I felt as though I could see the shadow of death surrounding my sweet little Derian. I was a fail-ure as a mother. How could I think such thoughts? I had to know I had done absolutely everything I could do to change this plan. I wanted prayers, like never before, for my son. They had to be powerful, and the people praying for him must be able to touch his hand as they prayed. I had to figure out a way.

Days later the boys were finger painting.

As I watched them, I knew what to do. I needed his handprint. I picked up a paintbrush, placed Derian's hand in mine, and I painted each fin-ger. Derian giggled from the tickle of the paintbrush. As I stared at the wet handprint, I envisioned it on a card next to a picture of Derian. The cards would request a victory for Derian. People could press their hand into Derian's, and look at his face while they prayed for him. Within the next few days I brought my mock-up prayer card sample to Lana, a friend from high school whose family owned a print shop. I told her what was going on and shared my idea for the cards. She was greatly touched and told me there would be no charge for this job. I was honored they would do this work for me. The job had to be done with love and special care; it wasn't just a printing job. This was my plea for my son's life.

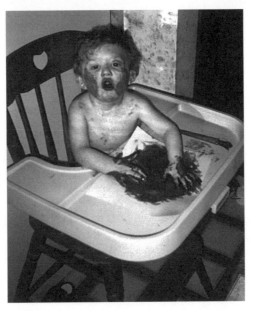

Chapter 43

The Easter Bunny came to our house that morning and set up a tent in the living room. When the boys peeked inside and found the baskets, they went wild. Within minutes of their arrival into the tent, candy and cellophane grass exploded. They danced, laughed, and pigged out before church. They were so happy being together; they were truly soul twins. I wondered if between the two of them they also knew what lay ahead.

Monday morning came and I went back to work. It was hard to listen to the recap of everyone's Easter break when I was convinced Dr. Hesslein would tell us in the next few days that Derian needed another surgery. Fear was at an all-time high as I ate lunch with my friends that day. I listened to their vacation stories in hope the fear would just go away. Finally, I couldn't hold it in any longer. I blurted out, "Derian is going in for another heart catheter Thursday and I know he is going to die if he has to have another surgery." I asked them, "Can you please pray I'm wrong and that Derian will be just fine?" The bell rang. We ended lunch with Kleenex and hugs. It was hard to switch gears and get excited about teaching a lesson on how to write a good speech introduction.

What was God trying to tell me? I had to get some peace and some answers at the same time. But whom could I speak with and share this horrible secret without them dismissing what I knew to be true. I was selective in choosing my confidant. I needed to speak to the minister of the church Robb and I attended when we first were married. His secretary scheduled me for an appointment the following day.

I had fond memories of Reverend Arnie and our days in his church. He was an English man with a heavy accent. It was delightful to listen to him, and evident he knew God. I trusted him. I couldn't wait for school to end so I could see him and rest my anxious heart. I had never been to his new church. It was huge, ivy covering its brick walls and the pointed peaks of the doors creating an English atmosphere. The warm colored brick gave the room a cozy feel. I was in the right place.

Arnie opened his office door and smiled the same smile I remembered from years before. In his English accent he greeted me, "Hello, Patsy." Hearing him say my name brought me back to another life. I caught him up on the last few years and focused the rest of the conversation on what was staring me in the face.

"Arnie, have you ever known something to be true before it came to be?"

"What do you know, Patsy?"

"I am certain Derian will have another heart surgery and he will not survive. I imagine being at his funeral and I see Robb, Connor, and me moving through life without him and smiling. What kind of mother thinks such things? What does all this mean? Why would I know all this?"

He handed me some Kleenex and soothingly said, "Patsy, sometimes God sends us gifts to prepare us for the future. I think God is preparing you for Derian's death. Perhaps the message God is sending you is to use your time wisely." He allowed me to explore the scenario of finding out that Derian needed surgery, the day of the surgery, Derian dying shortly afterwards, and moving through a life without him. As we did this exercise, I knew Derian was not going to be ours much longer. Instead of thinking of me as an awful mother giving up on her son, he told me, "Patsy, you are a strong woman to be able to look into the future and face whatever lies ahead. I'm confident that should you need to face Derian's death, you will hold your family together, and create something beautiful with your life."

I pondered heavy thoughts as I drove home. How do I look at my child with this knowledge? How do I work or do anything except play with him and spend an entire lifetime in a short time span? I felt dishonest knowing the future and being too ashamed to tell anyone. As I opened the front door, both boys ran to me and gave me great hugs. Derian's hug was especially tight. He hugged me in a way that I knew he was relieved I knew the truth. We hugged for a long time. Such a jewel. How would I be able to let him go? We danced so well to life and the bond we shared was intense. It was as if while he grew inside me, our souls grew together.

Derian was especially close to me the next day. I recall holding both boys one night on the couch, watching TV. My arms were stretched beyond their limits. Dan, a friend who was visiting, came into the living room and we began to talk. I asked him if he could take one of the boys for me. Connor was awake, but Derian was zoned. He came over to the couch and carefully tried to remove Derian from my arms without waking him. Derian felt the touch of different hands and woke up tiredly saying, "Onnor." "Take Onnor." Derian seemed to want as much time as he could with his mom.

Chapter 44

April 11, 1996

We had to be at the hospital early. This would be the day we would find out if Derian needed another surgery. Robb and I knew the routine and how the day would evolve. We knew we would have lots of sitting time while the doctors and staff were in the catheter lab with Derian. We filled backpacks with items such as magazines, books, snacks, papers to correct—anything to keep busy. We would be at the hospital for at least 12 hours, or we'd stay overnight if they ballooned his heart.

As we checked in, the windows of the children's gift shop distracted Derian. He squealed and pointed excitedly to each Sesame Street character. It seemed this distraction was a trick designed to lure him farther into the hospital. Why couldn't he be just be a little kid, worrying about not getting something from the store rather than if his heart was working? Why couldn't he have been blessed with a healthy body?

We were directed to the Same Day Surgery part of the hospital with Derian's admittance items: papers, armbands, and insurance information. The nurses swooned over Derian. They were impressed with how big he had gotten in the last few months. Derian loved this kind of attention! Soon he was blowing them kisses, dancing, twirling around, and smiling at them. As often as he was in the hospital, he should have been terrified of this place and the people who worked there. Not Derian. This was partially his home. He accepted this at a young age. He must have felt this was how life was supposed to be. He wasn't afraid. He knew the routine well.

The nurse listened to his heart while he moved the stethoscope around his chest for her. He knew to hold out his arm for the blood pressure cuff. The nurse let Derian push the button that started the machine. He didn't seem to mind as much when he was controlling the machine. After all his vitals were done, they prepped him for the catheter. This was the hardest part. The nurse he felt safe with, along with his parents, now held him down and placed a cold white cream in his warm crotch. He cried streams of tears while the fighter within him moved with the force of a champion. He was so strong. Eventually he surrendered his body.

Once the cream was in place, he would need to keep his leg straight until it was time to go to the procedure. This wait could be anywhere from half an hour to two hours. Not surprisingly this was the longest part of the day for us. How does one entertain a 2 1/2-year-old for that amount of time *and* make sure his leg is in a straight position? We colored, watched Barney, read books, looked at all the objects in the room, and even counted the ceiling tiles. After only one half-hour, I couldn't think of one more thing to entertain him.

When they called his name, we moved quickly with our nurse through the double doors that led to the heart lab. The team waited outside the door for him. They looked friendly and promised to take good care of him. Robb and I squeezed Derian in the middle of us and gave him a hero's kiss before handing him over. Derian cried sad cries as we walked down the hall that seemed so much longer now. My stomach clamped together. God, I hated leaving him. I knew he was afraid. What adult wouldn't? Imagine what it would be like for a small child to have 4-5 adults hovering over with masks and puffy hairnets. Poor Derian. Robb gave me a hug before we walked through the now-closed double doors. We hugged a lot in the hospital. It was an easy way to express our feelings of helplessness and fear while supporting each other.

The cardiac nurses were great about coming by with hourly updates on his progress. They played a huge role in Derian's life since his birth. We chatted about Derian and Connor and caught up on anything that was new from our last meeting. During the middle of the procedure, Dr. Hesslein left the heart lab and came to see us. This had never happened before. He was his usual upbeat self, but grew serious as he spoke. "The pressures in Derian's heart are higher than they have ever been."

I could feel my stomach twist. I knew what was coming before Dr. Hesslein even said it. "I'd like to try and open up the artery by ballooning the catheter and see if that won't reduce the pressure. However, that will require Derian to stay the night so we can keep an eye on him."

I never minded being in the hospital when Derian's condition seemed fragile. I preferred to have him under someone else's watch on those occasions. After Dr. Hesslein left, we called our parents with the "Derian Daily" and made arrangements for Connor. Luckily, we could bunk in the parent center. Robb went home to get a few items we needed.

Dr. Hesslein came out of the lab right after Robb left. He looked exhausted. I met him in the hall and we put our arms around each other and walked into the waiting room. He was honest enough to tell me he wasn't exactly sure what was going on. As frightening as that is to hear as a parent, I trusted Dr. Hesslein. There had to be someone in this world that would know about Derian's condition, and I was convinced Dr. Hesslein would find that person. He didn't have an ego problem and I knew he would get help when it was time. He told me he was too tired to put all the pieces to this new puzzle together that night. He wanted to sleep on it and confer with a few other cardiologists before he could tell us what was best for Derian. He apologized and understood it was disappointing to wait so long without getting any answers. His gentleness caught me in a net of security.

When Robb returned I told him about Dr. Hesslein's report. Together we generated our own list of questions to ask him the following morning. Our parents had a few questions of their own as well. Our heads spun as we thought about what was ahead for this little boy.

Derian was unusually crabby after waking up from the anesthesia. His movements were disjointed, delayed, and lethargic. I hoped he would be able to sleep it off. It would make it easier on all of us. I rocked him for hours before he eventually drifted into a deep sleep. Before I went to sleep myself, I asked the nurse to ring our room if Derian were to wake up. The nurses always did a great job of listening to our needs and wants. I appreciated their support.

I went to sleep in my clothes, just in case I would get a call. I must have fallen asleep as soon as my head hit the pillow. It had been a long, hard, unanswerable day. A few hours later the phone rang. Robb sat up abruptly. I held my breath as I timidly answered. "Keechs' room" *Was Derian in trouble? Were things going as planned? Did he wake up?* My stomach relaxed once the voice on the other end of the phone said, "Derian woke up. He's crying." I hung up the phone and told Robb. We had been conditioned to expect fear. I stumbled to the sink, wet my face, put a hat on, felt around the counter until I found my glasses, grabbed the key, and headed toward the ICU.

They say a mother can recognize her baby's cry. It's true. As soon as I turned the corner in the ICU I could hear Derian's panicky cry. As soon as I entered the room, he reached for me. I wrapped him in his blanket and rocked him in the hospital rocker. His eyes were still dull—looking and his balance was unstable. It took him a while before he could calm down and relax in my arms. He cried as he pointed to the IV in his arm. How much more would this sweet baby have to endure?

When Derian quieted, I looked around the ICU. Directly across from us was a baby girl who had heart surgery the day before. I talked to her parents and they shared that Dr. Hesslein had told them if she made it through the night, she would have a good chance of surviving. She must have been in really big trouble if Dr. Hesslein, the most optimistic doctor, gave them that report. I prayed all day for that little girl. Now in the middle of the night, I found my eyes locked on her crib. She was stretched out spread eagle; blue-crinkled tubes protruded out of her chest and white tape pulled her cheeks together to keep the ventilator in place. At the head of her bed was the young doctor responsible for her this night. Watching her chest rise and fall, he stood guard over her, ready to act immediately if her next breath did not follow.

The beauty in this scene struck me. This was not a routine medical scene. This was a doctor who cared, truly cared, about this little girl's fate. Struggling to stay awake, he was putting in extra hours to care for her. What were his thoughts? Did he wonder what she would be like as she grew up? Was he afraid he would lose her during the night? Or, was he praying to God asking Him to help save her? I marveled at his dedication, and hoped if Derian were ever in that same fate, he would have a doctor like him. I've never been able to forget this scene of tenderness.

Her mother and father sat next to her bedside stroking her tiny feet. So much love surrounded her. *I knew that if only love could heal her, she would be fine.*

The next day Lana called me from the print shop and let me know the prayer cards were done. I had to get those before Robb left for work. The prayer cards were Derian's only hope. I needed to pull out all the stops for a possible surgery.

Prayer Card
for
Derian Richard Keech

"Victory is through the Lord"

**Thanks for praying for a victory
for Derian.**

Sincerely,
Patsy, Robb, Derian & Connor
Keech

The cards looked beautiful. I passed them out to Lana's family immediately. We needed a flood of prayers. I couldn't care for Derian and pray for him at the same time. I completely relied on my family, friends, and church to pray for me. The prayer cards were a new step toward changing the situation. They were coming directly from me, in the most powerful way I could think of. I couldn't fail Derian. He counted on me.

Lana gave me a hug and asked me to call her after Dr. Hesslein's report. I was fearful of life and fearful of death. The answer was getting closer; I was weak thinking about what blow would be dealt to Derian…and to us.

Robb had to leave, so Derian and I waited with our box of prayer cards for Dr. Hesslein. Derian was in a good mood and sang along to the songs on the Barney tape. He must have sensed my fears, though, for he kept patting me on the shoulder. He was so wise. Did he know what was ahead? Was he an ordinary kid or did he have a little bit of heaven in him that was never lost?

He was offering me peace, telling me it was okay. Derian wove his magic and melted the gaps of fate. I looked in his eyes, sure of what I saw in his future, and he looked back at me with reassurance that things would be okay—that my life would not stop, even with his death. Why did Reverend Arnie say this was a gift? I felt cursed knowing this future, and ashamed for thinking he could die. What kind of mother rehearses her child's funeral in her mind or thinks about what it would be like to live without that child? And if that weren't bad enough, I knew I would still find things to make me smile, laugh, and feel joy after he was gone. What kind of evil lived inside me? I was afraid of my future and of myself.

Dr. Hesslein finally came into the room and delivered the news I expected…Derian needed heart surgery. Dr. Hesslein wasn't sure if Derian could wait until school was out for the summer. I didn't even care about taking more time off work or how this would affect Connor and our budget. I couldn't put life on hold for one more month. I told Dr. Hesslein I wanted to do the surgery sooner than later. He understood and told me to call his receptionist to set up a date.

Before Dr. Hesslein left, I gave him one of Derian's prayer cards. He looked at it as if he was pleased to know he wasn't the only one we were asking to save our child. He asked for a few more for his church and the nurses in his office. I was a surprised by his reaction.

The last thing I asked him is whether we should take Derian on a trip to Fond du Lac, to visit Robb's sister, Heather. I knew Derian's leg was sore from the catheter and would need to be kept straight for a few hours. Perhaps a six-hour car ride would be unfair to him. Robb was determined to go, providing Dr. Hesslein said it was okay, which he did.

When Robb arrived home that night we packed and headed for Fond du Lac.

Movement Five—

Playful Spirit

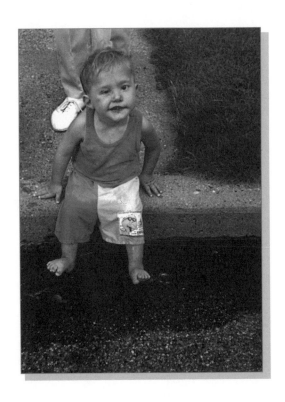

Chapter 45

The car ride went much better than expected. We didn't have to break up any fights or worry about Derian getting hurt. We met Robb's parents for dinner on the way to Heather's. Over dinner we relayed what Dr. Hesslein told us. Their silence communicated their disappointment of Derian's upcoming surgery. Since words couldn't change anything, silence was a comfortable solution. I had come to learn at this point on our journey with Derian that as hard as all of this was on Robb and me, it affected our parents two-fold. They felt badly for Derian and for us. I knew they worried a lot on their own.

The boys fell asleep once we got back on the road. While they slept, Robb and I talked about Derian's upcoming surgery. Robb decided he should be the one to take time off from work and stay in the hospital with Derian. As much as I appreciated his offer, I wondered how he expected me to leave Derian after I had always been the one who stayed in the hospital.

It was eleven by the time we finally arrived in Fond du Lac and quietly carried the kids into Heather's house. We were hopeful to pull this off without waking the boys, but our original plan failed. Heather's dog barked uncontrolably to announce our arrival. Startled by its bark, the boys awoke. Their eyes opened to discover a room full of new toys. Curiosity shifted into high gear; the two of them leaped out of our arms and began acquainting themselves. With the barking dog and the boys whooping it up, sleeping one-year-old Madeline didn't stand a chance. She soon walked out of her room holding a teddy bear and rubbing her sleepy eyes. She curled up in her daddy's lap and just watched the guys for a while before joining in.

Once the kids decided it was safe to interact, they began chasing each other throughout the house. Not wanting to miss out of any fun the dog joined in. Within minutes the house was electric. Madeline tried so hard to keep up with Derian and Connor. After a few hours, the kids settled down, and we all crashed for the evening.

The next day, as we sat around and watched the kids play, Robb informed his family about Derian's upcoming surgery. I remember this because it struck me as strange. No questions or discussion. Everyone kept eating and casually drifted off into new conversations. Not another word was said about it. Looking back, we wondered if they also knew this would be Derian's last surgery or if everyone else accepted that this lifestyle was normal for us.

In addition to balancing the heavy trauma in our lives, we were up to our armpits in sibling rivalry. We had just started doing time-outs in our house, mainly with Connor. He would get wild and push Derian out of his way. Since Derian's balance was never very steady, one push from Connor could do real damage. Connor had a temper and a flare for dramatics. That weekend, I caught Connor pushing Derian into a wall. I picked him up, set him on a chair in the living room and firmly said, "Sit here until I tell you to move!" Of course, I chose to do this in front of onlookers. Connor started to wiggle his way out of the chair, so I put my face right in front of him and said, "NO! When I tell you that you can get up, you need to give Derian a hug and tell him you're sorry."

Had I lost my mind? That scene reminded me of engaging in a power struggle with a student in front of a class. Everyone was watching to see who would win this battle. Connor carried on in the chair for a few minutes. Once he was on the verge of calming down, I approached him and told him to give his brother a hug and say he was sorry. My spectators were doubtful Connor could do what I asked, but I stayed firm. In a perfect moment, Connor went over to Derian, gave him a sweet little kiss, and said "Orry." This was a miracle, a complete act of God. I covered the truth up by acting like I was the perfect parent and this little scene was typical of my parenting skills.

Before we left Heather and Glenn's that weekend, I gave Heather some of the prayer cards and asked her to pass them out. Heather had a group of people she had asked to pray for Derian on many occasions. Motherhood had created a bond between Heather and me.

We returned home and began our 25-day wait; I never counted the days in between surgery dates as days of my life. Frankly, life meant nothing during those times. I was unproductive at work, forgetful, and annoyed with anyone who thought they had a problem. Knowing our entire world could be torn apart with the slip of the surgeon's knife made me unsympathetic toward anyone whose problems didn't revolved around life and death. Everything else seemed trite and solvable.

Our days were filled with doctor appointments, work, and arguments about who was going to watch Derian. Robb and I had never fought about this before. I thought he was being cruel, expecting me to work

when Derian was in the hospital. Derian had been my primary job since he was born. How could I leave him now? How would he function without me?

My dad was the only one able to give blood for Derian. He didn't enjoy this but was honored to do it for his grandson. He used to pray that his blood would be good enough to make Derian well. Dad's favorite part of the whole deal was the snacks. "Free Snacks," he'd say, and dig in. I appreciated his willingness to give this gift to Derian.

Chapter 46

As the surgery date neared, I tried to spend our time together wisely by relaxing and watching the boys play together. How I loved that. They would run back and forth from the kitchen to the end of the hallway. They both loved being chased. When they played this game, they could never tell who was the chaser and who was the one being chased.

There were so many things to organize and get ready for May 9th. As I packed Connor's clothes, I felt cheated. I would miss several days of getting him dressed in the morning or tucking him in at night. How would I ever make up all that lost time with him? Robb reached for me as I climbed into bed. He pulled me close and we snuggled. "Are you worried?" he asked.

"Yes, are you?"

"I'm waiting for Derian's angel to come and talk to us again. Has he spoken with you?"

Where was that angel? I would love to talk to him and get the same message Robb got. Or had he already been speaking to me?

May 8—Derian's Pre-operation day

It seemed this day would never come, and yet it came way too soon. As I drove to school that morning, a song about a little boy who went to heaven came on the radio. Would Derian be singing that same song tomorrow? Would he be leaving us? Would two and a half years be all the time we would have with him?

By the time I got to school, my makeup was beyond repair. How would I be able to teach? I should have taken the whole day off. We should have all spent the day together! This could be the last day of our son's life. Why in God's name were we spending the day working? Why, Why, Why? Unfortunately, I knew the answer. I didn't have any days to take off. Robb had finally convinced me it was financially wiser for him to use his sick time in order to keep one paycheck coming in. I hated having to deal with financial realities on top of everything else.

I had always kept my students informed about Derian; they all knew he was having surgery the following day. At the end of the hour I asked each class to think of Derian that evening, and if they prayed, to offer a prayer for him. Once my classes were over, I packed up some work from my desk and became overwhelmed with a sense that within the next 24 hours, I would become a different person. Good-bye to the Patsy Keech who didn't know about death, good-bye to being a mother of two, good-bye to Derian

Mary, our daycare mom, had Derian dressed and ready to go by the time I pulled into her driveway. This was going to be the boys' last day at Mary's. She was required to reduce the number of children in her care due to some state law. One more good-bye. I snuck in and grabbed Derian without Connor seeing me. My mom was going to pick Connor up later and keep him overnight. Mary gave Derian a kiss and then handed him a balloon that said, "You will be missed." I knew which good-bye the balloon was intended for, but it knocked the wind out of me. *God really was going to take Derian away tomorrow.* Mary gave me a hug and asked me to keep her informed about Derian's surgery. She would be praying for him throughout the day. Mary loved my boys!

I put Derian's things in the car and returned for him. He met me at the door with his usual smile. I gave him a squeeze and carried him to the car. As I buckled him in the car seat he looked at me with questioning eyes. "Where's Connor?" He wanted to know why Connor wasn't coming with us. I addressed his concern. "You and I are going to see Dr. Hesslein." Derian clapped his hands; he was one of his buddies.

When we arrived at Dr. Hesslein office, his secretary handed me a large envelope that listed the Pre-Opt tests Derian needed. She warned me it would take hours to get everything done. She wasn't kidding. He needed blood work, an EEG, chest x-ray, and a urine sample. Each of these tests was done in separate parts of the hospital.

Our first stop was the EEG lab. This test was pretty simple, due to the fact that Derian enjoyed wearing stickers. However, once he realized wires were attached to the ends of each sticker, he decided he wasn't going to wear them anymore. I tried to make a game out of this, but he was too wise. Frustrated, he began to pull off the stickers. The technician was just as frustrated, pulling Derian's hands away. It was a full-fledged battle. These tests had to be done and that was all that was to it! Therefore, I turned off my feelings and did the best I could to help him get through it. If I could turn something into a game, I did it. If I could soothe him by stroking his hair, I would do it. If only I could take it all away, I would do it.

Derian was thrilled to have that test finished and to get back into the stroller. The blood lab was our next stop. This was one of the most difficult tests. It always took several pokes before anyone could find a vein. Derian cried as soon as he smelled the alcohol. He knew exactly what was going on. He screamed and cried big wet tears before the needle came into view. All I could do was stroke his sweaty hair and tell him how brave he was. To our good fortune, the technician who consistently got a vein on the first try was working.

Once the nurse was done, it was my job to calm him down. To make up for the trauma she caused, she offered Derian a sticker. He couldn't hold a grudge or pass up a sticker, so within seconds he was choosing his stickers, one for himself, one for Connor, Daddy, and me. It was amazing that he wanted to do something kind after enduring all he had.

X-rays were our last stop before heading back to Dr. Hesslein. I never knew which was worse for Derian, having blood drawn or x-rays. For as many x-rays as he'd had over the years, you'd think they wouldn't be a big deal. Not so. Derian was terrified of them. He hated being strapped down, unable to defend himself.

But on that day Derian didn't cry or fight at all. Perhaps he was too tired. He willingly allowed the tech to strap his arms over his head and then strap his feet down. Derian turned his head to look at me behind the sheet of lead glass. His thin body breathed a deep breath and let out a sigh that said, "This is the last time I need to do this." Tears blurred my vision. I didn't want to believe it, and yet, I knew Derian knew he would never take another x-ray. When the technician peeled away the Velcro straps, I gave Derian a big hug and reassured him he was "All done!" He smiled heroically as he reached his arms into his shirtsleeves. The x-ray tech gave Derian another sticker for his collection. Derian blew him a kiss bye-bye.

The x-rays would take 45 minutes to be developed. *I forgot how long all this took.* Derian was hungry. While we waited for the x-ray, we went to the gift shop to get a snack. Derian took his time choosing his treat. He walked back and forth eyeing each item in the display case before he looked up at me as if to say, "Can I have one of each?"

"Only one."

Derian finally settled on M&Ms and confidently carried his selection to the counter so he could pay for it himself. The sales lady smiled and made a big deal about the stickers he was wearing. Before we knew it, he pulled a sticker off and handed it to her. She thanked him and commented on what a sweet boy he was.

We picked up the x-rays and walked down the long, isolated, tunnel that would bring us back to Dr. Hesslein's office. Walking through the tunnel, I couldn't help but think of how often we'd been in this hall with this child. Midway though the tunnel, a set of automatic doors opened up and a woman with a huge balloon bouquet passed. I recognized her as someone I used to work with. As we spoke Derian pointed and waved his hands as he reached for a balloon. *Nothing like hinting, Derian.* Noticing his admiration, Pam took a balloon out of the bouquet and gave it to him. Derian grabbed the balloon and signed "thank you", then "more." We cut our conversation short. She would need to replace the entire bouquet if we continued talking.

By the time we arrived at Dr. Hesslein's office, my fingers felt as though they would break off from the weight of stuff I was carrying. We had accomplished a whole lot in those few hours. Now we would wait to see Dr. Hesslein and his nurses and go over the plan for tomorrow. I really needed to be reassured about this surgery. Derian loved to play with the dinosaurs in Dr. Hesslein's office. Observant of his play, I noticed the color of each toy he was drawn to and listened to his squeals as he pushed a little turtle toy across the carpet. Derian was a special child enchanted by the many diversions of fun that passed his troubled path.

He was strong in his spirit and would fight to be a little boy in the midst of it all.

Finally, the nurse called our name. Derian was a good sport about leaving his toys behind him and energetically followed the nurse to our room. He walked in like he owned the place and quickly found something new to entertain himself. In between his play, the nurse took his vitals. Derian took an active part in caring for his own body. He carefully placed the stethoscope on his chest and moved it around and then puffed his chest out to show us what a big boy he was. He was so proud of himself. I watched him in amazement as he went with the flow. No fear. No hesitation. No sense of pity. I wanted to be like him. I learned so much about how to live from him. He never gave up and he faced each crisis (and maybe even death) with grace and a lively spirit. *God, please let me be wrong about tomorrow. It can't happen. It can't.* An hour later, Dr. Hesslein popped into the room. He looked frazzled and admitted it had been a crazy day. He would review Derian's tests and send a nurse back with his report. He had another patient waiting on an exam table in another part of the hospital. He apologized for not being able to spend more time with us and left.

I couldn't believe this! I needed his time more than the other person. I was sure of it. Dr. Hesslein always calmed me down and reassured me everything would be okay. I needed to know my thoughts were just craziness and nothing else. The hospital that housed us for so many stays suddenly felt like an unfamiliar place. The hours in the day were going by quickly and no one could give me a peek into tomorrow. Why wasn't anybody there? Damn it, I needed to talk to someone!

Derian sat on my hip as we left the office; the two of us arrived home to an empty house. Robb was working late that night and Connor was spending the evening with my parents. My brother Tom insisted on coming over for dinner with his wife, Cathy. There was a sense of urgency in his voice. Did he know what I did?

Cathy and I sat at the table talking, while Tom lay on the floor next to Derian, watching Derian's favorite video. Derian rested in his arms and soaked up his uncle's attention. The two of them laughed and did any actions the Sesame Street characters asked them to do. When the video was over, Derian began fussing. He was trying to tell me something, but I couldn't figure it out. *Did he have something special in mind for this night? Did he just want to be held? What? What did he want me to understand? Was he disappointed Connor wasn't there to play with him?*

Not wanting to interfere with Derian's bedtime, Tom and Cathy decided to leave. They reached out and gave me a hug as they wished us luck tomorrow, then knelt down and gave Derian a kiss. Derian hugged them back and blew kisses as they left.

Now that they were gone, my thoughts were free to race around.

Where was Robb? We never spent the evening before a surgery apart. What if this was truly Derian's last night with us? Maybe Connor should have stayed home. What if the boys would never see each other again? Was he trying to tell me he wanted to see his brother and his daddy?

A few minutes later, the doorbell rang. It was Barb and Cossette, co-workers from school. They stopped to drop off a care package filled with goodies and time fillers. Derian was immediately drawn to the goodies and began pulling them out of the neatly arranged basket, scattering them to the floor. Barb and Cossette smiled and laughed at Derian's enthusiasm. Their eyes focused on him the entire time. Were they admiring his hearty little spirit? Did they feel sorry for him? Could they see the death's shadow hovering near him?

Looking back I wonder if everyone sensed what I did. I have heard many stories where people could smell and feel the presence of death within a loved one.

They kept their visit brief, gave me a hug, and reassured me they would be praying for us. Derian gave each of them a kiss and wildly waved bye-bye.

The house was now quiet. I savored the hours that belonged to us. When it was time for bed, I dressed Derian in his pjs, wrapped him in his blankie, gave him his bottle, lit a candle, and turned out the lights. I stroked his hair to the rhythm of the rocker, listening to the sucking sounds he made as he drank his bottle. Derian looked at me with wise eyes. Both our hearts knew the truth about tomorrow. This evening was filled with a million lasts.

As I held his sleeping toddler body, I asked God to take him while he slept. *God, if you must take him, please do it before the surgery. Don't make him go through all that pain just to take him away.* Hours later, I carried him into our bedroom so he could to sleep next to us. I wanted to listen to the sound of his breathing, smell his breath on my face, and feel his arm tucked under my neck. Watching Derian sleep, I wondered how to spend my last hours being his mom. *What do I do? Do I memorize the curves of his face and engrave them into my mind. Do I hold his hand, hoping our spirits melt together? Do I sleep with him in my arms? How do I absorb enough of him to last a lifetime? How do I say good-bye to my baby?*

The kitchen door opened and shut. Robb was finally home. He came into our room and picked up his sleeping boy. From the moon's glow, I could see the shadow of Robb's fingers trace over the curves of Derian's nose. He silently cradled him rocking his body back and forth, saying good-bye to his son. We slept with connected hearts. The hours moved forward and brought forth the next day.

Chapter 47

The sun's rays peeked through the blinds and woke us up; it was time to face the day. I took my shower, got dressed, woke Robb, and packed a few bags of time fillers. The clock sped up and suddenly we were rushing around the house. We were going to be late for surgery.

Derian didn't suspect a thing as I woke him. He opened his brown eyes and flashed me a bright red-lipped smile as he did every morning. We discussed the plan for the day as I changed his diaper, combed his hair, and carried him to the car. Something felt different as I buckled Derian into his car seat. The dangle of my mother's necklace that Robb had given me was missing. I wore this necklace every day. Leaving the house without it was not an option.

Without telling Robb why, I reopened the house and ran into our room. My heart pounded in the furor of lateness. Thankfully, it was on the dresser. When I grabbed the necklace, the charm that represented Derian fell from the chain and landed on the floor. Shivers shot through my heart as I picked it up. This was another sign of what today would bring. Despite Robb's blowing the horn, I took my time getting back into the car. I pushed aside Robb's comments about being late. *Why would being late matter today? These could be the last moments we have with Derian. Why should they be rushed?*

Robb drove as quickly as he could. We were supposed to have been checked in ten minutes ago. I decided I was going to enjoy this ride, no matter what. Thankfully, Derian wasn't that upset about not getting a bottle. He was in a great mood. The sun shone on him as we made our way to the hospital.

The admittance person was waiting at the door for us and told us that she had received a call wondering if we had checked in. I've been late to most everything in my life, but surgery was never one of them. Knowing that the entire staff was annoyed with us didn't make me feel very responsible or comfortable.

We passed the hospital gift shop on our way to the elevator. Even though we were in a hurry, I decided to let Derian peek into the window at his favorite Sesame Street characters. I coaxed him to the elevator by promising him he could push the buttons. This excited him, and within a few seconds, he ran ahead of Robb and me. Once we walked out of the elevator we were in the land of no control. Derian pushed the number three button.

The three of us hurried off the elevator, briskly walked to the pre-op section of the hospital, and checked in. The nurse was waiting for us and hurried us along. We'd no sooner gotten into the room when she asked us to strip Derian and she scrubbed him with Betadine. Derian was out of sorts with the rushed feeling that hung in the air. Thankfully, Barney was on and helped distract him enough so I could lay him down and do the wash. Why was it that on the one day that we were late, the entire hospital was running on schedule, scrambling to make up for those lousy 10 minutes the Keechs weren't there? Typically we were the ones who waited for the hospital to get moving. I was annoyed with the comments and the rushing.

Once the wash was complete, I dressed Derian in the ugly yellow hospital pjs while the nurse checked his vitals. As she took Derian's temp and checked his blood pressure, she rapidly rattled off the list of pre-surgery questions. This woman was making me nervous. These questions were important, and I couldn't shoot back the answers as quickly as she wanted. She barely listened to my last answer before she rushed us out of the room and directed us to the elevator that would take us to the holding room. Derian hopped in and pushed the number two on the elevator panel. The doors opened and we followed the signs. Once we were there, two nurses greeted us. They wore scrubs and informed us that they were part of the surgical team that would be working on Derian.

Minutes later, the anesthesiologist entered with his assistant and he discussed Derian's health history, the procedure, etc. All the pre-operating procedures were the same, except for one. Derian was sitting on my lap listening, and flirting with the anesthesiologist. He was a tall man with a kind personality. In fact, he was the only person that morning that slowed down time. He picked up his stethoscope and asked us if we wanted to listen to Derian's heart. In all the times we had procedures pertaining to Derian's heart, we had never listened to the sound of it. I felt privileged to have such an opportunity. The anesthesiologist placed the stethoscope in the correct position so Robb and I could take turns listening to the "swish, swish, boom, boom" we had heard so much about.

When I was done, he had me listen to my own heart. I placed the stethoscope to my heart and heard nothing. The anesthesiologist looked at me and smiled, "Patsy, your heart is on the other side." I smiled back, embarrassed. It was Robb's turn next. Derian had had it with all the heart stuff. There were cool things to play with in this room, so he wiggled down and began exploring the toy box.

While Derian played, Dr. Nichols entered the room and went over the procedure with us one more time. He asked if we had questions and then handed us a clipboard and a surgery permit. Now that the surgeon had left, it was only a matter of moments before we would turn Derian over to them. The anesthesiologist re-entered the room and asked, "Mom, do want to come into the operating room and help us get Derian to sleep?" I was never given that option before.

"Yes, I'd like that." He handed me some scrubs, a hairnet, and slippers to cover my shoes.

"You'll have to hurry." I quickly pulled the scrubs over my clothes. While I was rushing, Robb held onto the moment with Derian. He pulled Derian into a hug and pressed his face next to him. In a low tone I could hear him say, "Derian, we really need you to be brave today. I know you will do just fine. I love you so much, son."

When I was ready, Robb handed Derian to me and the nurse hurried us out of the room. Derian waved bye-bye to his daddy. Robb walked out into the hallway and signed "I love you" to Derian in slow motion.

God, I just wanted a moment to feel something. It was all going so fast. I was surprised by the gym-like appearance of the operating room. The anesthesiologist led me to a chair at the head of the operating table. Derian and I sat down and cuddled. "Mom, which flavor would be Derian's favorite to smell: bubblegum, grape, or orange?"

"Grape."

Within seconds a clear plastic mask was placed over Derian face. He looked scared and began to pull at it before taking a breath. He must have liked the smell. He took a second breath and sank into my arms. *Was this the last time I would see him alive? God, please bless the people in this room and bring Derian back to me.*

"Mom, it's time to go." I kissed him one more time before handing his limp body to the anesthesiologist. I backed out of the room until my back was pressed against the door. My eyes rested on the anesthesiologist holding my boy. As the door was closing, someone from the team said, "Mom, we'll take good care of him." The door clicked shut.

What had I done? Why did I give my baby to them? A nurse placed her arm around me. "That must have been really hard." Gulping back tears, I nodded. *Robb, where is my Robb?* I walked into the room where Derian was moments earlier. Robb was sitting on a chair, crying, holding the last toy Derian played with. God, this was so hard. Robb and I sat next to each other and cried. We didn't need to rush anymore. The room was ours for as long as we wanted. I kept looking at all the toys Derian touched before he left. *God please, please bring him back to us. It just can't be all over yet. Not yet.* When we were composed enough to meet Robb's parents and my mom, we left the holding room and went to the family waiting room. My dad was in the middle of a roofing job and would call for updates throughout the day.

Nancy was our cardiac nurse that day. Each time she stopped in she had a positive report. Wouldn't it be great if I were wrong! How wonderful it would be to be wrong! When the eight-hour surgery was completed, Dr. Nichols came in to debrief us. He shook his head from side to side and said, "He's had a lot of surgery, a lot of surgery." His voice indicated there was something to be afraid of. I always imagined that if something bad were to happen, it would be during surgery. Everything should be fine now. All fear was put aside. Another victory was achieved. The prayer cards must have worked.

Nancy moved us to the waiting room on third floor so we could watch as they moved Derian to the PICU unit. Since everything was okay, Robb's dad went back to work. Robb was having a caffeine attack and went in search of a soda machine. Minutes later, Nancy walked into the room. "Patsy, Derian's heart stopped. He has been returned to surgery. They are massaging his heart right now."

I stood stiff-kneed, frozen, unable to breathe. Before I knew it, I dropped to the floor and screamed into the chair in front of me. My feet stung from slapping them on the carpet. "No, God, please bring him back to me. Please God, please, please, please." The arms of both of our moms wrapped around me.

Robb walked into the room. "What's going on?" *Oh my God, he didn't even know.*

I picked myself up. "Derian's in trouble, they brought him back to surgery." We embraced in a desperate hug. The door opened, it was a social worker. She shook her head and said in a flat voice, "Nancy called from the operating room; it doesn't look good."

"Ahhh! God, help him!" My insides felt as if each organ was being tied together. The air grew chunky—too thick to breathe. The social worker asked, "Should I call for a priest?" *A priest? This meant we were giving up.* Someone said "yes" and she left the room.

My mom called me over to the phone. It was my dad. "Dad, Derian's heart stopped." *My dad gasped.* "Please come to the hospital, Dad. Please come quick."

"I'll be right there. I'll say the rosary on the way over."

The social worker returned. "I just received another call from the operating room. It's not looking good. Not at all." I screamed. My body doubled over, my heart pounded as fear shook through me. My child, whom I protected from falls and danger, was now on the verge of dying, and I could do nothing.

Pacing, kneeling, jumping, and screaming didn't bring any comfort. Cold, it was so cold! I breathed in breaths of sorrow focusing on Derian and his toughest battle. Suddenly, I noticed the air became lighter; breathing was easier. As I absorbed those breaths, I could feel droplets of tranquillity drip down my back, arms, and shoulders. Each clenched part of my body went limp. Fear gave way to peace.

I surrendered. I let go.

It was then that God allowed me to witness our son's struggle between heaven and earth. I could see in my mind's eye a sharp, clear, bright light and felt its warmth. My brown-eyed little boy looked unsure as to which way he should go, toward the light or back to the operating table. He teetering back and forth as if he were playing a game of chase and wanted me to run after him. With the softest gentleness, I could feel his hands on both sides of my face, pulling my head toward him. He wanted to tell me something, "Mom, I'm not going to leave you, I am never going to leave you."

Ring…Ring…"Hello?"

"Patsy, Nancy. We got him back—he's okay now." Derian kept his promise. Robb and I grabbed each other. Relief exploded into the room. Derian had pulled it off once again.

We waited for Dr. Hesslein like soldiers pulled away from battle waiting for their leader. Our family members had been called and would be arriving soon. The hospital staff knew Derian drew a large crowd, so the social worker made arrangements to move us into a private room. This room was a few feet from Derian. I had walked past it many times before and noticed its beauty, but had never been in it. The ceiling was raised and the large windows overlooked the busy streets of St. Paul. There were many couches to relax in, plenty of chairs, and a private bathroom. One by one, our families and Pastor George arrived.

Dr. Hesslein's report was unsettling; he couldn't account for what had happened. We were in for a long night. If they didn't know what was wrong, Derian could easily get into trouble again. Dr. Hesslein also told us there could be side effects from the long arrest Derian had. During the next few hours, he would be looking for signs for kidney, liver, and brain damage. Part of me didn't care so long as he was alive; the other part was sinking. He may never be the same little boy we brought to the hospital hours earlier. For as many problems as Derian had, I was always thankful his brain was healthy. I couldn't deal with anything new on top of everything else.

Dr. Hesslein suggested moving outside of the room so we could see Derian. Machines rolled heavily over the carpeted floor. Derian was on his way. A four-person team pushed Derian and pulled several machines behind the gurney he was resting on. This sight always disturbed me, to think his life was dependent on the functioning of those machines. But at that moment, I didn't care about the machines. Hell, I was grateful for them! Derian was like an Olympic runner approaching the finish line. His family lined the final stretch, cheering him on to a victory. Robb and I greeted him with a kiss on the cheek as family members said things like, "We love you. We are so proud of you, Derian."

Loud clashing thoughts penetrated my mind. *How can we go on living this way? Why does Derian need to give us so many scares? When is he going to get a break? Thank you, God, for sending him back to us!* We were filled with fear and thanksgiving at the same time. Robb pulled me into his arms and gave me one of his we'll-get-through-this-together hugs.

After several hours, Pastor George left. An hour passed before the social worker returned. "Derian's heart stopped. He's in trouble again. Should I call Pastor George and ask him to return?"

"Yes, please call him." The door closed behind her. The room was filled with a tortuous silence. No one said anything, no one breathed, no one moved. I knew Derian was going to leave this time. "God, I give you my son."

Robb gave me a hard nudge, "Patsy, don't give up on him."

"Robb, God is going to do what He wants, so we might as well let Him."

After a long silence my sister leaned over and asked, "Patsy, do you want us to say an Our Father?" I couldn't speak. My body caved in from despair. Time ticking away was the only sound I heard. I went to the bathroom to escape it. Nancy met me in the hallway. "Patsy, we've been working on Derian for 35 minutes. We have to stop soon. At this point the damage is irreversible."

"You mean you are giving up?" *Giving up* and *Derian* had never been used in the same sentence. What was she was saying?

I went into the center of the room to tell everyone what Nancy had said. Gasps, cries, and wailing finally drowned out the ticking of the clock. I lay on the floor and beat my fists onto it saying, "Please don't take my Derian, don't take my little boy." I could feel hands on me and heard both of our mothers whisper, "Patsy, you were the best mom Derian could have asked for." Robb punched his fist into a door and ran out of the room to Derian. Too distraught to move, Nancy's words ran through my mind. "In a few more minutes, we have to quit." Energy seized me. I only had a few minutes to say good-bye. *He can't die before I say good-bye.* I ran down the hall, turned the corner and saw a large group of nurses in blue scrubs standing in a "V" that stemmed from Derian's bed. The nurse closest to Derian said, "Mom, come and hold his foot." I stood next to Robb and picked up Derian's limp, blue foot

"1—2—3—machine check." Nothing.

"Mom and Dad, I need to inject adrenaline directly into his heart." I squeezed Derian's foot as she gave the injection. I had to look away from Derian. I looked up into the eyes of the strangers that surrounded us. Their hands were at their sides and tears rolled from their cheeks. There was nothing they could do. It was time for Derian to go. I looked back at Derian; he looked like a pale, spineless doll. The stitches had been ruptured from the chest compressions and blood dripped from his wound. His eyes were rolling back into his head. Robb and I looked at each other. We both knew what was best for Derian. "Let him go, just let him go," we said.

We fell onto his body and cried before backing away and witnessing Derian's transformation from a little boy to an angel. "God, he's the best gift we could give you." As Derian's spirit left, a vision of a puffed dandelion gently dispersing in the breeze was captured in my mind. We immediately sensed joy. Derian was happy, he was with God, and he could now have a perfect life. What more could a parent ask for her child?

The doctor who gave Derian CPR was the same man I had watched care for a little girl one night. All I could say to him was "Thank you. Thank you for helping my boy. I know you did everything you could do for him. Thank you for all the sacrifices you made to be a good doctor." He stood in perfect stillness and let his tears fall.

Loud quick footsteps ran down the hall…Dr. Hesslein. Who would have ever guessed Derian was going to die today? Certainly not Dr. Hesslein. He gave me a sweet kiss on the cheek and hugged Robb. His voice was deeper and mellower than I had ever heard it. "You know, Derian was like a son to me." We always knew Dr. Hesslein doctored Derian with both medical knowledge and love.

When Derian was disconnected from the machines, a nurse asked if we wanted to hold him one more time. How could I hold him when he was no longer mine? He was God's. My only hope was that He would share him with me from time to time. I walked away for some alone time to make phone calls.

When I re-entered the ICU unit, a light-blue tent surrounded Derian's body. Robb, his parents and Pastor George were in the tent talking about burial plans. After what seemed like an incredibly long discussion, we decided on the following arrangements. We would have a closed casket memorial on Sunday, Mother's Day evening, a private family burial on Monday afternoon, and the funeral that evening.

Robb and I left that conversation and found Dr. Hesslein, who was filling out forms. "Dr. Hesslein, Patsy and I would like to donate some of Derian's organs." Dr. Hesslein listened respectfully to our wishes and told us of our options. We decided to donate his corneas in hopes that another child might see the flowers Derian enjoyed smelling. We gave his heart to Dr. Hesslein for research.

Robb and I wanted to have one more moment as a family with Derian. While we gathered everyone, the hospital staff dismantled equipment and freed Derian.

When the bluish tent was opened, I was struck by the change—not a machine or tube in sight. The light was dim and blue hues cast from the curtain created a mood of serenity. Derian was at the center of all this, covered with a white baby blanket. Peace surrounded him. His spirit coaxed me to touch his body. His cool hand went limp in mine, and then an electrical shock ignited our touch. Our spirits mixed. When I laid his hand down I knew the individual spirit of Patsy Keech was gone. I would live the rest of my life with a blended spirit, his and mine. I was proud Derian fought so hard, proud of who he was, and proud to have been his mother, even for a short while.

As our family gathered around Derian, I was struck by the light feeling in the air. The sorrow wasn't as heavy as it had been moments earlier. We joined hands and Pastor George led us in prayer. Once he opened the prayer, a conversation expanded into stories and special moments shared with Derian. I asked our family members to prepare a gift for Derian using their talents. Robb let go of Derian's hand and said, "If Derian were here, I think he'd want to say this." He gracefully signed one last time, "I love you Grandma, Grandpa, Mom and Dad. I love you all." My eyes became teary as he began to cry. I respected Robb for sharing his emotions. He didn't do it very often, but it was always a privilege when he did. He had been a role model to many men. I always hoped he would pass his tenderness on to our sons.

George ended the prayer. Derian received farewell kisses from each of us.

Chapter 45

Our bodies were feeling the toll of a twelve-hour emotional workout. We were exhausted. My thoughts focused on Connor. I couldn't wait to hold him. As Robb and I packed our things, the hospital social worker stopped in and handed us a folder with materials on grieving.

As I entered the elevator and pushed button one from the elevator panel, I thought of Derian. Just twelve hours earlier he had been in this same elevator pushing the buttons for us. As difficult as it was to bring him back to the hospital, it was far worse to leave this part of our life behind. The next thing to look forward to was years of grief.

Oh God, now we had to deal with grief! I had taken classes on that in college. It was supposed to take ten years to get through all the steps of grief. Now I was really mad at God. *You mean all the trauma and heart-break was just a prologue to grief? God, I know you never give us more than we are supposed to be able to handle, but has it ever occurred to you that I might be terrific at handling FUN? I'm sick of dealing with the tough stuff in life. I have worked hard to keep my chin up and keep up a good attitude through everything we have gone through. God, you owe me! I want a break on this grief stuff—one year max! And I want "grief light" because we've lived "grief heavy." I'm serious God, you have to listen to me on this one.*

Our family members were standing in the lobby as the elevator doors opened. We hugged one last time before Robb and I took our final walk out of the hospital.

We had walked down this hall many times in the last two and a half years. We knew the lightheartedness of packing up after a long hospital stay, the frustration and fear that accompanied a surgery, the anguished hours of waiting for test results, and the harbored feelings of running away. We saw it all, the good and the bad. As hard as some of those days were, we were incredibly sorry they were over. No longer would we walk up and down these halls. No longer did we need this place. We no longer had our brown-eyed Derian.

We walked to the car alone, carrying only a folder with instructions on grief and a formal condolence letter. The hospital that had become our home and the staff that carried us through all the moments prior to facing death were gone. I guess when your child dies, their job is over. They don't do dead kids.

The street light near the car shone on Derian's car seat. He would never sit in the back seat with Connor again. Robb slipped the seat belt off and carefully placed Derian's car seat in the back of the station wagon.

Chapter 49

I wasn't sure as I rang the doorbell if our friends knew Derian had died. By the way they answered the door and greeted us it was obvious they had been told. Connor squealed as we stepped into the room, grabbed his jacket from the floor, and was ready for home. His liveliness was a welcomed sight.

A wise twenty-month-old Connor looked at the spot where Derian's car seat was supposed to be. When he spied it in the back of the station wagon he looked confused. As I looked at his toddler face, I wondered how we'd explain his buddy wasn't coming home.

We arrived home to a full house. Our neighbors would not let us come home to an empty, silent home. They got busy and cleaned and made a wonderful meal for us. We hadn't eaten since breakfast. That evening, I learned the importance of embracing people in the midst of their sorrows. They taught me what to do for someone else.

Connor was fussing, and seemed overwhelmed and confused. I excused myself and went to get him ready for bed. One of the neighbors had taken the picture of a guardian angel watching over children off the wall and laid it on Derian's bed. It was a comforting reminder that Derian was safe.

Maggie and my soulmate Linda stopped by. They were there to find out how I wanted to handle things at school the next day. Obviously, I wasn't going to be there, and my students needed more than a lesson from a substitute. Even though I was mentally prepared for the loss of Derian, as I thought of my students praying for him, I was mad God hadn't given us our miracle. He could have convinced my young students how amazing He was. Little did I know that a greater miracle would evolve as a result of Derian's death.

Linda and Maggie would spend the day in my classroom with my students. "Patsy, you know the students will want to do something for you. Is their anything you would like me to suggest?" Maggie asked.

This was easy…I knew exactly what I needed from those kids. I needed them to write me a letter and tell me what they learned about life from Derian. I needed to know if they would take a part of Derian into their lives. If they would, then Derian would continue to live in a little corner of the world. Before Maggie and Linda left, they told me the night might not be a restful one. They made me promise I would call them anytime during the night if I wanted to talk. I was lucky to have such good friends.

Chapter 50

The three of us huddled in bed as we faced our first evening without Derian. As exhausted as I was, I was determined to see the end of the last day that belonged to Derian. The numbers on the clock flipped to the twelfth hour. The new day was as comforting as a steel door slamming shut on a prisoner serving a life sentence. How do I go on living without him? How do I face this new day knowing I will never hold my child again? Life without Derian was unimaginable. The hand of grief pinned me to the sheets. I couldn't breathe deep enough for my swollen heart; I was going to explode. My head kept playing and replaying the events that took place the day before. In a panic, I began searching for the spot Derian had laid on the bed that morning. *God, Why? Why did you take Derian from me? How do you expect me to go on? I can't do this, I can't.*

Dawn filtered though our bedroom blind. This would be the day we would choose a casket for our son. I looked at Robb, our hands met, and we wiped away each other's tears. Connor awoke and lay still under the bridge of our arms. We needed to tell him something. He was entitled to know the reason his mom and dad were so sad. Robb and I pieced the story together for him.

"Connor, Doo-doo had an owie in his heart that couldn't be fixed with bandages or doctors. Doo-doo went to heaven to be with Jesus. Doo-doo lives in Jesus's house now, but Jesus will share Doo-doo with us. Doo-doo will wink at us through twinkling stars and smile through the sun. Doo-doo will watch over us from heaven." Connor began to repeat our explanation, "Doo-doo angel?" He seemed thrilled to know Derian was in heaven—and seemed excited for Derian's heavenly adventure. Perhaps he remembered what heaven was like and was glad Derian could be there once again.

Chapter 51

Several visitors stopped by that morning with food, stuffed animals for Connor, flowers, hugs, and lots of company. We were expected to be at the funeral home by 11 a.m. With so many guests, I was running late. Mindlessly, I ran into the boys' room to grab something. Once there, I couldn't remember what it was I needed. Looking around, hoping to get a clue, I noticed a neatly folded pile of clothes next to the picture of the angel on Derian's bed. His shoes rested on the top of it. It was Derian's Cookie Monster outfit. We had decided to have him buried in it. Looking at the lifeless pile, I realized I would never dress him in that outfit again, in any outfit again…ever! I would never tie his shoes again, put him in his car seat…nothing. Jolted by the finality of death I knelt next to his bed and began to wail.

Alarmed, people ran into the room. Robb picked me up and held me tight. I always felt safe in his arms. People in the doorway were crying. So much pain for so many people. How could we ever move on from this? Would we ever be able to smile again?

"We've got to get going to the funeral home. We're going to be late," someone said. *Who the hell cares if we're late? What were they going to do, cancel the funeral?*

A few minutes later, three cars were off to the funeral home. Strange, as close as Robb and I were moments earlier, he rode with his family and I rode with mine. I wondered why we weren't riding together? Years later, I understood why. We both needed to be cared for. Who could do it better at that moment than our parents, our own families?

On the way to the funeral home I noticed a woman on a motorcycle wearing a T-shirt that said, "The pride will outlive the pain." Can that really be true?

At end of the funeral home appointment, Robb reached under his chair and handed the man a bag with Derian's clothes and his picture. They needed a picture so they could make him up right. I knew how to do it. I didn't even need a picture. Why couldn't I dress him? Why couldn't I fix his hair? The mortuary man was trespassing. He didn't know Derian. Would he dress him lovingly the last time? Would he do it like I did? I had to force my mouth shut. I wanted so badly to ask if I could get him dressed, fix his hair, and be his mom for just a few more minutes. I felt guilty for all the times I had hurried to dress him as we rushed off somewhere.

The squeals of Connor and Madeline welcomed us home. Connor ran to the door and jumped into Robb's arms. Connor was his child. Robb was the one who took care of him while I cared for Derian. I really didn't know Connor. God, what a mess! I was given a healthy child and not much of an opportunity to be his mommy. Derian took everything from me. Did he know he was only going to be mine for a short time? Is that why he was so protective of his "mom time"?

Over the course of that day, I watched Robb and Connor interact. They were a team. I no longer had a place in our family. The roles we once played wouldn't work in a family of three. We were meant to work in fours. Would Connor and I ever develop a relationship? Would he ever need me? It became obvious that Derian's death would affect every aspect of our lives. Death doesn't just take away the person who dies, but the life of the survivor as well. I wished I could die too. It would be so much easier than living.

Friday and Saturday moved in slow motion. The only thing I could concentrate on was making sure Derian had a beautiful send-off. This would be the last thing I would plan for him and I wanted it to be all about Derian. Family members as well as friends helped me put my ideas together. I asked the man who did our wedding pictures to make a video from a collection of photos. A friend brought over Twila Paris' song, *A Visitor from Heaven*. We wept as we listened to it.

"Airplane" was the last word Derian learned to say—it would be so "Derian" to have an airplane kite lead the procession into the church. I found the perfect yellow model airplane for the job, and a talented friend put it together.

The plans, the time, and the company all were overwhelming. Loneliness singled me out amongst the crowd that surrounded me. Sharp pains attacked my chest. God, could you spare me some pain by letting me have a massive heart attack?

Chapter 52

Someone new was staring back at me when I looked in the mirror. I didn't recognize this Patsy: droopy eyes, gray skin tones, gaunt face. I looked horrible. I would not attend my son's wake and funeral looking this awful. Perhaps getting something new to wear would make me feel and look better.

My sister Colleen offered to take me shopping at my favorite department store. Robb thought it was a good idea and stayed home with Connor. The lift I was hoping for couldn't distract me from the pain. As I moved through the mall, people walked by smiling, laughing, and carrying large shopping bags. Anger welled within me; it was shocking to think that the entire world wasn't slowing down because Derian died. How could life be moving on for all these people? Maybe they'd understand if I introduced them to my pain, stuck it right under their noses. That's exactly what I did to the sales clerk.

"Excuse me, can I help you find something?"

"I'm looking for something to wear to my son's funeral."

It was a terrible thing to say to someone who was trying to help. Her smile faded; she stood expressionless, unsure what to say. Ashamed for making her feel so uncomfortable, I decided I would have to figure out a way to cope with my loss and still respect others.

If it were not for my sister, I would have come home empty-handed. The world I once belonged to, where clothes and style were important was insignificant. Wandering aimlessly through the store racks, I realized I was incapable of making a decision.

"Colleen, will you just find something for me?"

"Sure. I'll meet you in the dressing room."

I lay down on the bench in the dressing room and waited. Within minutes she brought in an armful of dresses. Standing lifelessly in the center of the dressing room, I lifted my arms up while Colleen dressed and undressed me. I grimaced when I looked in the mirror. Colleen picked out two outfits, one for the wake on Sunday and one for the funeral on Monday.

The next 48 hours were knit together with a variety of emotions: anger, peace, frustration, love, and confusion. Everything changed so rapidly. I was a stranger in my own life; my mind was painted with the effects of amnesia. The actions of others gave me a glimmer of the relevance of a past life.

My dad and brothers stopped by after a hard day of roofing. The three of them stood together as my brother Tim handed me a check. My dad spoke on behalf of the men in my family. "Patsy, we did a job today and offered our work up for Derian. At the end of the job, the homeowner asked us who he should make the check out to and we gave him your name."

I was proud to receive this gift. Not only did the fruits of their labor benefit us, but blessed the homeowner that lived under that roof.

Chapter 53

Mother's Day evening

Our families met on the funeral home lawn and walked in together. Robb and I held hands as we moved to the room where Derian's body lay. We took a deep breath before entering. I kept my eyes on the floor; I didn't want to be there. I didn't want to see him dead, or lying in a casket. We all stood frozen in the middle of the room. No one could bring himself or herself to move up to the casket. Connor was oblivious to what all this meant. For him it was just another room to explore. He ran wildly up and down the rectangular room, laughing and squealing. I could just see him running into the casket and knocking Derian out of it. We kicked into parent mode and followed Connor to the front of the room for both boys' protection.

Derian was so still—never except in death do you see a little one that still. His hair was clean and wispy, parted to one side. The paleness in his face made him look peaceful. His glow and radiance couldn't be captured in the makeup used by the funeral home staff. The baby blanket I made for him was tucked around his legs, his hands were folded, and a pastel wooden rosary rested between his fingers.

Joe, Colleen's husband, stepped forward and shared his homemade offering. He had spent the day making a wooden heart. On top of the heart was Derian's name; carved underneath it was the last names of the in-laws, then an equals sign, and then the word "LOVE." It was a beautiful gift; one I knew Derian would have been proud of. Glued on the back of it was something Colleen wrote and shared with us.

Derian's Parade

I remember when Derian first learned to wave. As he was with all of his accomplishments, Derian was extremely proud of himself and needed to share this new source of joy with others, family, friends and strangers.

Patsy took Derian to the shopping mall to "show his stuff" and as always, Derian embraced the opportunity. As the stroller wheels began to spin, Derian's little arm got in position. He waved to fellow shoppers, to children, and to workers with such incredible style that people were moved. People wanted to watch Derian. They wanted to stop and chat with this joyful little boy. They were taken in by Derian's overwhelming charm and sense of wonder.

Waving was one way that Derian found to connect with people.

He soon became a master of hugging, blowing kisses and holding hands. These new tricks provided him with a variety of ways to reach out to others, to give all of himself, to increase another's joy.

This was Derian's lifetime mission.

Derian led a parade of kindness. As a child he had already grasped what many adults have not. He understood that love is the essential ingredient in life and he relished in both the giving and receiving of it. Derian called us to join him in his mission of kindness, to join his parade. He now continues to call for us to "show a little Derian" in our words and actions.

In his memory, we are asked to march.

A proud follower,
Auntie Colleen

The room was filled with emotions by the time Colleen finished her piece. Derian left behind two families that bonded together with hugs, tears, memories, and Connor. Connor was desperate to add a plus to the minus we shared. He was the little brother who would continue life with us, shouting his presence, making himself known…in many ways for the first time.

When we were ready, the funeral director covered Derian's face and closed the casket. The click of the latch was a period at the end of a life. The funeral home personnel wheeled Derian out to the hearse that would bring him to the church.

Connor left the funeral home with Heather. She was going to take both Connor and Madeline to the home of one of my students who offered to watch the kids during the wake and the celebration service the next day. When Robb and I arrived at the church, a potted tree decorated with colorful Sesame Street characters greeted us. The Birth-Through-Three team created it from pieces of Derian's favorite game. Robb and I held each other and recalled the delight Derian found in that game. As the wind blew, the pieces magically danced on the tree.

We walked together into the church and took a deep breath as we looked around. It looked like a celebration was going on; bright, robust balloons lined the entrance of the church. A clear vase filled with sunflowers, tulips, and daisies sat on the altar. Next to the vase was a child size director's chair with Derian's name; a single balloon was tied to its arm. There were several posters filled with pictures of Derian and lots of angel statues. Our favorite bouquet was a stand up Cookie Monster decorated with blue carnations. Derian would have loved it! He would have been so happy to join this service. The people who decorated knew what brought joy to Derian Richard Keech.

The spring sun shone brightly through the skylights and cast a heavenly appearance around Derian's casket. He was there; his spirit filled up the church.

Before we knew it, the evening service began. People arrived at the church in droves, leaving their own Mother's Day celebration to honor Derian and support us. I remember each person who attended that evening. Their presence diminished our grief—at least for awhile. The hugs we received that night offered enough support to help us get through the next few days. Robb told me later that night that people were comparing the line to get into the church to the lines to get concert tickets. How profound to think Derian could touch so many people in such a short time.

In the depth of sadness, a welcomed relief of humor came as I hugged one of my sister's friends. I felt something fall down my shirt. I looked up and noticed she was missing an earring; I pulled her close to me and whispered, "Jenny, I think your earring is in my shirt." I shook my entire body for a second and then it fell to the floor. I picked it up and the two of us giggled uncontrollably. I laughed so hard I cried. No doubt the people in line waiting to greet us thought I was having a grief attack.

Connor returned to the church near the end of the wake. Excitement ran through him as he ran up and down the aisles dragging bouquets of balloons behind him, squealing and smiling a magical smile. His energy was captivating. It was clear that Connor would be our thrust back into life again.

Pastor George allowed Derian to lie in state that night. We were glad Derian would spend the evening in a place he knew. George brought in a night light for him, a kind gesture that softened death.

Chapter 54

Once again we were running late; this time to the cemetery. When we arrived, we got out of the car and greeted the people waiting for us. I wanted to introduce Connor to a relative who hadn't seen him for a while. I assumed Connor was with Robb but he was not. Robb thought he was with me. We began calling his name, no response. Panic set in and soon everyone was looking for him. This was unbelievable! We were about to bury one of our sons and we'd lost the other in the process. "Patsy, did you leave him in the car?" asked my sister.

"I'm sure, Colleen. How could we forget to get him out of the car?"

"Well, you do have a few things on your mind. I didn't see him with you when you first came. I'm going to go look." Sure enough, Connor was patiently waiting in his car seat for someone to let him out. Once we got our act together, we proceeded to the gravesite. Pastor George mentioned that a man who came to church that morning composed a song for Derian and called it *Opus Derian.* I was intrigued, to say the least, but couldn't think of anything other than getting through the next few days. I tucked it all away in my mind, knowing someday I would meet this stranger and hear Derian's song.

As we threw handfuls of dirt onto the casket, we sang "How Much is That Doggie in the Window." I was glad the final service was tonight and all this would be over. I was so tired.

A stream of sunlight shone through the skylights. A serene glow filled the church. Derian would have a joyful send off! Reality veiled my heart. I could observe what was going on and understand what this night was about, but my emotions were blocked.

We waited with our families for the service to begin. A few minutes before 7 p.m. I peeked into the church—it was full. So many people came to honor our son! My knees felt weak.

Colleen and Joe had the music for the service and had not yet arrived. What were we going to do? Each song was carefully picked and needed to be a part of Derian's send off. The person running the sound system was getting nervous—he had no idea what to play when. *Where were they?*

Once they arrived, Colleen handed off the music arrangements to the sound system person. Within minutes, the mourning sound of bagpipes wailed through the church. Joe grabbed the stick with the airplane kite and began the procession. Robb took my hand and the two of us walked down the aisle of the church. It was a strange walk; we were not a new bride and bridegroom, or an attendant in someone's wedding. We walked behind an object that represented something that gave Derian great joy. Joe led the dancing red, blue and green tail of the kite from side to side over the heads of our friends. Watching the kite zip though the air reminded me of the joyous way Derian would shout "airplane, airplane."

We took our seats at the front of the church. Pastor George began the service with an invocation and a welcome. When the readings were finished, the women's choir sang, "What Matters Most" from *The Champ*.

Then time for sharing…

It was almost as if I was lifted off the chair; this was the last time I would speak on Derian's behalf.

> *Today would be a great day to be mad at God; but instead of being angry, I choose to be thankful for the time I was able to be Derian's mom. Please allow me a few minutes to tell you about my son.*
>
> *Derian was a person who included everyone. If we were singing a song which had actions that went with it, Derian would make sure each person was involved. When he played Ring-Around-the-Rosy, he would frantically run around the room to make sure everyone was in the circle playing this wonderful game.*
>
> *Derian was open and honest with his love and affection. Derian would kiss and hug everyone! People he knew and people he didn't. People who were sad, people who were*

happy. Even the doctors and nurses, who, in caring for him, would need to do yucky things to him. He never left the office or let them leave the room without blowing a kiss or giving them a hug.

Derian was all spirit. His spirit was happy, lively and joyful. I remember what it was like getting Derian out of his car seat. He always had this look of excitement in his eyes like, "Whew, what's here?" "What's today going to be like?"

Derian loved to cheer people on. If someone were doing something cool or just plain weird, Derian would clap his little hands together and let out a cheer.

Derian loved babies. In fact, "baby" was the first word he learned to sign. He'd bring his arms together like he was carefully cradling a baby and then he would say "baby" ever so reverently. He would pet them gently and loved to kiss their soft baby skin. He was a protector and a lover of babies. He knew they couldn't do as many things as he could, but he enjoyed the things they could do: hold his hand, smile, giggle, and coo.

In some way I know he has passed this love to all of you. I know I will continue to find Derian living in someone else when I see a hand stretched out to invite someone into a circle of friends, a game that's being played, welcoming someone into a family, and people holding hands.

I have felt Derian in the many hugs I have received in the past few days. He put all his strength into a hug, kind of a baby-bear hug. His hugs always meant something—they were refreshing and all giving.

I will find Derian's spirit in people each time I hear the excitement in a voice that speaks about a new baby, a trip, finding love or learning something new. I will also hear Derian's supportive cheers when I hear a room full of people applauding someone's success.

Derian loved all babies—healthy babies and the babies he met in the hospital that were sick. I believe he has passed his pro-

tectiveness of those babies on to me. You can help me protect babies like Derian by writing to government officials and sending the message that these kids are important! They are expensive, but how can dollars be a deciding issue over a life? We must get the word out to our future political leaders that LIFE IS LIFE and MONEY IS MONEY. Cost effectiveness should never start with our health.

Derian has accomplished so much in the two-and-a-half years we were privileged enough to have him. I find comfort as his mother to know he lived out his mission. He did every-thing he was supposed to do in his lifetime. It's up to all of us to carry on what he started:

- *Maybe he was sent here to help us love better*

- *To help us accept challenges*

- *To open our hearts to others*

- *To celebrate each day*

- *To bring new passion to our lives*

On the evening of May 9, we asked to donate Derian's organs to someone else. As we mentally went down the list of items that Derian could pass on, we realized the best thing about Derian was his heart. Thanks so much for listening, may you always have a heart like Derian.

Caroline, my mom-friend from the hospital, approached the podium.

"I remember the first time I met Derian Keech. It was in the hospital and I was losing hope for my own son. I saw Derian and saw energy and life and a very special person, and I turned around and saw my own son in a couple of years. I understood for the first time how precious life can be if you live it to the fullest. I regained hope.

I visited that brown-eyed little boy a few days ago and was once again impressed by his natural tenderness and affection. I knew that his heart was weak but his capacity for love was incredible. I looked into his eyes and saw his soul and I swear that he spoke to me about being open to others. Derian always gave hugs and kisses and showed such wonderful attention to everyone around him.

In many ways Derian had to struggle to communicate, but he always found a way around the obstacles that life had thrown to him. He communicated with his eyes, body language, sign language, and whatever else he could find. He found a way to be one with Connor on many occasions through team playing, showing by example, or mimicry. My husband and I visited the Keech family a few months ago. Connor decided that he wanted to play a new game called Run to the Big Basket, Hold On and Scream as Loud as You Can. Derian watched him and decided to join in. They had the best time ever running to the basket, holding on, and screaming their heads off together. The joy and fun they were having together was written all over their faces. Siblings everywhere should emulate their relationship. Connor and Derian were so lucky to have one another over the last few years.

Derian watched over my son, Scott, on the occasions they were together. Just the other day he and Scott were watching TV together and Scott was moving everywhere and grabbing for Derian. Derian made sure that Scott had enough room to move and didn't find it at all frustrating that Scott kept reaching out for his face or other body parts. I felt safe when Derian was with Scott. I knew that he would handle him with care and affection.

I believe that he was sent to us to teach us about things we wouldn't have otherwise learned. We need to learn to love unconditionally, work hard to achieve our goals, and strive to bring families together and make them strong. Derian did all of these things in just two and a half years. Thank you Derian for all that you gave to us.

We softly say good-bye to you and know in our hearts how empty this world will be without you. We love you. I can't wait to meet you in heaven."

Gail, my friend and midwife, came forward.

"Derian led a perfect life, because Derian lived in joy.

Patsy and Robb invited me into their life during their first pregnancy. I'm a doula, a birth assistant, like a birth mentor. Patsy calls me her midwife.

Patsy, Robb and I delighted over the movements of the child within her. Some people have such a presence that you know when they enter a room before you see them. Derian had such a presence in the womb. I felt his strong spirit emanating through the curtain of Patsy's skin. One quiet time I felt Derian rolling in her womb while I listened to his heart. Through I heard nothing unusual, I felt moved to ask, "Is this the first grandchild?" Derian was the first grandchild on both sides of the family. I saw the great anticipation and expectations for this child. Plans were being made for many years in the future. Something made me wonder if this large expectant family could accept this baby if he wasn't up to those expectations. HOW LITTLE DID I KNOW THIS FAMILY!

Patsy and Robb were due in mid July, two weeks before my wedding. We thought—no problem. But Derian was cozy where he was. The first sign of labor was four days before my wedding. I sat with Patsy in her early labor three days before my wedding, then two days before. The morning of my wedding I said a sad good-bye and left Patsy and Robb in the capable care of Dr. Matt and Rolla, my substitute. Derian birthed while we dined with our wedding guests.

Derian's life was a life of joy. A life of joy from Derian's perspective. I feel I can say that from watching him laugh and play so hard. Even between medical treatments! Two weeks ago I laughed with Derian and Connor as they danced amidst 12 bright helium balloons. Pure joy enraptured us all.

Facing Derian's death makes us all face more of our mortality. I'm getting to the age where I'm assessing my life. Thinking about cashing in my chips, I doubt I've done enough in this life to confidently face my maker. A dozen doubts actu-

ally come up. What worth has my life been? These are things adults worry about. Not Derian.

This two-and-a-half year old knew only love and a fight for life. He threw himself into every exploration. Every climb, every run, every balloon. As much as he suffered his physical pain, he quickly forgave his doctors, nurses, and his parents because he sensed they worked for his best interest. He got right back to the joy.

That's why I say his life was perfect. He never knew shame or guilt. He never knew regret or resentment. These aren't the worries of toddlers. He loved life. He met God with the joy of a new exploration.

He taught and continues to teach us so much. Look at all he offered healing to, getting us together in so many ways. Jesus' little brother, Derian.

Our friend Dan came forward and read a letter written by Dr. Hesslein.

Dear Robb and Patsy,

Somehow, I never imagined I would be writing you this kind of letter. As complicated as Derian's medical situation was, and as frequent as Derian had unexpected, even dangerous complications, Derian seemed indestructible. He was like the Energizer Bunny, in constant motion, someone you could count on even when reason suggested he should have long since run out of energy.

From time to time, life gives us a lesson in the most surprising way. Derian was just such a lesson from the very start. Derian was faced with numerous problems, any one of which could have been insurmountable. But it never really slowed him down. His spirit gave us all the will and the courage to strive for him, without complaint or even a sense of obligation. It wasn't fair that a little guy should have to deal with so much, or that his parents should be burdened with such responsibilities and helplessness all at once. But Derian never really seemed to mind, and you never appeared crushed by the load. You three just rolled up your sleeves and got to work, building a life. (Derian was so small that he also had to roll up his cuffs a bit.) Derian blossomed in your care. Derian was fortunate to have you for parents. I, in turn, have been blessed with the privilege of working with him, and with you.

I remember once, this past winter, when Derian had been hospitalized a long time with a bloodstream infection. He finally was discharged, only to return a day or two later with a complication. I bumped into you and Derian in the hall as you arrived that day, and Derian was signing that he was now "home" again. My first reaction was to feel sad, because Derian had spent so much time with us, that he regarded the hospital as home. But Derian wasn't at all unhappy. He was a person who felt at home no matter where he was, and he succeeded in turning even a hospital into a home. You two also helped to make the hospital into a warm, caring, home-like place. Tempting as it must have been to leave the place behind you whenever you could, you instead offered yourselves to other families in need, and even became politically active to smooth the way for sick children and their families.

I will never forget Derian's little body, careening around the room, constantly busy, never bothered by bumping into things, climbing onto the examination table to let me look in his ears or mouth, helping me to place the stethoscope on his chest. It has been a privilege for me to get close to such a spirited soul, and to become a part of your lives in the process. I hope you will allow me to remain so.

Derian's life, however short, has real meaning for us all. I wish I could join you on Monday evening to celebrate that life, but rest assured my thoughts are with you always.

My mother came forward and shared her thoughts about Derian. This was her gift to him.

Derian…

From the moment I first met you, I felt a sense of awe and reverence for you—you were a special child. It was only through the goodness of God, technology, and your strong spirit that we had you as long as we have. In your short years you have taught everyone who had contact with you a little bit about how to live. It seems so incredible to me that without ever having spoken a single sentence, you have taught so much.

You taught us how to love.

Your love included and reached out to everyone you met with hugs and kisses, smiles, a wave, or even a handshake. Without a word, you communicated to each person the value you saw in him or her.

You taught us to be fully alive.

With limited hearing, you loved music and enjoyed it by clapping your hands or dancing with a delightful abandonment —there were no inhibitions with Derian.

You taught us to persevere and not feel sorry for ourselves.

When playing you ran as fast as you could, or did whatever you were doing with gusto—even though it often meant falling and getting bumps and bruises because of your trouble with balance. You would just pick yourself up, cry if you needed to and go right back to what you were doing.

You taught us how to comfort.

During your hospital stays, you comforted the family as we came up to see you. Often we would find you walking up and down the halls, with an IV in your arm, and Mommy or Daddy pushing the pole it was attached to behind you. You would stop at the nurse's station, wave to them enthusiastically and rapidly move on down the hall, excited about the next person or thing you would see. At night I know there were many times while you were there that you snuggled up to Mommy or Daddy, held them, and got them through another night. At Christmas time, when the hospital had a special Christmas show for the children who were there—you were in the front row clapping your hands, shaking your body to the music and totally enjoyed the show. Seeing how happy you were helped the rest of us get through that time.

You taught us to be joyful.

When you woke up in the morning, you were instantly awake and ready to face the new day. You were enthusiastic about breakfast, watching a Barney video, and what clothes you were going to wear. Each little thing was important and to be enjoyed.

You taught us to take time and enjoy the little things.

Since last July, when you first gained your sense of smell, you always stopped to smell the flowers when there were any in sight. Along with that, your sense of taste improved, and you loved to eat. You would always say "yummy" when things tasted good to you and would sign for more of your favorites.

You taught us to look after each other.

You assumed the role of big brother to Connor and looked after him. Of course, there were the times to fight and push, too. But so often I would see you put your arm around him, pat him when he was crying, and be so relieved when someone looked after Connor, whatever his needs were.

You taught us how to live without fear.

You could have been a little boy afraid of everything, especially after all the scary things you've been through, but instead you lived without fear. Instead of being afraid of the bad times, you truly enjoyed all the good times. What a powerful example that is for us.

Derian, we thank you for the gifts you shared with us and for all you have taught us about the simple and most important things of life—without even a sentence of instruction. I hope I

*can always remember them. Patsy and Robb, you have done
a superb job of parenting and I thank both of you for sharing
him with us—because of your generosity, you allowed us to
have time with him so we could truly get to know him and
treasure him.*

*Derian, you are an angel who whisked through our lives. How
blessed we are to have had this time with you. Derian, we love
you so."*

My dad was the last to speak. Nervousness about a public presentation,
combined with the sadness of the night, made it especially difficult for
him to speak. The sound of sorrow cracked in his voice. It was difficult
to listen to him because I could hear his pain. The others were perhaps
more experienced speakers, each with a tender message, and were able
to hide the pain a little better.

*"This is the first time that such heart-piercing sorrow has vis-
ited our family. It has made me appreciate all of the healthy
bodies and clear minds we do have but more importantly, the
loving, caring spirit of these people. Immediately all differ-
ences were set aside and "What can I do to help" was fore-
most on everyone's mind.*

*The closing ranks, unity and moral support have made this
tragedy bearable. I have never been more proud of this family.*

*Yes, Derian, in your death as in your life, you have made a
positive and lasting difference.*

*With God's help and our own angel, we will all be better
people."*

Following my dad's words the church grew dark and the projector was
turned on. Twila Paris' song, "A Visitor from Heaven," began to fill the
church while pictures of Derian were shown on a screen.

The last song sung that night was "If You're Happy and You Know It."
We asked everyone to sing it loudly for Derian. It is impossible to sing
this song and cry at the same time. The entire church felt happy.

The closing prayer meant this night of Derian was over. This was the
last time all these people would ever be gathered together for him. I

hung on to the words of the Irish Blessing as it was sung and signed by Mary, Derian's teacher. The closing blessing meant it was time to resume our positions behind the swaying airplane.

Once again, we walked down the aisle. I looked into the faces of the people we passed as we left the church, hopeful that they learned more about who our little boy was.

There were cookies and treats following the service. Several of my students came to the service with their parents. My students honored my request and composed an entire booklet filled with testimonies for what they learned from Derian. This booklet is tucked away in a special spot.

When people had a chance to get a snack, Colleen and Joe called everyone back into the church. Joe explained the reason they were late. "On the way to the church we were listening to the radio when Celine Dion's song, "Because You Love Me" came on. As we listened to the song, Colleen and I looked at each other and knew this was what Derian wanted Patsy and Robb to know."

They turned down the lights and we all listened to the words of "Because You Love Me."

Listening to the song brought back memories of picking Derian up so he could reach, being his eyes when he couldn't see, being strong when he was weak, being his voice when he couldn't speak, and the faith he gave me through it all. It almost seemed as if this song were written especially for him. Robb and I sat down in the pew, holding each other. From that point on, "Because You Love Me" was Derian's song.

Connor returned to the church and once again he ran through the balloons squealing joyfully. Connor would take the front seat of our lives from this point on. Thank God for him.

by Connor Keech

Chapter 55

Those first days without Derian...

The growl of emptiness roared through me. It could not be filled with food, drink, talk, or memories. Nothing could quiet the howl that echoed through me. I was like a caterpillar that could not fill itself up. Each morning I awoke with an empty heart. Life seemed an impossible thing to do, and yet it hadn't stopped.

I took an extra three days off from work and, for the first time in days, I was left alone. Robb and my parents went back to work. Everyone else had a world to go back to, but the life I once knew was over. There was nothing to go back to. We had a future with no familiar ground to stand on, and a body with no spirit. I wanted to pull the covers over my head and feel the steel cover of a coffin seal me from the rest of the world. The world had betrayed us, and more insultingly, life was going to move forward—with or without me.

Connor was up; I could hear his little feet slapping across the floor as he crossed the hall into our room. Panic set in. I had never totally been this child's mother. He was seventeen months old and I didn't really know who he was. Would he ever accept me as his mom?

Connor reached his little hands up to me. I pulled him up into our bed and snuggled with him. I felt clumsy, unsure of how to mother Connor. We were like two new dancers approaching the floor, dancing for the first time. Who would lead? Who would follow? What was the tempo of the melody we would dance? Connor lay so still that I could feel the beating of his heart next to mine. *What was he thinking? Was he wondering where Derian was? Would being an only child be okay with him?*

During the course of the day, I studied Connor for cues about his thoughts and feelings.

Connor and I spent the day walking aimlessly through town. We had no destination. Connor squealed each time he spotted a squirrel scamper by, noticed an airplane overhead, or felt a gust of gentle spring wind. The day was warm and inviting, the kind of day perfect for playing hooky. The heaviness of my thoughts excluded me from being carefree. I wondered if Derian was watching us. Connor and I ate lunch and we both lay down for a nap.

I awoke to the sound of little hands slapping. Connor was yelling, "No! No! No!" I ran to the bathroom and found a young toddler in as much pain as me. Connor was standing next to the life-sized Sesame Street shower curtain hitting the characters on it yelling, "No, No." He and Derian had spent hours together in the bathroom, talking to characters on the shower curtain. I knelt down next to him, unsure what I should do. *Do I let him cry? Do I let him hit this curtain until he works out some of the anger? Do I hold him and love him through it?*

I sat on the floor and asked him, "What's wrong, Connor?"

"Doo-doo come. Doo-doo come," he answered.

He fell into my arms as I reached out to him. Little Connor was grieving and didn't have a vocabulary of words that could express how he felt. We swayed back and forth on the bathroom floor. The shower curtain and all the matching accessories would have to go. Sesame Street was something we shared with Derian. It was too painful to look at now.

"Connor, do you want to watch a movie about Doo–doo?" I had the memorial tape that we had used at the service and a few others of the two boys playing together. Connor nodded his head. The two of us sat next to each other on the couch and watched it. Connor's face was pale and his eyes were serious as we watched one picture fade into the next. We never spoke or looked at each other once the tape began.

When the tape was over, Connor signed, "More." We watched it again. As soon as the tape was finished, Connor got off my lap and began to play on his own. He was done putting his energy into sadness and quickly threw himself into his toys.

When Connor seemed okay, I phoned Robb and told him what happened. In the rawness of his own grief, Robb was able to reach out to

Connor. That evening he came home with a white shower curtain and hung it. We would start out tomorrow differently. I would miss having Sesame Street as part of our life.

Movement Six—

Now My Soul Can Rest and Sing to You

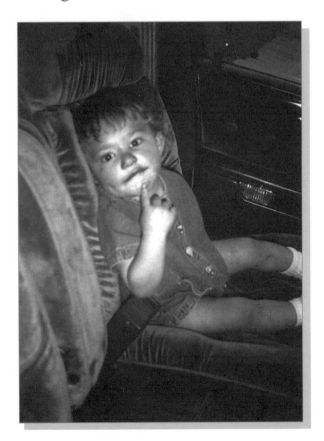

Chapter 56

Hot water dripped from the showerhead, steam circled the room, and the smell of shampoo unleashed into the air. I was lathering the thick shampoo into my hair when I was shocked with a high voltage message. "Call the man who wrote the song." *Good idea, I'll do it later.* The voltage increased, "CALL THE MAN WHO WROTE THE SONG." *Okay, I'm listening.* I obediently got out of the shower, wrapped the towel around me, and went to the phone and called the secretary from church. She knew who I was talking about and rattled off his number. I stared at that number for a few minutes before I called. Who was this man? He had gotten a message from Derian. I wanted to hear the song he heard.

Breathing brave, faith-filled breaths I dialed the phone. A man with an energetic voice answered, "Hello."

"Hello? may I speak to Steven C. Anderson?"

"Speaking."

"Hi, I'm Patsy Keech, Derian's mom. George Martin from St. Martha and Mary's Church told me you wrote a melody about my son the morning of his funeral. I was wondering if I could hear it."

His voice smiled as he said, "I'm glad you called. Your son's melody is burning in my head. It has great purpose, but I can't finish it until I know who he is."

"Would you like a picture of him?"

"Yes, that would be very helpful. I'd love to meet your son."

We agreed to meet at his Summit Avenue home the next afternoon. Summit Avenue is a grand part of St. Paul. The street is lined with stately old mansions. I got nervous driving down Summit Avenue looking for Steven's house. Steven lived on the same block as the Governor of Minnesota. Wealth and power surrounded me. *Why would this guy even care about some middle-class woman's need to hear her son's song? Who was I in this prosperous mass? Why did Derian choose such a successful person to speak through?* When I found Steven's castle, I was tempted to turn around and retreat to my little home. But my desire to hear Derian's song gave me the courage I needed to get out of the car. No doubt this meeting was prearranged.

I took Connor out of the car seat and carried him up the curved driveway, over the grassy hill, to the sidewalk that led to Steven's home. Sitting on the front porch was a young man wearing a baseball cap, T-shirt, and shorts with holes in them. He smiled warmly, extended his hand, and welcomed Connor and me into his home.

The double doors opened into a huge room that shot off in three different directions, revealing a tall ceiling, large windows with long flowing curtains, three enormous fireplaces, a grand wooden staircase, and wooden floors dressed with beautiful ornate rugs. Steven gave me a few minutes to absorb the beauty before leading me down a narrow hallway into the kitchen/family room. His wife, Diane was sitting in a rocking chair nursing their infant, Grace. Four-year-old Mattie stood next to her.

Steven introduced us, and then led me down the hallway again to the front of the house. Connor fell asleep in my arms. With so many sights to absorb, in addition to the awesome fate of our meeting, I was overwhelmed but yet comfortable. Derian and God were behind the thread that joined us. There was some reason for our meeting.

We spoke of many things that sunny afternoon. Steven seemed so regular to me. He dressed and acted much the way my brothers did. Yet, there was a sparkle to him that made me understand why Derian had picked Steven for his message. Steven was a mover and a shaker, creative, successful, and had big ideas. The big ideas in that house were contagious.

I remember telling Steven that someday, I would write a book that would be made into a movie directed by Steven Spielberg. Steven asked me, "What will you do with all the money you will make?"

Being as broke as we had been for so long, the question was humorous. The thought of ever having an abundant supply of money was somewhat entertaining. The answer to that question fell from my lips, "I want to help the families who continue to live the life we did with Derian."

Where did that come from? I had never even thought that before. Spiritual energy twirled around the two of us throughout that meeting. Was it Derian dancing, rejoicing in the union he created? When our conversation was over, Steven asked if I wanted to hear the beginning of "Opus Derian." Just as he pulled out the piano bench, Connor woke up. I unbuckled him from the car seat, lifted him into my arms, and placed his blanket around his face, hoping he'd fall back to sleep. Steven waited with the patience of a new father for us to get settled near the piano. Steven looked at Connor and said, "I'm sure this little guy has no idea of the significance of this song, but someday he will."

As Steven played "Opus Derian" with bold, unyielding passion, reflections from the past came to life. I could feel the grip of Derian's hands on the sides of my face, see his smile, and feel his energy whirling in the masterpiece Steven created. The suffering and pain was echoed in the mystery of F sharp. My heart opened and thanked God for the blessing of this gift. How lucky we were to have a song of Derian's to play when we were lonely. This performance was recorded on a tiny handheld recorder so I could share it with Robb, and everyone else I knew. I left Steven and Diane's with the knowledge that there was a purpose to Derian's melody.

Steven kept us updated on the progress of "Opus Derian." This divine masterpiece was our tug into the future. The "Opus Derian" project was more than creating a CD or a song; it united people, pulling others into it. It was like Derian.

The more I played "Opus Derian," the more I reflected on our experiences with Derian, the kindness bestowed upon us during those tough times, and the relief a mortgage payment brought, it became clear to me what we needed to do. We needed to help families, who continue to struggle with the trials of an ill child, cope in the same ways others helped us. We understood the financial pressures and strain that come from hospital life and what is most helpful. Paying the kindness forward was the thing to do. I had visions of Robb and I working together, building an organization that would pay a mortgage for families.

As I shared these visions with Robb and invited him to be the father of this organization, life began to make sense in an odd sort of way. Neither of us had a background in non-profits. We got busy and researched what was involved in starting a non-profit, interviewed leaders of existing non-profits, recruited board members, filed legal papers, and kept our eyes open to opportunities to share our vision with others. We named our organization "The Spare Key Foundation." We chose this name because everyone would understand the feeling of being locked out of something and the relief of discovering a spare key. And since we would be helping families who were locked out of life, it all made sense.

Spare Key became a spiritual product of our grief that kept Robb and I united in Derian's message. The ups and downs of building Spare Key often felt like a re-run of our journey with Derian. So many unknowns, letdowns, unbelievably lucky breaks, moments of giving up, unbridled joy, and signs—mystical, wonderful signs—made us forge ahead.

Something powerful rested in our thoughts that night. We were being led to a new place and we embraced the change. I awoke the next morning with the feeling that Derian had been there the night before. My heart felt a familiar wholeness to it, and our home had a radiant glow.

Chapter 57

As much as Robb and I had gone through together as spouses and parents, learning to live without Derian was something we would each have to do our own. We would have to find our own ways to fill the "Derian void" we carried. Even though others reached out, no one knew our pain the way we did. No matter how many cards were sent, positive stories were read, and flowers were given, it couldn't begin to chip through the pain that chilled our hearts. We each had to find a way through this maze of grief.

It took me awhile to figure this out. In the beginning I was trying to help Connor, then Robb. And oddly enough, others were looking to me for strength. I was drowning, and yet they kept holding onto me for support.

Writing was the way I kept my head above the surface. Thoughts and feelings would wake me in the middle of the night and beckon me to write the words down. Words poured through the pen, pencil, or crayon and onto the page. I never thought about what was being written, it just flew out page after page. When my emotional binge was complete, I would read what surfaced on the page. These writings helped me sort through my feelings.

Doing things correctly is the curse of the first-born—grief was no exception. I was convinced that if I didn't grieve "correctly," I would end up with some disease due to toxic emotions being stuffed into my body. Writing was one way to free the surplus of emotion.

Summer and writing provided me with much-needed solitude. However, when I re-entered the high-energy, high-speed world of teaching, my balance was lost. I was sinking, crashing, and on the verge of breaking down. Escaping the pain sounded appealing, but there were two men in my life to whom I had pledged my loyalty. They were counting on me and I couldn't let them down. I needed help!

I cornered the school psychologist one day. "Help me, please help me. I need some help. Who is the best person in the field for grief? I need to talk to someone." She was startled by my desperation. A few names popped into her mind. She gave me their phone numbers. I raced back to my office and began calling.

"I need to make an appointment today. Is John in?"

The cheerful secretary's voice said, "No, I'm sorry he won't be in until next week."

"Next week? I won't be able to wait that long." With sheer desperation I responded. "I need to see someone today or I'm going to have a breakdown. Please help me!"

"Come in at four this afternoon."

Immediate relief. The bell ringing after each class let me know I was closer to help. Four more hours, then three, two and one. I left school with the directions to the Grief Center tightly in my hand. The most relaxing part of the trip was when I parked the car.

The elevator opened up to a mint-green carpeted floor that reflected off the bright white walls. This was the entrance to my oasis. The office numbers led me down the hall to The Grief Center. When I opened the door, "Because You Loved Me" was playing over the office speaker. Derian was with me. I felt as though he were saying, "Mom, you made it!"

I was given a packet of paperwork to fill out prior to my appointment. Countless questions asked about my relationships with parents, siblings, and one even asked if I was hearing voices. I didn't care about the past. The past was fine. It was the future that was in trouble. I needed help finding a future again. In the section where I could fill in the blanks with comments, I wrote: ***Help me; I'm drowning with grief!***

The woman I met that day helped me piece the fragments of my life. Cathy became my anchor. The first blessing I received in my grief was to meet this woman.

Chapter 58

Writing and my meetings with Cathy held me together, but Robb was having a hard time finding something to fill the void. One day he leveled with me. "Patsy, you have your book and your writing to help you think of Derian. I don't have anything. I need to have my own place with Derian and I've found something that could give me that. I'd like to buy a canoe, so I can float under the heavens and have my own quiet time with my angel boy."

We bought the boat that afternoon.

And for Connor, having a mom and dad all to himself seemed to be a great consolation. The three of us were meshed into the rebuilding of our family. Connor was our cheerleader back into life. Life was something he knew very well. Connor became our firefly, twinkling his light amidst the darkness.

Firefly

I was in a dark forest.
The sky was lined with the darkest shade of black.
I was cold, alone, and scared.
I shivered at the thought of living in this doom.
I longed to relive the past.

I craved to feel the love that little hands bring.
I missed being called "Momma."
I missed having a place, a role, and a relationship.

Then from the darkness, a tiny light cast forth.
It happily scooted its joyful body across the sky.
Its little twinkle pulled me into its light.
I focused on the spark, and its brightness.
I was given relief from the darkness that swallowed me.

I waited for the next twinkle and delighted in its joy.
I jumped to the sky to catch this magic little twinkle.
I wanted to catch it and keep it for my own.
Try as I could, I could not capture the happy little wink.
It wasn't meant to be captured, just to be enjoyed,
And bring a new spark to a life that was darkened.

That firefly was you, Connor Keech.
Thank you for your quickness in lighting my ways,
For the happy, magic light that sparks within you.
I love you and look forward to sharing in the journey of
your life.
You are my little firefly.

—Mom, July 29, 1997

Chapter 59

In October...the son of a woman I worked with died suddenly on a hunting trip. He was in his early thirties, married, and had one child with another on the way. I had known his mother Betty for many years. To intimately know the pain she would carry deeply saddened me.

I went to the grocery store to pick up some food for their visitors who would be arriving during the next week. The road to the store was extremely familiar; my eyes could watch the road while my mind explored the pool of emotions trapped in my thoughts:

One more angel
One more new playmate for Derian.
One more tree planted in memory of a son.
One more set of parents with a crack in their heart.
No more holidays with all the kids together.
A baby who would never know its father.
A wife that would never sleep in with her husband again.
A three-year-old whose daddy wouldn't get to teach him
how to ride a bike.

Betty's sadness mixed with my own. It had been four months since we'd buried Derian and began our walk down this path. Derian felt so far away that day. I scolded him saying, "Derian, where are you? I never hear your song on the radio anymore. I don't feel you by my side. Have you left me? Will I ever feel you close to me again? Could I feel you in an earthly way just one more time?" When I returned with my groceries, I started the car and when the radio came on, "Because You Loved Me" was playing. Derian had responded.

A few days later, a letter arrived from a county social worker who worked with us. We really didn't know him all that well so I was surprised when we received the letter. It was dated the day I'd asked for an earthly sign from Derian.

Dear Patsy,

Greetings! I've been thinking of you and your family. A while back, I had a dream about Derian and I couldn't quite put into words some of the (what I call) energy exchange, and light-smiles. My attempt goes as follows:

> *I listened to a little wind-wisp of light/wind today…almost as if it were encouraging me to write my thoughts…or perhaps to capture the wind-wisp's spirit of thought…like a whisper…tell them, tell them.*

> *And I got that this was Derian…*

> *"Hey mom, it's pretty cool…like, Heaven is closer than we ever thought. And you know, it's like everything I got to learn and experience and be was a direct result of unconditional love…"*

> *"It's like we're all really mirrors of one another's hearts. What I learn and give, I see/experience others learning and giving. There's a permission and a love! There's like a heart-key…and I learned to give this away 'cuz I got so much of it from you and others."*

> *"I got to fly, cuz people around me fly! I got to play cuz those around me play. I got to love wholly without condition cuz that's what surrounded me! We are such mirrors!"*

> *"In the miracle of an eyeblink, or a lifetime…God said it was good!"*

> *"Thanks for being my mirrors…my teachers…my playmates…my loves!"*

> *Then glee as if to say, "Yippee, Yahoo, Yahoo!" and "I love you forever-always!"*

I mentioned this dream to Becky (Derian's early education teacher) when we were talking about another matter and she suggested I send it to you. So here this is. There was another aspect to my dream-experience too. Initially the contact or touch felt like a 'smiling, knock-knock' as if to get me to pay attention and listen to the light-energy. It was after that moment that I 'sensed' or 'understood' the light-energy was Derian or light representing Derian and then there was the 'flurry' of energy exchanges, which I included above.

Enjoy!
Thinking of you!
Nick

I dropped the letter. It truly was a sign from Derian.

Other signs continued to come from Derian in written words…

Steven C. thought his "Opus Derian" was complete but his wife Diane began to hear lyrics echoing through the notes. She found herself writing down words as they came to her and wove them into the music. She quietly worked on the lyrics under the guidance of Derian's spirit.

Steven and Diane invited Robb and me to join them in the studio for the unveiling of the new "Opus Derian." We were thrilled to be included in this final part of the project. Diane held a picture of Derian as she sang. How lucky we were to share him with them! They were Derian's spiritual parents, and we his birth parents.

Each one of these incredible gifts offered a quiet hope and ignited a passion that was leading me to a place where I would be able to fly. In letting go of my own agenda, I discovered the plan for my life.

Chapter 60

It was fall parent/teacher conferences. In the middle of the conversation with a parent, the mom said, "I bet you could use a year off."

"That would be great." I dismissed it.

After a few more conferences were concluded, the next parent said, "I bet you could use a year off."

I listened a little closer this time. "A year off? What does this mean?"

That evening I went to see Cathy, my anchor. During the course of our conversation she said. "I wish you could have a year off."

Okay, I'm listening! Three times in one evening must mean something. As I drove home I thought about what life would be like if I didn't have to teach. Hmmm…I could hang out with Connor, spend more time with Robb, and I could do some more writing, perhaps finish my book. After saying it out loud, it became clear to me that the three most important things to me were Robb, Connor, and finishing my book about Derian. If I had a year off, I could devote a great deal of time and energy into my life again. *"Well, that would be great, God, but how can I ever afford it? It's a little unrealistic."* But a seed was planted that evening.

A few weeks later, I was going through the bills, totaling up what we owed and to whom. If only we could get rid of some of this debt, maybe I would be able to take part of a year off. When Robb went in for his annual work review the next day he replayed this scene to me.

"Robb, there's been a slight problem this year with bonuses."

Robb's heart sank into a familiar hole as he thought, "Please don't tell me we aren't going to get a bonus this year."

His boss continued, "The problem is we haven't been paying you enough, and therefore, your bonus will be five thousand dollars more than you expected."

I wish I could have seen Robb's face. When he called to tell me, it was a high-voltage explosion on the other end. This money could pay off a good portion of our bills! In fact, with this boost, we might be able to survive financially if I took the following year off. That meant a sabbatical leave, so that I could still receive half of my salary and benefits.

People kept telling me they thought I would be able to apply my book, in some way, towards a master's degree. So I called Mankato State University and spoke to a professor (who later became my advisor). I told him about my experience and desire to share it in a book and asked if my project could earn credits toward a Masters in Experiential Education. He thought it was a great idea and told me I could earn up to 27 independent credits towards my master's with such a project.

This was perfect! I could do what I wanted, get paid, and have a full year off all at the same time. After many discussions, Robb and I agreed it was worth a try. He believed in my book and was willing to support it any way he could, even if it meant pinching pennies for a year. How lucky I was to have married him. I never could have reached the heights I had striven for without his willingness to let me fly. Robb's mom, Lois, volunteered to watch Connor two days a week so I could work and we could save some money on daycare. That gave me 48 hours a week to write and a built-in play day with Connor each week.

It was almost as though God had planned this out for me years in advance.

Applying for sabbatical was my first step in breaking into a new life. I was fearful of how we would cope financially. What if Robb got sick of being broke and resented me for taking this risk? Maybe I'd fail school by fooling myself into thinking I could write. Once I received the following letter I was committed; there was no turning back. I would have to move forward even if I were afraid.

March 12, 1997

Dear Ms. Keech,

We're pleased to notify you that the school board approved your application for sabbatical leave for the 1997-1998 school year.

Sincerely,

Superintendent of Schools, Independent School District 196

The Journey of Change

My paddle is in the water, I said my good-byes
I know I'm leaving a good place.
As I push off and drift out in new waters,
the shore hauntingly whispers—come back…
we'll see you soon.

My heart races with the excitement
this uncharted trip will bring.
Where will I go?
Who will I meet on my travels?
What new experience will catch my sail
and blow me in a new direction.

I see the dock fading from my sight
and I see a wide-open body of water
pressed against the sky.
So much to explore
So much to discover.

God, I offer you the rudder in my boat.
Steer me on my course.
Guide me with the closeness of your breath.
Help me set ablaze this newfound passion
and let me guide others to your light.

—Patsy Keech, May 1997

(This poem was later dedicated to Pastor George)

Chapter 61

One year later—My Butterfly Summer

Seven months into our non-profit venture, we hosted our first fundraiser, Derian's Dash, a 5K Run/Walk. Oddly enough, we chose this type of event even though none of us were runners. Our thinking was…"How hard can a run be? Organize a course and people run on it. Plus, how many volunteers do you need to host a run?" By the end of that event, we learned volumes!

Derian's Dash was to take place the day before Derian's fifth birthday— it felt like a pseudo- birthday party. Due to the date, I felt we needed to include something that would capture Derian's joy-filled spirit. Butterflies kept coming to mind. I imagined releasing hundreds of monarch butterflies into the sky at the start of the event. Great idea, but I would have to go find someone who raised butterflies. Our board members didn't mind working hard for Spare Key but mandatory butterfly catching was beyond their volunteer duties.

After talking to numerous people, I found out that the University of Minnesota had a program called **Monarchs in the Classroom**. We could purchase butterflies from them. I explained to Karen, the director of the program, how we wanted to incorporate the butterflies into our event. She thought it was a great idea! Then she told me the price of my idea—$5 a butterfly. Since we were a non-profit organization, there was no way we could justify spending $500 on butterflies for a fundraiser—that amount could make a mortgage payment! There must be some other way we could get butterflies that would be less expensive. Karen sensed my disappointment with that dollar amount and suggested we raise them ourselves. Larvae were only 50 cents. Now that was in my price range. I ordered a hundred of them.

The larva pick-up date was scheduled for July 13, 1998. According to Karen, larva at that stage would emerge into butterflies by August 1, the date of the Derian's Dash. Karen sent me information about raising butterflies prior to my pickup date. Reading the information invoked strong reactions within me. Part of me was excited about trying my hand at this; the other part was unsure whether I could pull this off. Visions of wearing boots, pants, and long sleeved-shirt, spending hours in snake-infested fields looking for milkweed—caterpillar food—spooked me. As my July pickup date approached, I lost confidence in my ability to play "Mother Nature." Fearful of defeat and disaster, I decreased my order to 50 larvae.

Three-year-old Connor came with me to pick up our new little pets. Karen sensed my hesitation and gave Connor and me a tour through the University's caterpillar lab. We saw hundreds of caterpillars in different stages of development. Some so tiny we could hardly see them, others were medium size with black and yellow stripes circling their body, and some were fat, blackish *J*'s hanging on top of the screen cage. Connor pointed at each screened container and excitedly chanted, "Butterfly. Caterpillar." Karen picked up on his enthusiasm and offered to put a caterpillar on his hand. Sheer wonder flashed across his face as he felt the suction of caterpillar feet walking across his hand. When he looked up at me with his little boy eyes, I knew we could do this. Sharing the miracle of the butterfly with Connor was an incredible opportunity. While this project was ultimately for the run, the experience itself would be extremely rewarding for our family.

I left the University with an excited three-year-old, 133 larvae, and a feeling of satisfaction. On the way home, Connor and I discussed names for the butterflies.

Robb hurried home that evening to help get the caterpillars settled. Connor spewed out everything he learned about butterflies that morning. The two of us were charmed by his enthusiasm. The three plastic caterpillar containers were given a place of honor in our home—the kitchen table.

The next morning we awoke and headed straight for the kitchen, not for breakfast, but to check on the caterpillars. It was amazing to see how much they had grown and eaten during the course of the evening, not to mention the amount of caterpillar droppings that had accumulated. Piles of tiny rabbit-like pellets spilled from the folds of the milkweed onto the floor of the container. The first job of the morning was to take all the plants and caterpillars out of the container, shake out the droppings, wash, return the plants and caterpillars, and add fresh milkweed.

As the caterpillars grew, they ate even more. *The Hungry Caterpillar* storybook was not exaggerated! We used to joke with Connor, "One morning the caterpillars might wake you up by knocking on your door and asking you to get more milkweed." Connor kept an even closer watch on them.

When the house was quiet, we could actually hear the caterpillars munching. The caterpillars were soon referred to as "the boys." Each morning the three of us began our day by hunting for fresh milkweed for "the boys." Around the ninth day, several caterpillars crawled to the top of their cage, and began to hang and looked like a letter *J*. During the course of a day, their green and yellow stripes began to turn black. Change was on the horizon.

I peeked in on "the boys" later that afternoon and noticed a few green-shaped chrysalises hanging where the *J*-shaped caterpillars used to be. Elation! It was working, we did it! Everything was going according to butterfly time.

Then it happened. One of the caterpillars split before my eyes. The entire black *J* peeled away and became an oval, jade green chrysalis wiggling from the top of the container's screen. The only remaining evidence of a caterpillar was the molting on the bottom of the container.

During the course of a few days, we watched many *J*s go through this process. The transformation was different for each caterpillar. Some wiggled out of their black skin and into their chrysalis quickly and easily; others moved slowly; some died in the process.

Days later, a thin gold thread appeared around the thickest part of the chrysalis. The base was speckled with gold flakes. "The boys" would be in their chrysalis for 10-12 days. One of the caterpillars was a few days ahead of the rest. He was due to emerge right around the time of our vacation. Before we left, I laid the lid horizontally over the container just in case he needed some flying room.

Chapter 62

As soon as we arrived home, we checked in on "the boys." They were still in their chrysalises, which was great. Derian's Dash would take place in three days. I looked for the chrysalis farthest along. All that was left was a clear shell of an empty chrysalis. I picked it up and showed Robb. "Does this mean that it died?"

"No, he emerged. He must be somewhere in the house!" The three us searched the house for the first butterfly. Minutes later Robb shouted, "Look, on the curtain. There it is!" Connor and I stood next to each other as we looked up at Robb's discovery. When the butterfly felt the weight of our stares, it responded and spread its beautiful multicolored orange and black wings.

Connor yelled with elation, "WE GOT A BUTTERFLY!" We celebrated our accomplishment with a family high-five. What a thrill to know we played a small role in making a butterfly. Connor called both of his grandparents that night, proclaiming the news. Somehow Connor got it into his head that the butterfly would sleep in his room. He cried as he naively explained his wish to have the butterfly sleep on his finger.

Robb and I smiled at his simple request and then explained, "Butterflies are not made for snuggling, or to stay inside. Butterflies need to be free, and by being free, they can make people smile." Considering his reaction with the first butterfly, I wondered what we were in for as the other 132 butterflies emerged. Robb and I re-emphasized, "Remember why we are raising the butterflies?"

"For Derian's party," he answered back.

"That's right. On that day, we will let them all go free so they can play."

Connor tearfully asked, "Will they ever come back?" This question touched my heart. When you love something, it is so hard to let it go.

Most of the chrysalises were black by the next evening. We could look inside the clear chrysalis walls and see the black, orange, and white patterns on the wings. It was amazing to think a butterfly could fit into such tight quarters. The butterflies' timing was perfect.

The morning before Derian's Dash, another butterfly emerged. Connor and I heard a tiny cracking noise from the corner of the container and sat down to watch. Which one?

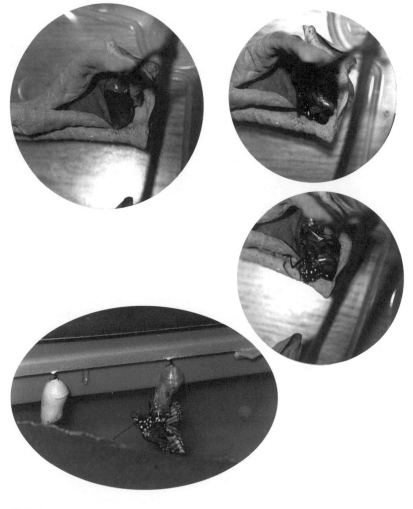

The head slowly popped out, then the legs, and then the body dropped out from the chrysalis. Only the wings remained in the chrysalis. To complete this final separation, the butterfly planted its feet on the base of the chrysalis and pulled out one wing at a time. The wrinkled virgin wings were wet with a darkish fluid.

Once the crumpled butterfly was freed, it attached itself to the shell of the chrysalis and hung upside down and pushed open each wing. When the wings were completely expanded, the butterfly opened and closed them. This beautiful creature took its time to acquaint itself with its new form. Connor and I witnessed the births of 75 butterflies that morning. How grateful I was to experience this with Connor. Having watched the entire process, Connor would, no doubt, always have a special spot in his heart for butterflies. What a gift!

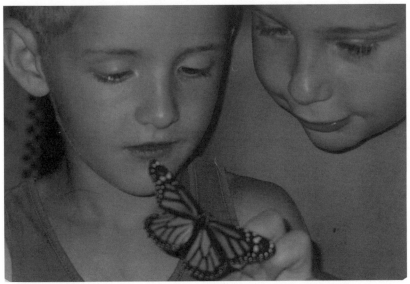

Connor and friend Cody

That evening, the butterflies were transferred to a tent we set up downstairs. From the top of the stairs we could hear the sounds of the butterflies' wings hitting the tent's sides. As I listened, I wondered if they remembered their days of being caterpillars. My pondering mirrored my journey with grief. The parallels between the transformations I had witnessed echoed the journey I began after Derian's death.

Chapter 63

The morning of Derian's Dash

The sun smiled over the two hundred people wearing their Derian's Dash t-shirts as they stretched out before the race. Volunteers answered questions and made sure everything ran smoothly. It was time for the race to begin.

"Welcome to Derian's Dash. The reason today's event is called Derian's Dash is because tomorrow would have been Derian's fifth birthday. I can't help but think that Derian and his angel friends must be smiling. The home-raised butterflies we release today symbolize our continued commitment to families of critically ill children. I would like to introduce Steven C. Anderson, a special friend of Spare Key. I would like to publicly thank Steven for his love of children and his ability to make music out of life."

As Steven began to play his portable piano, we released "the boys." One by one, the sky welcomed each colorful creature. The crowd was tearful and in awe of the wonderful sight. Victory pressed at my heart, for I intimately knew the butterflies' journey. We were not the ones who helped them on their journey to new life; rather, it was they who helped us on ours.

No matter how successful the day before, facing Derian's birthday without him was going to be difficult. As I wandered into the kitchen, I was blessed with a miraculous sight. Dangling from the outstretched toe of an angel figure that hung in the bay window was the last monarch to emerge. As I took in the sight, I couldn't help but think...I was the butterfly who had been safely nestled in the chrysalis and grew under the angelic eyes of Derian.

I had my own wings,

I was free to fly in my world…

and Derian in his.

Eda Hanson—One of Derian's nurses

Reading this book gave me much food for thought and opportunity for reflection. I realized, once again, the impact a nurse can have in the lives of children and families experiencing a critical illness.

The technical aspect of caring for a sick child is the easy part. Managing bells, whistles and physical problems is what we do. It's a concrete thing: a problem, a solution and an expected outcome.

The other part of our job is much less defined. Providing emotional support and a shoulder to lean (or cry) on is just as important, and far more complicated. It is not black and white and there are no textbook solutions. A sensitive, caring and supportive nurse can make a huge difference to families in crisis.

Patsy has heightened my awareness, touched my heart, and made me proud to have shared a small part of Derian's joyful life.

Dr. Peter Hesslein, Pediatric Cardiologist

Every young doctor entering Pediatrics is asked the same question a hundred times, by friends, classmates, and family: "We love children, too, but we could never bear to see a child who is in pain, or dying," they say. "How can you choose to deal with such sadness?" When that doctor becomes a pediatric cardiologist, dealing with some of the most deadly conditions in the most delicate of people, that question is asked again, and continually. It almost becomes an accusation.

How can we do it? How do we do it?

First, you deserve to know the whole truth about Pediatric Cardiology. Many of the children we see have nothing wrong with them! Innocent murmurs, dizzy spells, palpitations; almost all of them meaningless. Likewise, many of the real live heart conditions we see have the good sense to fix themselves. The joy we see when we share this news with frightened parents and nervous kids is an easy thrill for us, but one that never grows old.

Most of the rest of pediatric heart disease can be fixed by us, with surprisingly little risk, and with amazingly good results. There is little that can't be repaired, thanks to the boundless strength and resilience of a child's heart and to tremendous advances in knowledge and technical capabilities over the past 30 years or so. I needn't tell you what gratification we derive from helping such children reclaim a normal life.

And then there are the Derians of this world.

These are the kids our friends wondered about, and our parents warned us about. It doesn't happen often, only a few times a year, only a small fraction of our practice but every so often there comes a Derian, with heart disease that's so complicated, so challenging.

Derian was more than a challenge. At first a nameless baby, the son of frightened young parents, Derian soon began to exhibit his unique spirit. Patsy and Robb quickly got beyond their fear and their inexperience to do what parents do: they took charge. Meanwhile, Derian became a boy, laughing, careening down hallways, bouncing into our lives.

These are the kids who remind us that medicine is a serious business. And, when our best efforts aren't enough to save them, they remind us how much more there is to Medicine than effecting a cure. Long before there were pills and operations, before antibiotics and anesthetics, before doctors had the ability to treat diseases, they had to treat patients.

Pediatricians know that although their job may begin with the child, it encompasses the whole family. So it is that when a child dies, only a part of this amazing organism has been lost. The rest of the family unit, grievously wounded, needs intensive care to survive and surpass this horrible event. As for a person who has just lost an arm in a terrible accident, attention must shift from saving the limb to saving the person. This is the moment when a physician faces the greatest test, the greatest opportunity, and the greatest privilege.

How can so awful an event be an opportunity and a privilege? We generally take the "doctor-patient relationship" for granted, because we have all grown up with it. Who else, besides your loved ones and your clergy, is granted such intimacy? On the implicit promise of concern, gentleness and discretion, you bare your bodies and your secrets to us. You give us license to touch you as no one else can, and we respect the responsibility this implies.

When a child dies, it falls on us to explain what has happened. The family is never more vulnerable, and to be allowed into a family at such a moment is the deepest of privileges, not to be taken lightly. What the doctor says and does at this time will have lasting effects. It is the final opportunity to heal, even though a cure is out of the question.

But there's more to this privilege. Much more. People, it turns out, are stronger, more connected, more feeling than they generally appear, and their greatest moments come during times of greatest stress. To be invited into a family at a time such as this, to comfort and be comforted over the loss of someone that you, too, have come to love, is perhaps Medicine's greatest reward.

Derian was a special boy, as is will become clear in this book. He made better people of us all. Most notably, he has inspired his parents to good works in his name, and also to produce this memorial.

Why am I a pediatrician? This book answers that question.

Dr. Peter Hesslein

Reverend George H. Martin

Many days and moments in ministry blend into each other. Like a flat horizon without any defining structures or landscape, it can all start to look the same. But there are other days in ministry that remain rooted clearly in memory, almost as if they happened just yesterday. Such is my memory of the day I walked into that intensive care ward when Derian was less than a day old. My joy at his birth was quickly countered by the news that he needed heart surgery.

I still have a vivid picture in my mind. I sat with Robb and Patsy in a hospital room. With us was a marvelous cardiologist who used his own carefully crafted almost Van Gogh-like drawings of a heart to explain the surgery that would be done on a baby who had been with us for less than 24 hours. Our walk together began. Little did we know or could we possibly see the twists and turns of the long, dark, troubling nights and days we would share. Neither could we have known what joy we would know as we celebrated victories, bound together in Derian's fan club, watching this wonderful little boy smile throughout his all-too-short, but very intense ordeal.

Having watched Derian come through one huge dangerous surgery or hospitalization after another, I know I wasn't prepared for what turned out to be his last surgery. By this point in his short two-and-half years, this was supposed to be just another surgery. We weren't insensitive in thinking this way. We knew better than to take anything for granted though, and that's why we were with Patsy and Robb as we'd been with them so often. It was serious surgery, but by this time the word serious had taken on different shades of meaning. This surgery just wasn't supposed to be as monumental as others. Maybe that's why I wasn't at all prepared to deal with what I was always afraid of facing.

In my ministry, I've had to help other parents at a time of death. For me, at those times, I wished I might have chosen another profession. That wasn't an option on the day Derian died. All we knew was we had to put together some kind of service and something even beyond that moment that would help us and others hold onto the memory of Derian. Sad and distraught as we were, we also knew we needed to celebrate the gift of Derian in our lives.

The arrangements for the funeral included the tear-filled but still joyous service at the church. Derian's body in a casket. Hard to fathom, but he lay in state, much as so-called important people do.

Those who had been blessed with Derian in their lives knew, however, that he was quite an important person and deserved that status. Even so, I found myself apologizing, in a way, when I ushered in Steven Anderson the morning of the funeral. He was auditioning to play piano for a new jazz mass service. It was awkward, but it was the only time and place for the interview.

The "gift of Derian" was about to continue in an unseen way. Anderson's fingers touched the keys because this new father's heart was so touched by the thought of a little child's body in that casket. A wonderful, strange melody emerged from his fingers. He said, "I don't know where that came from. But that's Derian's song." Later he told me that the melody wouldn't let him go until he developed it fully. That song later became the foundation piece for the CD Anderson recorded when the Keech's family legacy to Derian, called Spare Key, got started.

In my years of being an Episcopal priest, I may have forgotten some of the people and events of my ministry, but the way in which little Derian entered my life is deeply and permanently etched into my memory. I have nothing but the highest admiration and appreciation for Derian's mom and dad, Patsy and Robb. Sometimes in ministry, I need to be the teacher, but in this instance, the roles have been reversed. I stand in awe of their love, their creativity, their courage, and their vision. They took the very worst thing that could have happened and started something that miraculously gives life again and again. We're all the better for their love and their story. Thank you, Lord, for sending Derian and making sure he had just the right parents.

The Rev. Dr. George H. Martin

Cathy Cammack, Therapist

The new client is sitting in the waiting room as she completes her intake information. I will have just a few minutes to look it over before she comes in for her session. All I know is that the issue is grief, and it must be recent. The appointment is an addition to my schedule; the client needs to be seen today. I am told she has finished her paperwork, so I will take just a second to read through it before inviting her in to the office. As always, I glance at the last question on the form: **what is the nature of the issue bringing you to counseling?** There is only one line scrawled in the space. It reads, *"Help me, I am drowning."*

Thus began my association with Patsy Keech. When I walked out to the waiting room that day, a feeling of such inadequacy came over me. Those few words had shaken me to the core of my soul. Who was I to think I had any answers or any magic wand to comfort so wounded an individual? When I introduced myself to Patsy, I was drawn to two things; one was her smile, and the other was the bright, tear-filled eyes that seemed to bore through me.

Patsy began to tell me her story…the story of Derian. An inner conflict was raging inside me. The therapist in me was trying hard to be objective, neutral. The mother in me was screaming, "How does a mother bury her child and live to tell of it?"

During the course of Patsy's work with me there were many highs and lows. One day she would come in filled with some wonderful adventure to share, some angelic occurrence to relay (these are common happenings with Patsy!). Other days she would grab for the tissues and tell me that she didn't know if she could continue. The turning point in her therapy came the day she shared one of her poems. In this poem she compared her grief to a great mountain that suddenly appeared on her journey through life. She said she examined her choices; she could try to go over the mountain, tunnel through it, walk around it, or dig beneath it. Instead, she said she decided to befriend it. She would no longer continue the adversarial relationship she had with it. She would embrace it. That was when I saw that Patsy was, indeed, not only going to survive; she would thrive. From that day on, her resiliency came into play. She turned to her gift of writing and let her poems, essays, and journal hold the pain that had wrapped itself around her heart. Later, she took those same words and shared them with others. She began to give presentations around the community and shared her story, and her son's story, with others who were in the throes of grief. Yes, Patsy continued to have the occasional "bad day," but she no longer gave in to it. She allowed the pain to wash over her as if it were a giant wave. She seemed secure in the knowledge that, just as a wave, her grief would crest, crash, and recede. Each time she would pick herself up, brush the sand and residue away, and start back on her path.

Patsy has a remarkable gift for drawing others to her. One cannot help but catch the enthusiasm whether she is telling of an angelic encounter, the raising of butterflies in her kitchen, or an appearance on television. She has a gift for taking her audience along with her. She shares abundantly her wisdom, her exuberance, but also her pain. She reminds us all that the human spirit is, indeed, resilient. We may stumble and fall, but we also get up, brush ourselves off, and begin again. Patsy's story is exactly that; it is a story of deep pain, intense mourning, and rebirth. She reminds us that if we focus only on the Crucifixion, we miss the glory of Easter. I feel so very honored to have been witness to her renewal. Even more, I feel honored to call her my friend.

Cathy J. Cammack

Individual, Couple, and Family Therapist

Spare Key Foundation

If in the course of reading this book, you needed to take a break from the intensity, please know that families living with a critically ill child do not have such a luxury. Perhaps you have become more appreciative of the gift of health. If so, please share your gratitude with a family who struggles by making a tax-deductible donation to the Spare Key Foundation.

A percentage of the profits of Mothering an Angel will go toward building an endowment fund for Spare Key.

Know that your donation will keep a child from being alone, repair a human spirit, offer hope, provide security, and bring relief. Your gift provides countless blessings. You will forever be a hero in the home of a stranger.

For more information, contact:

Spare Key Foundation
P.O. Box 612
South St. Paul, MN 55075
(651) 457-2607
www.sparekey.org

Have Patsy Keech Speak at Your Event

Patsy's combined life experiences make her a diverse speaker. She can inspire educators, students, medical personnel, parents of critically ill children, business groups, religious groups, dreamers, and people dealing with grief.

If you want a speaker that pulls at the heart, winks at hope, and delivers a message that lingers in the minds of an audience, call today and book Patsy as your speaker. She can be contacted at:

P. O. Box 612,
South St. Paul, MN 55075.
www.dreaminmyeye.com

$\mathcal{S}$omething to Note

The movements in Mothering an Angel coincide with the music of Steven C. Anderson's "Opus Derian," with lyrics written by Diane Anderson. The delicate yet majestic "Opus Derian" embraces the essence of Derian's extraordinary spirit. Check it out!

This CD can be ordered through the Spare Key Foundation at:

> P.O. Box 612
> So. St. Paul, MN 55075
> or through Spare Key's web site
> www.sparekey.org

All proceeds for "Opus Derian" go directly to The Spare Key Foundation.

You can contact the talented and giving Steven C. Anderson directly at www.stevencmusic.com

Acknowledgements

Mothering an Angel could not have been born without the support of many fine people. I would like to thank everyone who honored my dream and supported its completion.

I would like to thank:

My husband Robb for taking a risk and trusting this was the right thing to do. I am so lucky to be married to a man who listens to my dreams and supports the journey. The best decision I ever made was to say, "I do."

Our son Connor who rallied right behind me, especially on the tail end of this project. I hope this book serves as a reminder to "Think Big!" You are my favorite part of life! I am so happy to be your mom.

Our families for believing, supporting, and celebrating the milestones along the way. Thanks for always being there to baby-sit or help out. How lucky I am to be related to all of you! I am proud to share Connor with you and feel blessed that he has grown up with some of the best people I know.

My publisher, Milt Adams of Beaver's Pond Press, who connected me to all the right people and took *Mothering an Angel* under his wing. Milt has a way of making everyone feel like a winner.

My editor and friend Cindy Rogers. Thanks for helping create something I can be proud of.

Marianne Salter for the many hours put into making corrections. Without her help, the book never would have been finished.

The entire staff at Mori's Studio for their diligent work and the care they offered to *Mothering an Angel* and its author.

Minnesota State University, Mankato - Experiential Leadership, and Jasper Hunt, my advisor for granting me the opportunity to earn credit for this project.

All the friends who spent hours on the phone listening to me read huge chunks of text to them, ignoring the beeps of other callers. Special thanks go to Louise Mehr, Deb Rhody, Elaine Spurr, Diane Thayer-Peterson, and Gail Tully.

Reverend George Martin, Eda Hanson, Dr. Peter Hesslein, and Cathy Cammack for the impact they made in my life and for sharing their insights and wisdom with all of you.

Anita Moss for embracing this project with her creative artwork.

Jeff and Tracy Baker for believing me in the eleventh hour (you know what that means); Mary Molumby, Eda Hanson, Kip Courtemanche, Alison Heglund, Robyn and Mark Salter, Colleen Neary, Thomas Garvey, Maggie Gillard, and Mary Kanner for reading *Mothering an Angel* "in the rough"; and Kathleen Ehrreich at Southview Bank for making the impossible a reality!

Steven C. and Diane Anderson for inviting Derian into their family. Thanks for listening, sharing, and modeling your "all things are possible" attitude.

All the wonderful people who encouraged me along the way and believed in *Mothering an Angel*. You are a huge part of this project.

All the families who continue to live the life we once did. We will continue to be a strong voice for you.